The Family History Book

The Family History Book

A Guide to Tracing your Ancestors

STELLA COLWELL

Phaidon · Oxford

For my ancestors, known and unknown, but especially for my dear parents, William James Colwell and Elsie Irene Hartley Colwell, with love and thanks for everything.

Acknowledgements

This book was written during the period when the course of my life changed from being a professional genealogist to a law student. Consequently it will serve as my legacy to others interested in the subject of family history. It has been based purely on my personal experience of the sources and problems the genealogist will encounter, and will, I hope, give some indication of the tremendous fun and pleasure to be derived out of the pursuit of ancestors, whether your own or other people's.

I should like to take this opportunity to thank those who have helped me with their encouragement, advice and support over the years, and who passed on the torch of their own experience to the next generation: my history tutor at the University of Keele, Peter Spufford; my first genealogical mentor, Anthony Camp, Director of the Society of Genealogists; my principal at the College of Arms, John Brooke-Little, Norroy and Ulster King of Arms; my long-suffering tutor at the College of Law, Hilary Jackson; and Don Steel, Gerald Hamilton-Edwards, Derrick Emmison and Brian Fitzgerald-Moore, my guides and inspirations. I should particularly like to thank the following friends for all their help with offering tea and sympathy during the preparation of the book: Georgia Tennant, Valerie Bowyer, Celia Congdon, Sieglinde Alexander, Ann Cleary, Sara and Ian Andrews; and my best friends, my parents.

June Averill, Tony Attwood, John Brooke-Little and Charles Tucker helped me greatly with detailed items of research, Lena Parker and the Headmaster of Grasmere School helped in looking out old photographs of village life, and Mary Burkett and Sheila MacPherson gave considerable help in providing often elusive material.

Lastly I should like to thank Bernard Dod for encouraging and cajoling me to complete the book, and for all his valuable help and advice, cheerfully given.

The publishers would like to thank all the institutions and individuals, both in the UK and overseas, who helped with photographs and information, in particular Colin Harris, Mr and Mrs Donald Norman, the Estates Bursar of Jesus College, Oxford, and the Trustees of the Oxfordshire and Buckinghamshire Light Infantry Regimental Museum.

Phaidon Press Limited, Littlegate House, St Ebbe's Street; Oxford OX1 1SQ

First published 1980
© Stella Colwell 1980
Third impression 1986
First published in paperback 1984

British Library Cataloguing in Publication Data

Colwell, Stella
    The family history book.
    1. Genealogy – Amateur's manuals
    I. Title
    929'.1   CS16
    ISBN 0-7148-2074-1 Hbk
        0-7148-2372-4 Pbk

Printed in Italy by G. Canale & Co., Turin

Contents

Frontispiece. A family history collection. Acknowledgements are due to various members and friends of the Phaidon staff, and to the Headmaster and pupils of Grasmere School, whose centenary scrapbook (1954) is open at the back of the picture.

Introduction: What is Family History?

At the English Genealogical Congress, held at St Catharine's College, Cambridge, in 1978, Dennis Heath of Warwickshire was allocated a room next to Bill Marsh of Australia. Neither previously knew of the other's existence, but both were trying to trace the same ancestor. Mr Heath's mother's surname before marriage had been Marsh, and in the course of conversation he mentioned this to the Australian. The two discussed the distribution of the surname in East Anglia, and in one parish in particular. Mr Marsh told Mr Heath about his own forebear who had emigrated to Australia in the nineteenth century. He had succeeded in locating the date and place of his emigrant ancestor's baptism, and on the baptism certificate were the names

This printed 'table of descents' is in the John Johnson Collection in the Bodleian Library, Oxford. It shows the ancestors of John Stiles in both the male and female lines. Squares and circles represent male and female ancestors in the direct line, while octagons represent brothers and sisters. Such 'all-line' pedigrees expand very rapidly after the first few generations. (Oxford, Bodleian Library, John Johnson Collection, Genealogy Folder)

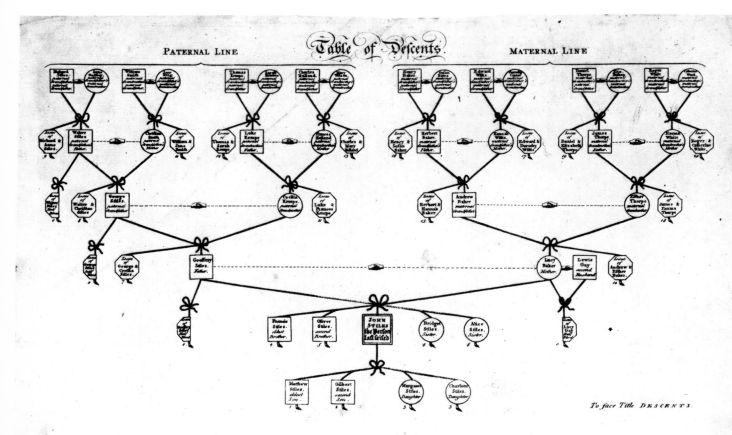

of the ancestor's parents. These names and dates seemed oddly familiar to Mr Heath, and when he returned to his room he looked through his notes and found that he, too, was descended from the same couple. This coincidence was featured in a local radio programme, and a listener contacted them to say that she was also a descendant. Not much more was learned about their ancestor's parents, but the distant cousins were able to build up a considerable body of facts about subsequent generations.

Dennis Heath and Bill Marsh met through sheer serendipity, but their meeting illustrates how a shared enthusiasm for family history can add much to the enjoyment of what can be a solitary pursuit. Family history involves the patient and resourceful study of sources for clues as to where to look next, and the piecing together of the evidence collected. It may also lead to the discovery of previously unknown relatives, to a wider family as it expands to take in collateral branches; beginning with the families of both parents, then of all four grandparents and so on, one moves into an ever-widening social milieu embracing families from different backgrounds and places. The searching and the analysis of the results make family history a fascinating and increasingly popular hobby.

The study of a family's history and origins is called genealogy, tracing back descent in a direct blood line, generation by generation, as far as it can be proved. Anyone who knows the names of his parents has a basic family tree, and, if he has children, is his children's ancestor. The genealogy of a family can be traced in both the male and female lines, although it is easier to trace the male ancestors of both parents because of the continuity of surname. Tracing descent through the female line produces a very complicated family history, as the woman takes her husband's name and the surname changes with every generation, but it does show the number and names of the families to which one belongs, however remotely.

A genealogical table, reciting the generations in order of descent, or back from the present generation, can take either a spoken or a written

Pedigree diagrams showing the direct male and female lines of ancestry. The black squares and circles represent male and female ancestors respectively in the direct line. Squares and circles with diagonals represent respective spouses, while open symbols represent brothers and sisters. The females take the surname of the husband in each succeeding generation, so there is no continuity of name.

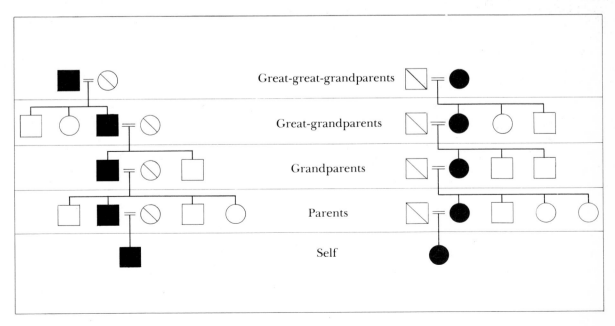

7

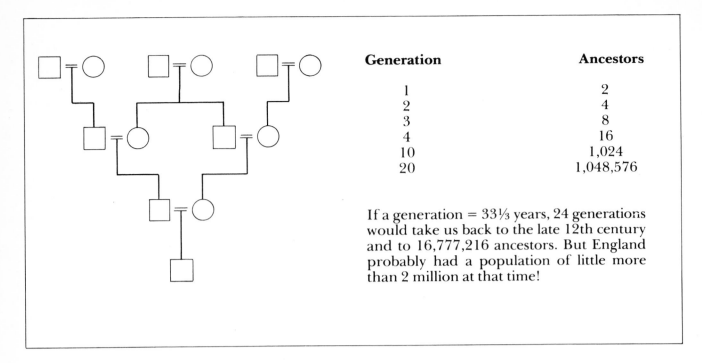

Generation	Ancestors
1	2
2	4
3	8
4	16
10	1,024
20	1,048,576

If a generation = 33⅓ years, 24 generations would take us back to the late 12th century and to 16,777,216 ancestors. But England probably had a population of little more than 2 million at that time!

form, and is known as a pedigree. This word derives from old French 'pied de grue', meaning a crane's foot, which the descent lines of many of the earliest pictorial pedigrees resembled. The sort of information included in them depends entirely on what sources were available to the compiler, and the purpose which the pedigrees served. They may range from mere chronicles of names to elaborate documents giving dates and places of birth, marriage and death, and details of land holdings, offices and titles. Genealogy has played and still does play an important role in societies all over the world.

Potentially the number of our ancestors doubles with each earlier generation, but the further we recede in time the smaller was the actual total population. This apparent paradox is explained by intermarriage; for example, if two cousins intermarry they have six grandparents between them, not eight. Such intermarriage over many generations greatly reduces the number of our actual ancestors, and it also means that many of us must be distantly interrelated without knowing how or when. Genealogical research into well-known pedigrees can reveal highly unsuspected connections. For example, H.M. Queen Elizabeth II has an ancestor in common with George Washington; she is also descended in the matrilineal line from Kuthen, Khan of the Kumans, who flourished in the thirteenth century; by 1911 there were over 80,000 descendants of Edward III of England in the legitimate and illegitimate line; the Dukes of Grafton and of St Albans descend from bastards of Charles II; the first Earl Ferrers, who died in 1717, left thirty bastards and twenty-seven legitimate children; U. S. Grant traced his ancestry back to William I of England; Thomas Jefferson to David I of Scotland; George Washington and Abraham Lincoln to Henry I of France; James Monroe to Robert Bruce of Scotland; and U. S. Grant, Quincy Adams, James Garfield, William Howard Taft, Henry Wadsworth Longfellow and Sir Winston Churchill were all descendants of passengers who sailed to North America on the *May-*

If two cousins marry, they only have six grandparents, as the diagram shows. This helps to explain the paradox that in theory the number of our ancestors doubles every generation, while the population of the country gets smaller the further back you go. In practice everybody must have an enormous number of very distant relatives with whom they have ancestors in common.

Right. Some remarkable connections. This table shows that Abraham Lincoln, George Washington, Sir Winston Churchill and H.M. Queen Elizabeth II all share a distant ancestor, namely King Edward I of England. Numbers in circles represent intervening generations.

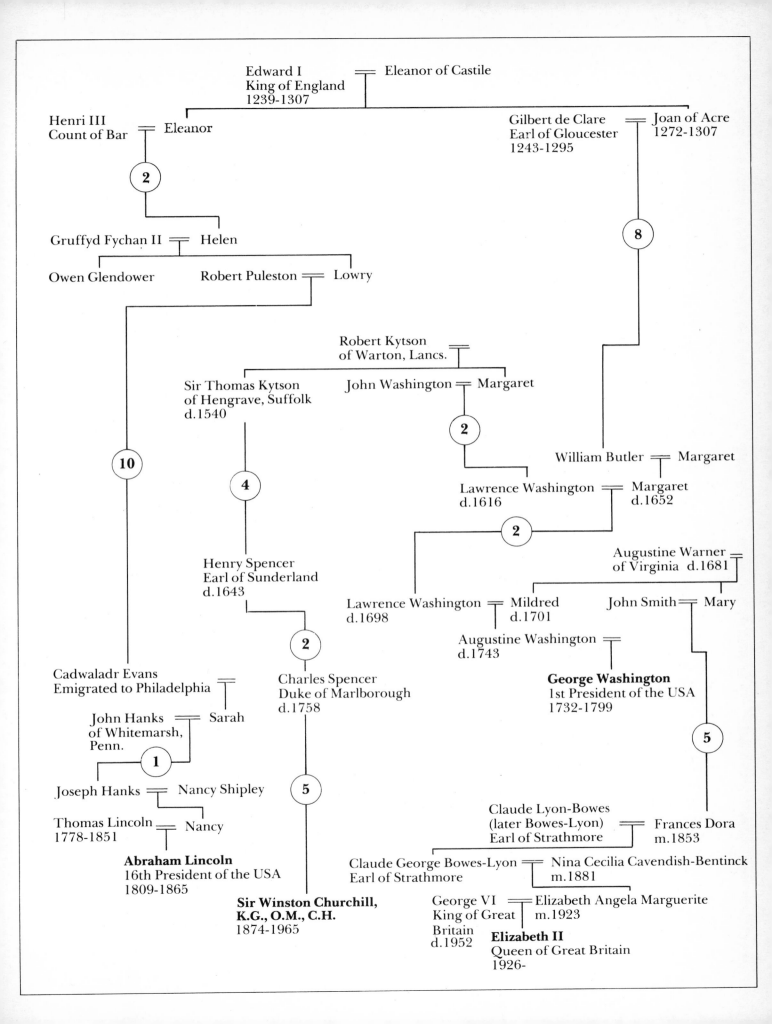

Edward I
King of England
1239-1307
=== Eleanor of Castile

Henri III
Count of Bar === Eleanor

Gilbert de Clare
Earl of Gloucester
1243-1295
=== Joan of Acre
1272-1307

(2)

(8)

Gruffyd Fychan II === Helen

Owen Glendower

Robert Puleston === Lowry

Robert Kytson
of Warton, Lancs.

Sir Thomas Kytson
of Hengrave, Suffolk
d.1540

John Washington === Margaret

(2)

William Butler === Margaret

(10)

(4)

Lawrence Washington
d.1616
=== Margaret
d.1652

Henry Spencer
Earl of Sunderland
d.1643

(2)

Augustine Warner
of Virginia d.1681 ===

Lawrence Washington
d.1698
=== Mildred
d.1701

John Smith === Mary

Augustine Washington
d.1743
===

Cadwaladr Evans
Emigrated to Philadelphia ===

John Hanks
of Whitemarsh,
Penn.
=== Sarah

Charles Spencer
Duke of Marlborough
d.1758

George Washington
1st President of the USA
1732-1799

(1)

(5)

Joseph Hanks === Nancy Shipley

(5)

Thomas Lincoln
1778-1851
=== Nancy

Claude Lyon-Bowes
(later Bowes-Lyon)
Earl of Strathmore
=== Frances Dora
m.1853

Abraham Lincoln
16th President of the USA
1809-1865

Claude George Bowes-Lyon
Earl of Strathmore
=== Nina Cecilia Cavendish-Bentinck
m.1881

**Sir Winston Churchill,
K.G., O.M., C.H.**
1874-1965

George VI
King of Great
Britain
d.1952
=== Elizabeth Angela Marguerite
m.1923

Elizabeth II
Queen of Great Britain
1926-

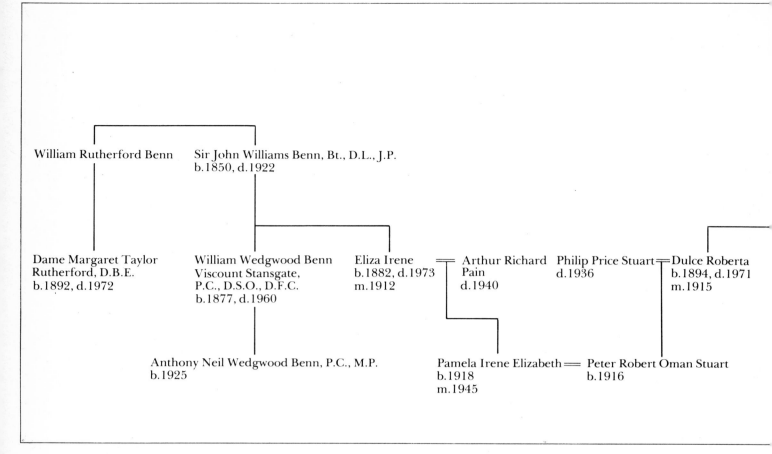

flower, in 1620. A large part of the fascination of studying one's own family history lies in the intriguing possibility of discovering such unexpected relationships. Some of the feelings that prompt people to investigate their ancestors and connections are well expressed by one of the characters in George Gissing's novel, *The Town Traveller*:

'I couldn't help thinking today ... what a strange assembly there would be if all a man's relatives came to his funeral. Nearly all of us must have such lots of distant connections that we know nothing about. Now a man like Bolsover—an aristocrat, with fifty or more acknowledged relatives in good position—think how many more there must be in out-of-the-way places, poor and unknown. Aye, and some of them not so very distant kinsfolk either. Think of the hosts of illegitimate children, for instance—some who know who they are, and some who don't. . . . It's a theory of mine . . . that every one of us, however poor, has some wealthy relative, if he could only be found . . . A little old man used to cobble my boots for me a few years ago in Ball's Pond Road. He had an idea that one of his brothers, who went out to New Zealand and was no more heard of, had made a great fortune; said he'd dreamt about it again and again, and couldn't get rid of the fancy. Well, now, the house in which he lived in took fire, and the poor chap was burned in his bed and so his name got into the newspapers. A day or two after I heard that his brother—the one he spoke of—had been living for some years scarcely a mile away, at

Lateral genealogy. This table represents another way of finding out surprising connections, by working sideways rather than backwards. This time H.M. the Queen's interesting relatives include Tony Benn and Roy Strong, Director of the Victoria and Albert Museum. Adapted from a pedigree made by Patric L. Dickinson.

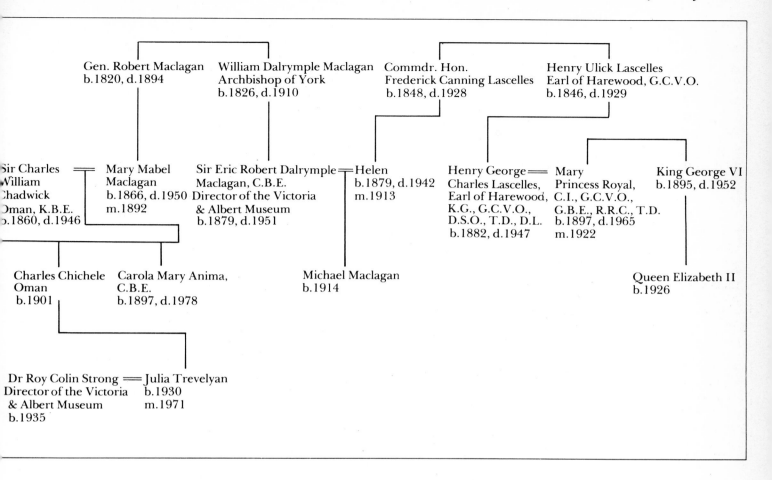

Stoke Newington—a man rolling in money, a director of the British and Colonial Bank.'

Family history is a means of understanding the past and appreciating the present, for each family is a part of society, and each family's history is a part of social and local history. If you take up this hobby you always have the incentive of a direct personal interest—it is *your* family and *your* background you are investigating. There is the additional stimulus of conducting original research and of not being able to predict its results. At the same time, you will uncover details about the social milieu in which your forebears lived, and prove or lay to rest such family traditions as 'money in Chancery', the right to bear a coat of arms, or a connection with a famous person or event. Perhaps your surname is unusual, in which case you may be able to trace its origin and its current distribution as well as unravel your own pedigree.

The art of tracing a family's history relies on a knowledge of what records exist, what they contain, for what dates and localities, their continuity and their accessibility. It is a fiction that only the nobility can be traced beyond a certain date. The very nature of our society allows for social mobility both up and down the scale, and genealogical research is full of surprises. It may be that your antecedents, however humble, can be traced at least to the Tudor period. Even before this they may have been recorded in land records as tenants, in wills as beneficiaries, and in taxation and legal records for obvious reasons. I

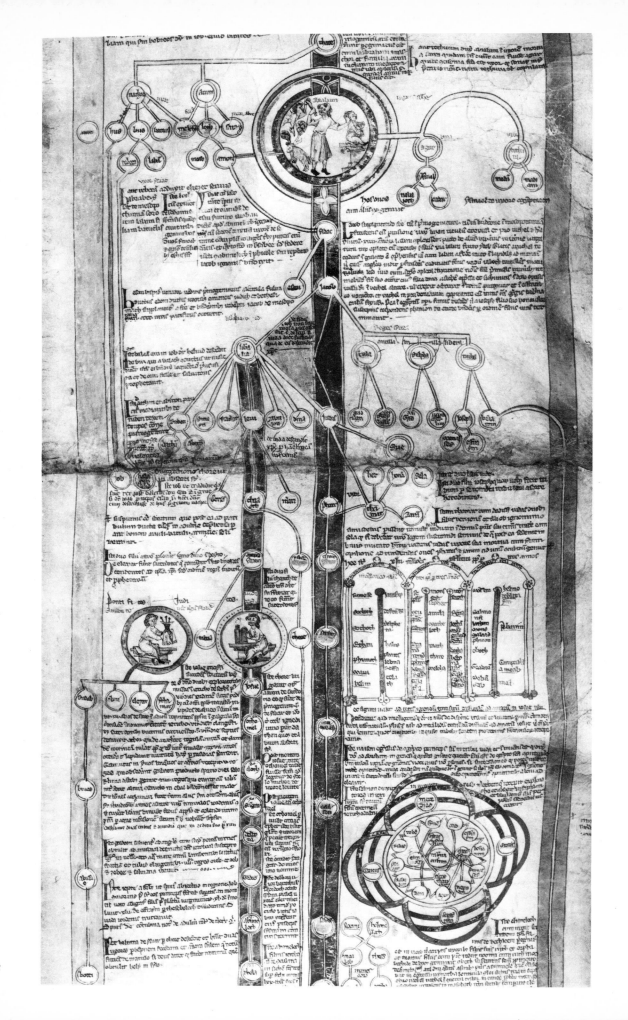

Biblical genealogy was a favourite subject in the Middle Ages. This example, dating from around 1300, shows part of the descent of Christ from Adam. The figures in the three roundels represent Abraham sacrificing Isaac, Aaron with the rod that budded, and Moses with the Tablets of the Law. (London, College of Arms, Muniment Room, MS. 9/58)

personally believe that careful and resourceful searching could extend many pedigrees which have faltered at this stage through lack of knowledge of what sources are available and how to use them. Many professional researchers balk at this point too, and the current guides for genealogists illustrate this ignorance. I have tried in this book to take the reader beyond the basic sources, and explore the public records in more depth.

In the last decade there has been an explosion of interest in family history, not of the gentry, or in pursuit of a noble forebear as in the past, but of the common man and his origins, however humble. The Society of Genealogists, founded in London in 1911, is one of the oldest associations of people who share this interest, but throughout the world many more recent national and local Family History Societies have been formed and flourish, particularly since the early 1970s. The hobby has reached boom proportions.

My main aim in this book is to give practical guidance to the beginner. In explaining the sources and how to use them I have assumed that many readers will be completely new to research involving original documents. A second aim is to place the subject of genealogy in a wider historical context, and to encourage readers to find out more about the lives of their ancestors and the society they lived in. Genealogy itself has a long history, and so chapter 1 opens the book with a short historical survey of genealogy and its uses. Chapters 2–4 provide the central core of the book, dealing with the basic sources and how to use them, while chapters 5–7 take up the three important subsidiary subjects of emigration and travel, names and heraldry. Finally, the chronological table at the end is again intended to provide a historical perspective against which a family pedigree can be viewed.

1 Genealogy in the Past and its Uses

My maternal great-grandfather, John Thexton, was a Lancastrian. He died around 1930 aged eighty-nine, and in his long life he would have read and heard of the Crimean War, the American Civil War, the Russian Revolution, the annexation by Britain of India, and the scramble for Africa. He would have had relatives and friends who were involved in the Boer and First World Wars. He would have endured the General Strike in 1926, and seen the extension of the franchise to women in 1928. He would have witnessed great technological advances such as the general use of electricity, the telephone, and the radio, and would have seen the first motor cars and have read of the first aeroplanes. One of his brothers emigrated to Canada and another to Australia, while he himself pursued several careers. He began as a prison warder, later being taken on as coachman to an Assize Circuit Judge, regularly transporting him over the Pennines to the York Assize Court, and he finally settled down as an insurance agent in Kendal, Westmorland, having raised a family of five children who became a chemist, a joiner, a librarian, a teacher, and his housekeeper. John was eventually elected a Town Alderman in Kendal, and was a devout Zion chapel elder. His first wife ran a Dame's school in the front parlour of their home, teaching girls and boys to read, write, do sums, knit and sew in exchange for a few pence a week. Throughout his life my great-grandfather kept in touch with his two brothers overseas. Their menfolk also returned to Britain to serve in both World Wars, and the link with the homeland was maintained down to my mother's generation.

John Thexton, the author's great-grandfather.

The life of this one man can be seen against its historical background, and reflects the opportunities open to a person of reasonable ambition. This connection with an individual makes history more personal, and this is one of the aims of family historical research today. The shift in emphasis from research into the pedigrees of notable families who dominated the social and political scene perhaps for generations, to the study of those with no special claim to distinction other than of mirroring the environments in which they lived, has opened up the field for the local historian and personal researcher alike in their pursuit of the past.

But the study of family history is not a recent phenomenon, for genealogies are amongst the earliest historical narratives, and certainly must have been preceded by a long period of oral transmission.

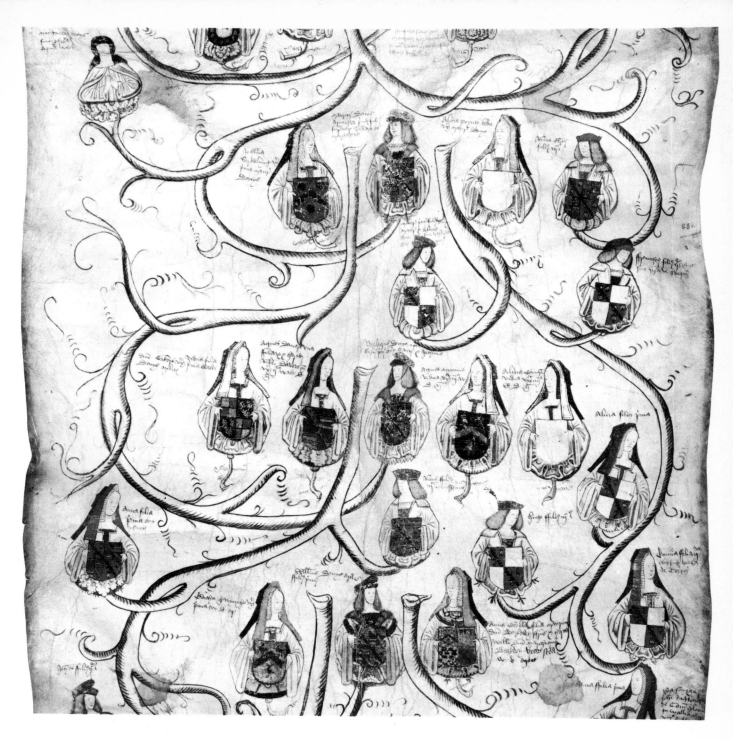

Part of a pictorial Tudor tree pedigree made around 1530. It records the Gloucestershire families of Denys and Russell. Note the heraldic shields carried by the figures. (London, College of Arms, Muniment Room, MS. 3/54)

Genealogy in the Ancient World

Genealogy in the ancient world is characterized by three main features: firstly by a preoccupation with a divine or heroic origin of an individual family, and of the race itself; secondly by a strong sense of kinship within groups; and thirdly by an obsession with maintaining the family's status, on which qualification for office, title or landownership often depended.

Surviving literature and archaeological evidence record a surprising number of pedigrees, however fragmentary, but they are often difficult to disentangle because of their use of mythological figures, their unre-

15

liability and contradictions, because of the purposes which they were intended to serve (to entitle a man to hereditary privileges, or to enhance the family's social prestige), and because of the lack of adequate outside evidence against which to test them. They do reflect current genealogical taste, and tell us much about the culture and traditions of ancient peoples. We may well chuckle at Julius Caesar's boast that he was a direct descendant of the goddess Venus through the Trojan Aeneas; or at the Greeks Hippocrates and Aristotle who both claimed Asclepius, the god of medicine, as their forebear; or at Solon, the sixth-century Athenian statesman and poet, who recognized the god Poseidon as the progenitor of his family. But even in the early part of this century Burke's *Peerage and Baronetage* was still publishing the serious claim of one noble family to be progeny of the Emperor Maximus, and its companion volume the *Landed Gentry* traced pedigrees back to the Battle of Hastings in 1066, giving such forebears as William I's grand master of artillery, his standard-bearer and cup-bearer, and several sets of brothers whose names were to be found in a fourteenth-century fabrication known as the Battle Abbey Roll (purporting to be a battle roster of Norman knights who landed with the Conqueror to fight the Anglo-Saxons). Such pedigrees may be seen as attempts to fix the family in an ancient and illustrious setting or to associate its members with the attributes of shadowy figures from history or legend. Parallels can be seen in the genealogies of the old nobility in China, Japan and Korea.

Surviving chronicles and histories contain genealogical material to illustrate the origins of nations and the descent of ruling houses. Herodotus, for example, in the fifth century BC, wrote the *Histories*, which incorporated the king list of Sparta, extending over forty monarchs, while the Greek Pausanias, in the second century AD, gave a list of the Athenian kings. It is important to remember that names in ancient genealogies may well be confused or transposed out of sequence; also, for the sake of continuity some of the earlier names may be inventions, just as the Biblical genealogies in Genesis merely serve to bridge vast periods. Other literature, such as the heroic epics of Homer and Virgil, depicts struggle between the gods as being perpetuated among their earthly descendants, the ruling houses of Greece and Troy. This literary convention had endless possibilities in showing how a feud might extend over many generations and to remote kinsmen of the main family; the same device can be seen echoed in the literature of the medieval and Tudor world, where it was used by Chaucer and Shakespeare. The genealogies of the gods themselves formed an important part of religious belief in the ancient world, and Hesiod's *Theogony* traced those of the Greek deities. There must have been many other similar compilations.

Respect for dead antecedents and a preoccupation with genealogy can be seen in the fine family tombs and monuments erected in the ancient world. These often include detailed inscriptions extolling not only the virtues of the dead but also their lineage and family connections. In ancient Egypt there was a cult of one's dead ancestors, for it was thought that the spirits of the dead were sure to return. Pride in a family's status and the privileges attendant upon it was also natural in ancient society where office was hereditary. Herodotus recorded that

A Roman family on a tombstone from the first century BC. *They are all members of the* Gens Furia, *one of the* gentes *or* clans *that reflect the tribal origins of Roman society. All the members of a* gens *claimed to be descended from a single ancestor, in this case Furius. (Rome, Lateran Museum)*

the Egyptian high priests erected statues to themselves in the high temple at Thebes, so that it was possible to discover not only the names of their forebears but the generation number of the present office holder. It was easier for the smooth functioning of government to rely on certain families for continuity and experience of office, and they were often allied by marriage to the ruling houses to bind them more closely together. The pedigrees of the Roman senatorial and imperial families illustrate the political and marital ties between them. Chronicles of the Fabii and Cornelii families survive, and others must have been compiled and circulated. Saint Paul, in the New Testament, warned of the numbers of family histories circulating in his day, just as the Greek traveller and historian Hecataeus of Miletus had examined and condemned the pedigrees of Greek noble families in his *Genealogiai*, written in the fifth century BC. Thus the practice of committing pedigrees to writing appears to have been widespread in the ancient world.

Genealogy also played a significant role in the ancient societies of the Far East. The Chinese Emperor Fu-Hi is said to have decreed that all his subjects should take a hereditary family name, as a means of distinguishing between families and of regulating marriages. All those of the same family name were considered to be descendants of the same progenitor, and therefore, as clansmen, could not intermarry. Each clan possessed its own village or part of a village. Descendants of younger sons of the direct line could establish new lines once five generations had passed. Most families maintained a Generation Book, giving names, births, marriages and deaths of its members, with the business histories of the males, as well as a record of the clan's origins and its collateral branches. It was held by the chairman of a board of editors, and was brought up to date about every thirty years. In ancient Japan a Government Office was instituted in AD 761 for the compilation of clan genealogies, and by the ninth century over 1,182 clans had been so recorded, mostly ascribing to themselves a divine royal or foreign progenitor.

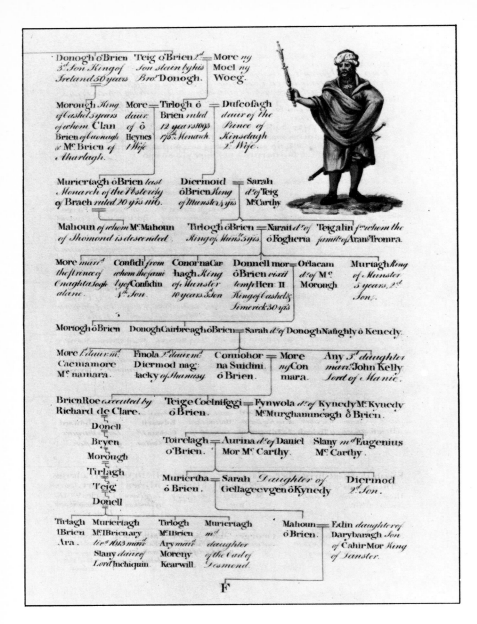

An Irish king list in the form of a pedigree, taken from the Bath Book *(1/101) in the College of Arms, London. It is part of the pedigree of William O'Brien, K. B., Earl of Inchiquin, compiled in 1812. The Earl traced his ancestry back to a Greek noble, Bracheus, who was said to have lived nearly 1500 years before Christ! Bracheus was father of Briggan, who founded Brigantia in Spain.*

In China, too, families set aside a room in their house, or a lodge of sorrow in their village, for wooden tablets to be erected and worshipped, each representing a dead ancestor whose biographical details were incised or painted on them. Filial piety in life and death were important to the Chinese, and this was a practical way of showing it.

After the Romans

In the hiatus between the fall of the Roman Empire in the West and the reassertion of settled government in the ninth century, the few contemporary records of life in Western Europe are in the form of vernacular heroic literature, annals, or archaeological artefacts. In England the most famous heroic poem is *Beowulf*, probably composed in the eighth century. There is also Bede's *Ecclesiastical History of the English Nation*, completed in 731, which contains a chapter on the origin of the race, while the *Anglo-Saxon Chronicle* records events retrospectively back to the Roman period. *Beowulf* depicts a society in which the bonds of kinship and personal loyalty were very strong, not only within the family but between lord and retainer, and in which tribes were united by marriage between leading families. The genealogies in the poem have no known historical counterparts: they are a literary convention, setting the scene for the story itself. Similar genealogies (some with a historical basis) can be seen in Norse literature, the Icelandic sagas, and the German epic, the *Nibelungenlied*.

One version of the *Anglo-Saxon Chronicle* probably ended in 855 with the ancestral table of the contemporary king of Wessex, Aethelwulf. The writer traced his descent back over forty-six generations to Adam, via Cerdic (who arrived in Britain with his brother in 495 and conquered the kingdom) and the Saxon god Woden. A compromise was reached between the heathen forebears of the Saxons and the Christian dogma of the monkish chronicler, by giving Woden an antecedent named Sceaf, said to be born in the Ark to Noah, Noah being recognized as one of Christ's forebears. Irish and Welsh king lists, too, were transmitted orally for many generations before finally being committed to writing in the eighth century. In the former case they can be historically proved back to at least the fourth century, and in the latter to a century later.

Geoffrey of Monmouth's *History of the Kings of Britain*, which appeared in the twelfth century, reflects current historical taste for forging links with the ancient world, and describes the Trojan Brutus as the progenitor of the British people. More useful historically are the Icelandic *Islendingabok* (Book of Icelanders) from the same period, and the *Landnamabok* (Book of Settlements) which contain details about ninth- and tenth-century Norwegian settlers in Iceland. The latter includes anecdotes about 400 chieftains and gives over 2,500 pedigrees of six or more generations. Thus the birth and growth of the Icelandic nation can be traced through these works, which also afford an accurate record of landownership and inheritance.

After the Norman Conquest a new social and political structure was superimposed on Anglo-Saxon society, the chief facet of which was the hereditary nature of office, title and landownership, which could only be extinguished by extinction of the family line, or by attainder or forfeit to the Crown after treasonable acts. Some of these hereditary positions still continue, albeit in rather a ceremonial form, like those of the Earl Marshal, Chief Butler, and Queen's Champion. Pedigrees of Norman families, especially those created hereditary barons, can easily be traced through the public records from the early medieval period. Many of these families had died out in the male line by the end of the Middle Ages or had lost touch with the junior branches who would have provided the next heir. The system of inheritance whereby the eldest son only was provided for meant that younger sons had to look to themselves for a living, so that their descendants ended up in an altogether different social group.

It was not only the higher echelons of society who were aware of their pedigrees. In the Middle Ages unfree tenants had no legal standing, and in order to bring a suit to a court of law they had to satisfy the assembly of their qualification to be heard. This proof took the form of genealogical evidence, sometimes giving names and relationships of collateral branches in an effort to show kinsmen of free status. The pleas

The Earl Marshal of England is a hereditary title that has been held by the Dukes of Norfolk since Norman times. Here Bernard, 16th Duke of Norfolk, is seen with the Duchess of Norfolk in ceremonial robes at the time of the coronation of H.M. Queen Elizabeth II in 1953. (Photo: The Illustrated London News Picture Library)

from the Curia Regis (King's Court) Rolls, later superseded by the Coram Rege (King's Bench) and De Banco (Common Pleas) Rolls in the Public Record Office, London, contain many extensive genealogies of ordinary people.

Tudor to Modern Times

Preoccupation with social status can be seen in the pedigree rolls constructed between the fifteenth and seventeenth century for the emergent merchant and professional families who replaced the ancient lines. They looked to the ancient world for suitable forebears, and the less imaginative to the pre-Norman period. For instance, in the early seventeenth century the Feilding family, of respectable yeoman stock in the fourteenth century, suddenly discovered that they were descended from the Counts of Hapsburgh. Even the royal line was not exempt from such fashionable fancy: the Maude Roll, inscribed in the fifteenth century, had shown Edward IV as a direct descendant of Brutus the Trojan and of Strepho, son of Japhet, the father of the northern inhabitants of the world and son of Noah. Both Elizabeth I and her successor were similarly portrayed.

The age of chivalry and romance gave wide scope for allusions to splendid ancestry. However, the Visitations of the heralds, taken in every English county at about twenty-year intervals from 1530 to 1688, were an attempt to regulate the use of coats of arms, and incidentally register the pedigrees of the gentry families, whether or not they had the right to bear arms. The heralds relied on family knowledge, tradition, and muniments as evidence, and few dates appear on their recorded pedigrees, but many of them extend over five or more generations back to the early medieval period, and because of their official status and objective scrutiny before enrolment they do not often reproduce the wilder genealogical theories. These Visitation pedigrees are an almost unique record of a particular stratum of society over 150 years, and are ripe for deeper social historical study. After 1688 the Visitation pedigrees were replaced by voluntary registration, and both series of records constitute a valuable source of information for the family historian. They are in the custody of the College of Arms in London and serve to trace emigrants, collateral branches, and mobility in and out of the shires. The College of Arms also has a series of peers', baronets' and knights' pedigrees, as well as pedigrees of many non-armigerous families. In addition, it has a collection of pedigrees submitted on behalf of young men seeking free entry to Oxford and Cambridge colleges as 'founder's kin'—for many of the original college statutes contain special provisions for students who could prove themselves to be related to the founder. Similarly benefactors set up private trusts for the support of their own kindred at specified colleges. In Scotland there is a Register of Genealogies dating from 1727, and from 1672 the Lyon Register records the matriculations of those claiming a right to display arms, often reciting pedigrees of several generations. These are retained by the Lyon Court, Edinburgh. The College of Arms has photographs of the registered Irish pedigrees and arms, the originals being in the Genealogical Office, Dublin.

Right. *A page of notes on heraldry as observed in the Oxfordshire village of Bradwell and noted by the seventeenth-century antiquarian Anthony Wood. Such notes, covering many places in the area and made over the years 1668–81, were later bound into a volume now in the Bodleian Library, Oxford. (Oxford, Bodleian Library, MS. Wood E1)*

Part of the Maude Roll, which traces the descent of King Edward IV from Adam. This section shows Adam and Eve (in the roundel at the top), and their descendants as far as Lamech. (London, College of Arms, MS. Arundel XXIII, pp. 2–3)

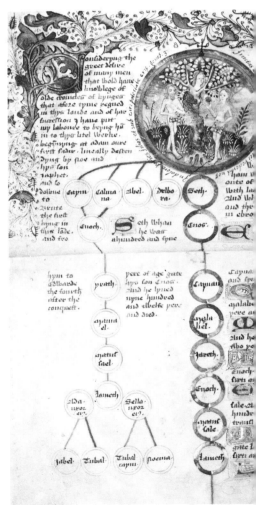

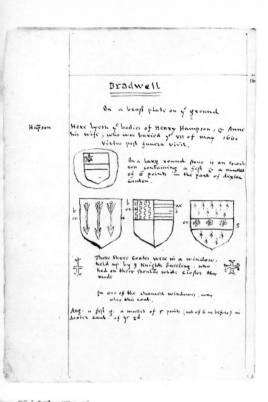

Counterparts to these genealogies also survive from Europe and Russia. Registers of noble and high-ranking families were kept in Poland, the Austro-Hungarian Empire and pre-Revolutionary France, while in 1685 an attempt was made to consolidate a list of all those Russian families holding rank and position in the army and civil service. This functioned as a useful directory to the Court. A similar registration is again found in the Far East, among the Samurai (warrior class) of Japan, whose pedigrees were collated in the 1640s and collected into twenty-two volumes. These registers were concerned with precedence, protocol, and the making of appointments.

In England in the late sixteenth and seventeenth centuries there was a growth of interest in antiquarian studies for their own sake, and some of the English heralds were pre-eminent among the early Fellows of the Society of Antiquaries. They used the opportunity afforded by the Visitations to note down abstracts of family charters and papers, to copy tombstone inscriptions and entries from monastic cartularies, and to sketch church monuments and heraldic stained glass. They also made private collections of pedigrees. Other early antiquarians collected manuscripts containing much genealogical material, some of it being amplified personal copies of the official records made by the herald painters accompanying the heralds. In the eighteenth and nineteenth centuries local and national historical and antiquarian societies were established, and some of these, such as the Harleian Society and the Camden Society, embarked on ambitious publishing programmes to make source material readily available. The Public Record Office was opened in 1858 and led to greater accessibility of original sources, as well as the production of printed calendars (summaries) of much early archive material.

The establishment of local Record Offices in each of the counties and many boroughs after the Second World War to collect, house and make available local records—comprising administrative, legal, ecclesiastical, territorial, personal, estate and business documents—has made the path much smoother for the prospective family historian. He can seek professional advice on what to search and where to look, while his nineteenth-century counterpart would have had to follow hunches and diffidently approach the great houses and public offices, to examine the often uncatalogued original sources. From the nineteenth century too, the pedigrees of many families have been recorded in print.

Some Uses of Genealogy

Originally transmitted orally, genealogies were a means of tracing the descent of a race or people through its ruling dynasty from a figure or deity from whom the race took its name. Many also recall a mass migration at a remote date, often from over the seas in the form of an invasion, and these events can prove to have a historical basis. They were often purely speculative about the earliest generations because of the artificial purpose they served—to show continuity from an illustrious ancestor to the present day. As well as tracing the origins of a race, the pedigree bound the members of it in a close sense of kinship, reinforced by its recitation on ceremonial occasions, normally in a poetic or chronicle form which was easy to memorize. The Ashanti and Yoruba tribes of West Africa, and the South Pacific Islanders of Samoa and Hawaii still have their own hereditary tribal historians whose function it is to preserve these genealogical traditions. In Scotland and Ireland, too, there were counterparts even into the nineteenth century, and in Scotland the Lord Lyon King of Arms remains the genealogist for all the clans.

A clan is composed of the descendants of an actual or mythical ancestor, the chief of the clan being the senior male descendant in the direct line. Clans are a feature of tribal societies, and have survived into historical times in many parts of the world, including Scotland and Ireland. Each clan was originally organized on a territorial basis, which helps the family historian to discover at least which part of the country his antecedents stemmed from. For a clan member a knowledge of his own genealogy and that of his chief was an integral part of his life, although no written record of it might exist. Family celebrations were the occasion for the recital of pedigrees to stress the unity and history of the line.

The sense of identity deriving from common ancestors can be found in many small communities. Even today, in the Outer Hebrides, rural Europe, and parts of Africa and India, it is possible for a person to remember the names of his antecedents over many generations. This habit seems to be ingrained. In my own village, Grasmere, in the Lake District, the few remaining representatives of long-settled families can record often complicated genealogies showing the lateral connections between them as families intermarried several times. This tradition will die out as the old farming families are replaced by hoteliers, shopkeepers and residents of no permanency.

Memorized pedigrees tend not to be written down until the need arises for precise documentation of legal rights, as in all modern literate societies. Genealogy alters from being the orally transmitted birthright of a whole community to being a matter of keeping official records for central government purposes. The colonial era produced interesting

Right. The gathering of the Maclean clan at Duart Castle on the Isle of Mull in 1912. Duart Castle was restored in 1912 by Sir Fitzroy Maclean, head of the Maclean clan, and this provided the occasion for the gathering. (Photo: Hulton Picture Library)

The author's home village of Grasmere, in the Lake District. Pavement End, home of the Green family (see below, p. 29), is in the centre. Until recently Grasmere was a settled agricultural community where families had lived and intermarried for many generations. In such communities family history is not a hobby but a living tradition, and complicated family trees can be memorized and handed down by word of mouth from one generation to the next. (Photo: Sanderson & Dixon Ltd., Ambleside)

confrontations between the old and the new approach; in the early part
of this century a Maori chieftain, staking his claim to his ancestral lands
before the New Zealand Land Commissioners, could detail from
memory his ancestry over thirty-four generations, including 1,400
names. However, in most societies pedigrees have long been committed
to writing, either in the form of literature or as records for reference in
case of future dispute. This is particularly important in societies where
claims and duties are hereditary.

The modern historian uses pedigrees to explain alliances between
ruling houses, the reasons for certain behaviour and attitudes, and the
influence which certain families have been able to bring to bear on the
political and social milieu in which they lived. The social historian is
interested in which families the financially exhausted landed houses
looked to for recruitment of brides to replenish their wealth in return
for social prestige. In a society where social and political influence
depended on family and rank, an ambitious man would be only too well
aware of the ramifications of his family connections. They afforded him
a means of patronage and opportunity, and a prudent marriage with
the scion of an influential family could ensure his advancement and his
children's social enhancement and security. Such matches were frequent in eighteenth-century England, as wealth in land gave way to
commercial and industrial affluence.

However, in more rigidly class-conscious societies like the Austro-
Hungarian Empire, pre-Revolutionary France, and Imperial Germany
alliances between families of different social status were regarded as
morganatic, meaning that the issue from them were excluded from
succession to their fathers' estates and titles. Precedence and status
followed strict rules, and proof of a family's nobility over a prescribed
period secured for its successors tax exemptions and entry to the army

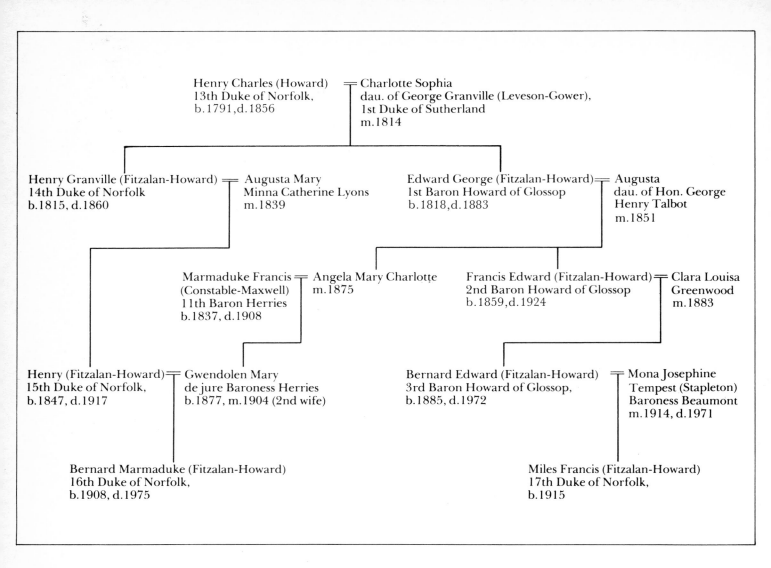

The relationship between Bernard, 16th Duke of Norfolk, and Miles, 17th Duke of Norfolk. In this case the succession to the title depended on a relationship going back four generations. Where a cousin or distant relative succeeds to a title, it has first to be proved that there are no surviving closer male relatives with a better claim.

or civil service at least at a certain minimum rank. Families were therefore tempted to forge splendid pedigrees in pursuit of privilege.

Claimants to hereditary titles in the United Kingdom are required to produce irrefutable proof that their representations are the best. Adjudication of the evidence lies with the Crown Office for peerage claims and the Home Office for baronetcies. Adequate documentation in the form of birth, marriage and death certificates, and other material showing filiation must detail the claimant's connection with the last holder of the title, even if it lies some generations back, and must eliminate all those male members of the family in nearer affinity by proving that they died without descendants who would have a better claim. The accepted claim is then enrolled in the relevant government department for future reference.

When someone dies without leaving a will and without known dependants, the Treasury Solicitor in England holds the estate funds and advertises in the national press for the kin of the deceased to notify him. The onus of proof lies with the family, who may not even know of the advertisement. Certain firms specialize in tracing the next of kin, and on payment of a percentage of the funds will provide potential claimants with sufficient documentation to allow them to present their case to the Treasury Solicitor.

Social and economic historians apply genealogical research to the reconstruction of whole communities. They examine and try to explain, for example, fluctuating family sizes, varying fertility rates, spacing between births, bastardy, infant mortality, age at marriage, age gaps between spouses, the incidence of subsequent marriages, the interval between marriages, intermarriage between families over several generations, age spans, and length of stay in a community. In an as yet unpublished study of Landbeach, in Cambridgeshire, Mrs Susan Stewart found that during the period 1560–1795 there were 432 different surnames in the parish registers of what was a small village. Only two of these were found continuously throughout those years, suggesting very high mobility rates in and out of the village. The site is in the Fenland, which is liable to frequent flooding, and malaria was once endemic there. Another study, of Wigston Magna, in Leicestershire, by Dr W. G. Hoskins revealed that the families of nearly half the population in the seventeenth century had been there for more than 100 years. Why? There the open field system required regular labour, so that work was assured and people stayed.

The study of a whole community of family units can thus reveal interesting patterns in the way our antecedents lived and in the ways they were affected by their environments. Such work helps to re-create the past of which our ancestors were part, and makes the individual family tree seem much less isolated. This is an area where family history branches out into social history.

An example of genealogy being used to record family mobility. The Spinneys were a family of Dorset blacksmiths, and the map shows the earliest dates at which the direct line of family can be traced in the registers of a group of parishes. To modern eyes the picture is one of remarkable stability.

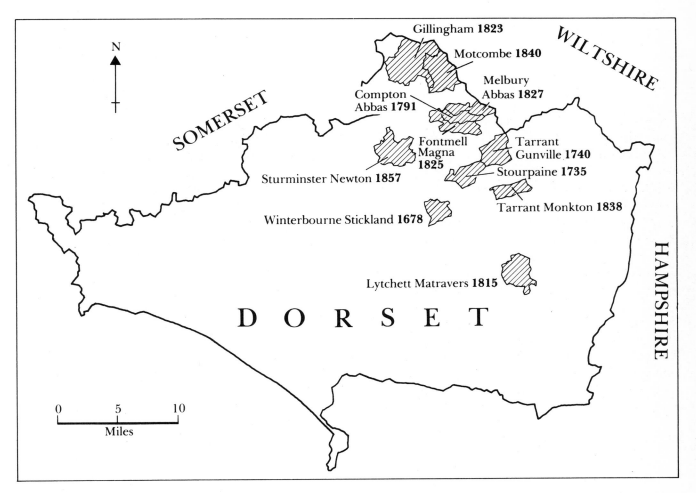

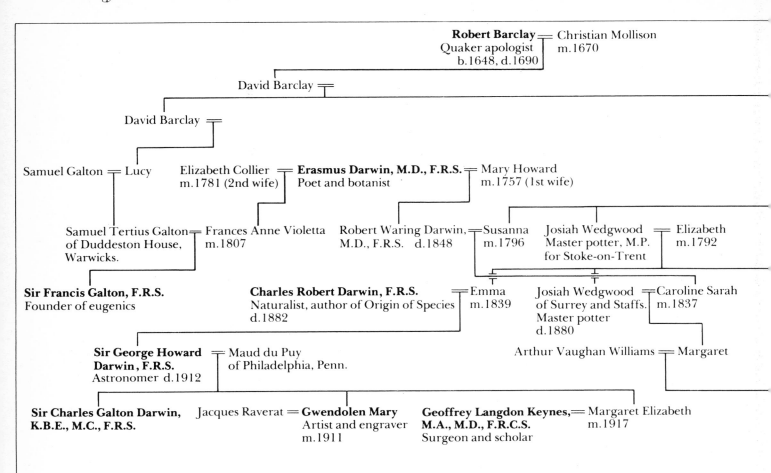

Robert Barclay ═ Christian Mollison
Quaker apologist   m.1670
b.1648, d.1690

David Barclay ═

David Barclay ═

Samuel Galton ═ Lucy   Elizabeth Collier ═ **Erasmus Darwin, M.D., F.R.S.** ═ Mary Howard
m.1781 (2nd wife)   Poet and botanist   m.1757 (1st wife)

Samuel Tertius Galton ═ Frances Anne Violetta   Robert Waring Darwin, ═ Susanna   Josiah Wedgwood ═ Elizabeth
of Duddeston House,   m.1807   M.D., F.R.S. d.1848   m.1796   Master potter, M.P.   m.1792
Warwicks.   for Stoke-on-Trent

Sir Francis Galton, F.R.S.   **Charles Robert Darwin, F.R.S.** ═ Emma   Josiah Wedgwood ═ Caroline Sarah
Founder of eugenics   Naturalist, author of Origin of Species   m.1839   of Surrey and Staffs.   m.1837
d.1882   Master potter
d.1880

Sir George Howard ═ Maud du Puy   Arthur Vaughan Williams ═ Margaret
Darwin, F.R.S.   of Philadelphia, Penn.
Astronomer d.1912

Sir Charles Galton Darwin,   Jacques Raverat ═ **Gwendolen Mary**   **Geoffrey Langdon Keynes,** ═ Margaret Elizabeth
K.B.E., M.C., F.R.S.   Artist and engraver   **M.A., M.D., F.R.C.S.**   m.1917
m.1911   Surgeon and scholar

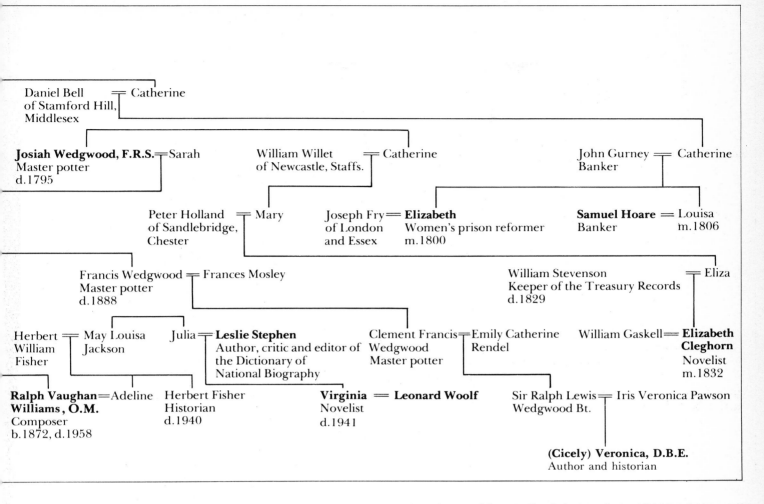

Above. *Heredity or environment? Sir Francis Galton, founder of the study of eugenics, believed that exceptional ability is inherited, and his own family connections provide interesting support for his argument.*

Left. *Family likenesses. The inheritance of family features is strikingly illustrated in these two pictures of Virginia Woolf and her mother. Virginia's mother, Julia (née Jackson), first married Herbert Duckworth. Virginia was born of her second marriage, to Sir Leslie Stephen, author, critic and editor of the* Dictionary of National Biography. *Mrs. Duckworth (left) was photographed by Julia Margaret Cameron, Virginia Woolf by C. C. Beresford.*

Family history is also the working tool of the student of eugenics (hereditary ability). In the nineteenth century the founder of this school, Sir Francis Galton, used examples of families with exceptional skills to further his argument. For instance, he showed that the Bachs exhibited high musical ability over eight generations from 1550, more than twenty individuals being famous musicians in the space of five generations. He also traced the pedigrees of elected Fellows of the Royal Society to discover the incidence of scientific genius amongst them, and might well have included his own, which showed not only links with the Darwins, but with bankers, industrialists, Quakers, educationalists, and writers, many of whom were distinguished in their own fields.

The term eugenics has fallen out of use nowadays, largely because of its association with Nazi notions about breeding a master race, but geneticists have continued to do much useful work in predicting the incidence of physical and mental defects and abnormalities, and of disease and possible resistance to it, by tracing family histories of those already affected. Insanity, haemophilia, porphyria, Huntington's chorea, diabetes, congenital blindness and deafness have been studied in this way, with valuable results. Geneticists can also predict the occurrence of twinning, and characteristics such as eye colouring, facial structure and baldness, by working on the genealogies of prospective parents.

2 Tracing your Ancestors

My father told me that my ancestors supplied shire horses to Queen Boadicea; that may be so, for all I can tell. More plausible was the information that our forebears were farmers in Co. Durham, and that for several generations the first son was always given the father's Christian names. My father showed me a broken decorated clay pipe, and a piece of ancient inscribed rubble which his father had brought back from Mesopotamia during the First World War. He told me about his own Sunderland childhood, his travels in South America when he was apprenticed to the Merchant Navy, and life on the family farm. I never paid much attention to his stories, but when he died and my mother and I went through his effects, we found albums full of unascribed and undated photographs, postcards he had received since childhood, diaries which he had kept for most of his life, medals, Highland Show judge's badges, Observer Corps badges, a Blood Donor's Gold Medal, his first driving licence, old Post Office savings books, his Penny Premium Insurance Policy, ration books and all his papers relating to the numerous societies and committees to which he had belonged. It was too late then to record what he could remember, and I have regretted it ever since, because in the days when he was ill he liked to recall the past. It was a salutary lesson to me not to put off till tomorrow what can be done today. As it is, I know a lot about other people's families but very little of my own.

While it can be interesting to read or hear about other people's genealogies, your own is personal to yourself—but which line do you try to trace? Usually it is the paternal line, because that is the surname you bear, though there is nothing to prevent you from searching for your mother's or your grandmother's antecedents. For convenience, it is better to concentrate on one family at a time.

Talking to Relatives

Begin by obtaining as much information as possible about your family from relatives, for they may produce a wealth of anecdotes and facts, family heirlooms and papers which can contribute much to the basic groundwork. One of the family may have already tried to discover the family's history, and have drawn up a pedigree chart of names and

The family tree of the Greens of Pavement (or Padmire) End, Grasmere. This pictorial tree was made nearly 100 years ago, and is now in the possession of Mr and Miss Rees-Davies of Taunton, Somerset, who are direct descendants of the Greens. Such a document, handed down within a family, can be invaluable as a starting-point for further research. Further records of the Green family, found through the clues on this pedigree, are printed below on pp. 39, 46 and 102.

The local school can be a valuable resource. The village school at Grasmere had no record of Greens of obvious relationship to this family among its pupils, but the school log-book's entry on Ada Usher (left) is a characteristic example of the rich details that school records can reveal. The photograph of the boys of the school in about 1887 (right), with the Headmaster, William Fuller, was kindly lent by Mrs Lena Parker, a local resident.

dates. Even though this may not be complete, or even reliable, it will at least be a guide for your own researches.

The first thing to do is to make a list of your known relatives, and write to each in turn, stating your interest in the family's history, and what you know already. Where possible ask to visit them to talk about the family, and ask to look at any papers, photographs, and mementos which might yield clues. Suggest a date for the visit and always enclose a stamped self-addressed envelope for a reply. Some members of the family may be reluctant to discuss such matters, or be completely uninterested, so that tact may be needed, and the sense to abandon the attempt if it becomes obvious that your approaches are not welcomed.

When talking to relatives it is important to coax out of them the essential data of the names, dates and places of birth, marriage, and death of each person discussed, whether they still have surviving descendants (and if so where they live), and what was their religious denomination, education and employment. It is this which will form the basis of the family tree, and on which you will rely for clues to source material like birth, marriage and death certificates, parish registers and wills. Dates and names may be inaccurate, but at least they can be checked against official documents if you know the places where your kinsmen lived and died, or the approximate year of birth, marriage or death. Relationships may also be confused and generations mixed up. It is therefore essential to talk to as many relatives as possible, because discrepancies may be resolved by further questioning of other relatives. Remember, though, that each person will tell you only what he wants to, and recollection of events of perhaps fifty years ago may be shaky. By talking to as many relatives as you can you should obtain a very detailed picture of the family's more recent history, probably spiced with lively anecdotes that bring the characters to life.

How do you record this information? Tape recorders can be inhibiting to a speaker not accustomed to their use, and an unaccomplished operator can make the situation worse. The thought of a record which can be played back is intimidating to some, but can also lead to garrulousness, which is equally disastrous. On the other hand, a recording does afford a sound archive. A small notebook is probably a better aid: it is unobtrusive, and you need only jot down names, dates and relationships, to be written out more fully when you are alone.

A skilful interviewer will have compiled a list of topics he wants discussed and will ensure that they are included in the course of the conversation. He may take along photographs of his own immediate family to encourage response, and exchange anecdotes about the old days, or past family celebrations and family characters. At the top of your account of each conversation do not forget to give the name and address of your informant and the date of the meeting, so that you know your source and can refer back to him later if necessary.

Having obtained your information, sort through it and try to construct a pictorial chart marking out each generation and incorporating the names, dates, places and other facts you have collected so far. Make a list of uncertainties which might be clarified by a second visit, and circulate a copy of this chart to each of your informants. It is surprising how it will jog memories into recalling more details, and correcting errors like nicknames substituted for baptismal ones. It is also a good

Above. *The kitchen at Townend, Troutbeck, Cumbria. This house contains a great deal of carved and fitted furniture made by the Brownes, a yeoman family, whose home it was at least from 1525 until 1944. (Photo: The National Trust)*

Below. *A modern photograph of the front of Pavement End, Grasmere, former home of the Green family. (Photo: Sanderson & Dixon Ltd., Ambleside)*

way of thanking your relatives for their help.

If you have no surviving relatives you will almost certainly have some leads to follow. For example, your parents may have told you something of their background, such as their birthplaces or where they spent their childhood: it is a good idea to visit these places, and to inspect the cemetery for gravestones erected to the family, and to study the Electoral Roll, usually found hanging in the church porch, to see if anyone of the same surname still resides there, and to arrange to call on them. Look at the local telephone directories to discover the distribution of the surname in the area, for the family may not have moved far away. Ask in the local hostelry if any of the older people remember the family, and if you know the street or house where they lived, ask the present occupants and neighbours for information, because they may know of their present whereabouts and still be in contact with them. Advertise in or write a letter to the local newspaper or magazine asking for details. The local Family History Society Journal is also useful for such appeals.

If the surname is unusual you can list all entries of it in the telephone directories covering a much wider area, and write a letter along the lines suggested before, detailing your own knowledge about the family and asking for further information. You may well discover kinsmen in this way.

The Attic Archivist

Visits to relatives give the perfect opportunity to examine family papers and ephemera such as wedding invitations, In Memoriam cards, postcards, letters, newspaper cuttings (often undated), family scrapbooks, photographs, the Family Bible, school certificates, war call-up papers, passports, prizes, children's handiwork, medals, badges, diaries, old parish magazines, embroideries, heirlooms, and woodwork—each with its own tale to tell.

A Family Bible was often presented by the parents of one of the parties on the occasion of their marriage, and in it were recorded the names of offspring and their dates (though often not the places) of birth, and their subsequent marriages and deaths. A photograph album may contain a feast of portraits, often entirely undated and unidentified. This is your opportunity to ensure that they are identified and dated, and to ask if you can make copies of them. Do not forget to label these copies, plus the name of the person from whom you borrowed the originals. Try also to make copies of other family archives, so that you can refer to them at leisure, and build up a centralized family record.

If one of your relatives lives in the old family home then there is a good chance that there lies a goldmine of information, not only in papers but also in the house furnishings. Ask if anyone else in the village or community has old photographs, for these may well supplement the collection, and may include views of the street or vicinity as it once was. Photograph the outside of the house as it is now, and the street in which it lies, because this will be of interest to your descendants one day. The local reference library may also have special collections of old photographs, and similarly if the school is an old one there may be old school photographs of pupils, including your relatives.

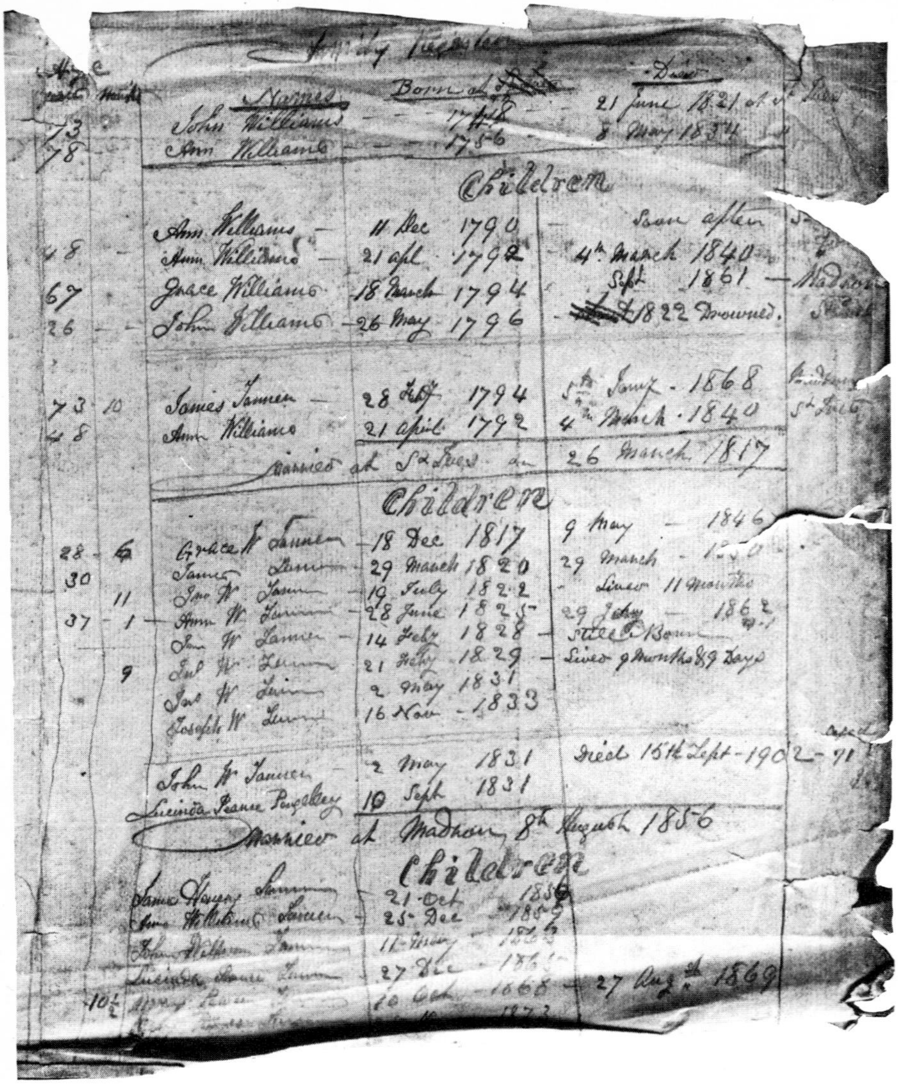

Family Register

Age		Names	Born	Died
73		John Williams	1748	21 June 1821
78		Ann Williams	1756	8 May 1834

Children

Age		Names	Born	Died
		Ann Williams	11 Dec 1790	Soon after
48		Ann Williams	21 April 1792	4th March 1840
67		Grace Williams	18 March 1794	Sept 1861
26		John Williams	26 May 1796	1822 Drowned
73	10	James Tanner	28 Feby 1794	5th Jany 1868
48		Ann Williams	21 April 1792	4th March 1840

Married at St Ives on 26 March 1817

Children

Age		Names	Born	Died
28	6	Grace W Tanner	18 Dec 1817	9 May 1846
30		James Tanner	29 March 1820	29 March 1850
	11	Jno W Tanner	19 July 1822	Lived 11 months
37	1	Ann W Tanner	28 June 1825	29 July 1862
		Jno W Tanner	14 Feby 1828	Still Born
	9	Jul W Tanner	21 Feby 1829	Lived 9 Months 29 Days
		Jno W Tanner	2 May 1831	
		Joseph W Tanner	16 Nov 1833	
		John W Tanner	2 May 1831	Died 15th Sept 1902
		Lucinda Pearce Pengelley	10 Sept 1831	

Married at Madron 8th August 1856

Children

Age	Names	Born	Died
	James Harvey Tanner	21 Oct 1858	
	Ann Williams Tanner	25 Dec 1859	
	John William Tanner	11 May	
	Lucinda Pearce Tanner	27 Dec 1861	
10½	Mary Pearce	10 Oct 1868	27 Aug 1869

Part of the Family Register in the family Bible of the Tanners, a family from St Ives in Cornwall. As the Register records, James Tanner married Ann Williams at St Ives on 26 March 1817. Further documents reproduced below follow the fortunes of members of the Tanner family (see pp. 34, 80, 116, 130), and you will notice also that some anomalies exist in the records (see p. 34). The Bible is now in the possession of a male line descendant living in Canada; another descendant, Mrs Peggy Norman of Middlesex, has had copies of each page made for her own archive, and several other documents reproduced in this book are from Mrs Norman's archive.

You are now beginning to put flesh onto the bare bones of the pedigree chart, by making the people come alive through the things which they treasured and wished to keep, and those which they forgot to discard. You should also now be able to amplify the information given orally.

Has it Been Done Before?

Even if no one in the family has tried to trace your ancestry, someone else may have done. You can check if this might be the case by referring to G. W. Marshall's *The Genealogist's Guide*, published in 1903, brought further up-to-date in 1953 by J. B. Whitmore as *A Genealogical Guide*, and in 1977 by G. B. Barrow, under its original title. These list known printed pedigrees and family histories in the British Isles. There is also T. R. Thomson's *Catalogue of British Family Histories*, brought up to date in 1976, and M. Stuart's *Scottish Family History*, published in 1930. In 1892 G. Gatfield compiled a *Guide to Printed Books and Manuscripts Relating to English and Foreign Heraldry and Genealogy*, and in 1965 F. R. Pryce published in a limited edition his thesis: *A Guide to European Genealogies Exclusive of the British Isles*. The Library of Congress in Washington has also printed a series of catalogues to American and

English genealogies in its possession. Many of the national and state historical and genealogical societies maintain libraries which hold manuscript pedigrees that do not appear in any published catalogue.

The quality of printed and manuscript pedigrees varies enormously, and they should always be treated with caution. However, they can be used as a basic guide for your own researches.

Cottages in Back Street East, St Ives, photographed around 1900. James Tanner is recorded in the 1861 Census as living in Back Street, and the scene will have changed little since he lived there. (Photo: Studio St Ives Ltd)

Central Registration

At this point, you will have exhausted your own family's archival resources and will have checked on possible printed and manuscript pedigrees. You now have to build on this knowledge by checking the earliest date you have found against official documents, and by filling in the gaps in subsequent generations. It is wise not to attempt too much at once, and I would advise that you concentrate on extending your pedigree backwards before returning to complete the later stages. The earliest date probably lies within the period of central registration of births, marriages and deaths, and in this case you need to obtain a sequence of birth, marriage and death certificates.

In England and Wales central registration of births, marriages and deaths began on 1 July 1837, and the records are held at the General Register Office in London. It is open Monday to Friday, but only the indexes are available to the public. It costs nothing to look through them, but a copy of each certificate will only be issued on payment of a fee. Postal inquiries can be dealt with for searches of restricted periods.

Central registration of births, marriages and deaths began in Scotland on 1 January 1855, and in Ireland on 1 January 1864 (although non-Catholic marriages were registered from 1 April 1845). You can search not only the indexes but also the actual registers containing the certified entries, in New Register House, in Edinburgh, on payment of a search fee. Records covering all Ireland up to 31 December 1921 are held at the General Register Office, Custom House, Dublin, and for Northern Ireland from 1 January 1922 at the General Register Office, Belfast.

The separate indexes of births, marriages and deaths at the General Register Office are arranged alphabetically, by quarter of the year, listing surname, Christian name(s), and registration district. This information is followed by the current registration district number and the page on which the relevant entry falls. All these details must be included on the application form for the issue of a certificate.

Your first search is likely to be for birth certificates, and there are certain points which you should bear in mind when searching the indexes to them. Firstly, the births had to be registered with the District Registrar where they occurred, which may not have been the parents' normal neighbourhood. Secondly, the birth had to be registered within thirty days, and thus may have been registered too late for inclusion in the index of the quarter in which it actually occurred, so do look in the subsequent index. Thirdly, Christian names in the index are not always a reliable guide: the names may be in reverse order to those by which the person was later known; names may have been dropped or added

Above left. The birth certificate of James, born 21 October 1856 in Penzance to Lucinda Pengilly, at that time unmarried. Lucinda later married John Williams Tanner and produced several more children, as can be seen from the page of the family Bible (p. 32 above). Note that there is an anomaly between the date of her marriage, recorded in the Bible as 8 August 1856, and the fact that the baby James, born on 21 October 1856, is officially registered as being fatherless. According to the General Register Office records, she in fact married on 8 August 1859. Her children recorded on her tombstone that she was 'the best of mothers'.

later, and thus differ from those on the birth certificate; the name you know a person by may only be a nickname; the child may have been registered under names which were subsequently altered at baptism (the certificate will advise you of this, but not the index); or a child may have been registered merely as 'male' or 'female'.

If you cannot identify the certificate you are searching for, possible causes should be considered. The parents may have defaulted in their duty to register their infant's birth, or the District Registrar may have omitted to copy the entry into his quarterly returns to the Registrar General in London. If you know where the child was born it would be sensible to write to the local District Registrar to see whether this was the case. You may have been given the wrong date of birth, and if so you should try scanning the indexes three years on either side of the alleged date. The birth may have been registered under a variant spelling of the surname, and again you should check all possible variations, making a note of those you have looked at. Finally, the child may have been registered under the mother's surname, either as an illegitimate off-spring, or as the fruit of an adulterous union during a previous existing marriage.

If you still have no success, then search a ten-year period around the expected year of birth and note all entries of the surname and its variants registered in the most likely district and apply for the certificate nearest to that date, requesting a check against the parents' names. A fee is still payable for such checks, but this will not be as costly as obtaining a certificate. After 1911 the birth indexes contain the former name of the mother.

The birth certificate itself gives the date and place of birth, the registered names of the child, its sex, parentage (including the mother's maiden or former name if married previously), the father's occupation, and the name and residence of the informant, who was usually a parent. This address may differ from the birthplace. The certificate therefore takes you back one more generation because it identifies the child's parents and introduces the mother's previous surname.

There is a separate series of Adoption certificates, dating from 1927, and indexed. Only the date of birth is given on the certificate, with the date of adoption, names of adoptive parents and the child's adoptive names.

Above. *A typical birth certificate. Frederick William Cowen was the great-grandfather of Geoff Cowen, Phaidon Press's sales manager. Note that Hannah Cowen was illiterate and signed her name with a mark. The birth certificate identifies both parents, thus enabling you to track down their marriage certificate.*

Below. *The marriage certificate of David Cowen and Hannah Geddes, who had been identified on their son's birth certificate reproduced above. This certificate identifies the fathers of both parties and gives their professions, thus taking the search for ancestors back one stage further. The details of the ages of the couple are in this case not very useful. David and Hannah Cowen are pictured below right, some years after their marriage.*

Irish birth certificates follow the English model, while the Scottish certificates are much more detailed. In 1855 only, the birth certificate gave, in addition to the names of the child's parents, their ages and birthplaces, their date and place of marriage, and whether there were any other offspring. These data were subsequently modified in 1856, omitting details of birth and marriage of the parents, and the totals of previous children. In 1861 the date and place of marriage were restored.

Generally the information on certificates in other countries varies between the English and the Scottish models. British subjects born in the colonies will be registered in those countries, but if they were born elsewhere they should have been registered with the British Consul, and the indexes to Consular Returns of births, marriages and deaths can be seen at the General Register Office in London, dating from 1849. If births abroad are not found in these indexes, then the corresponding Registration Offices of the countries concerned will have to be approached. Similar indexes to marine births and deaths covering both the Royal and merchant naval vessels begin in 1837, and Regimental Register indexes in 1761. The certificates contain the same details as the English ones. The combined births and baptisms, marriages, and combined deaths and burials of the British in India are recorded in the Ecclesiastical Returns at the India Office Library, in London, organized under the three presidencies and commencing in the late seventeenth century.

Just as the birth certificate gives the parents' names, the marriage certificate also yields essential genealogical clues. The quarterly registration marriage indexes are arranged by surname, Christian names, registration district, district number and page on which the marriage was registered. You need to look under both surnames to be sure that the details tally exactly, although after 1911 the indexes include a cross-reference to the surname and initials of the spouse against each entry. When searching marriage indexes it is a good idea to cover a period of at least fifteen years, and to note down the surname variants searched, and likely entries found but not matched with the expected surname of the spouse. If this fails, look at the indexes for the years after

[Printed by authority of the Registrar General]
CERTIFIED COPY of an **ENTRY OF MARRIAGE**
Pursuant to the **Marriage Act 1949**

T C 217531

M. Cert.
S.R.

Registration District			Oxford				
1852. Marriage solemnized at in the Register Office in the							
District of Oxford in the County of Oxford							

No.	When married	Name and surname	Age	Condition	Rank or profession	Residence at the time of marriage	Father's name and surname	Rank or profession of father
146	Second day of February 1852	Henry Francis Harris	Twenty one	Bachelor	Tailor	Church Street St. Ebbes	John Harris	Carpenter
		Ann Pavier	Twenty one	Spinster	—	Speedwel Street St. Ebbes	Charles Pavier	Smith

Married in the Register Office by before by me,

This marriage was solemnized between us { Henry Francis Harris / X The mark of Ann Pavier } in the presence of us { James Deacon / X The mark of Ann Maria Watson }

Henry Hatch
Registrar
John Thos. Dobney
Supt. Regr.

Certified to be a true copy of an entry in a register in my custody,

H. Wood Superintendent Registrar

30 MAR 1978 Date

CAUTION:—Any person who (1) falsifies any of the particulars on this certificate, or (2) uses a falsified certificate as true, knowing it to be false, is liable to prosecution.

An Oxford wedding, between Henry Harris and Ann Pavier. The Harrises were a family of Oxford tradesmen, one of whose descendants, Colin Harris, has traced the family back to the late eighteenth century. Colin, who works at the Bodleian Library at Oxford, is Henry Harris's great-great-grandson (see below, p. 78). This certificate was obtained from the local registry in Oxford, not from the General Register Office in London. It is common for certified copies of certificates to be typed these days. Further documents from Colin Harris's archive, tracing the history of the family, are reproduced on pp. 37, 101 and 108 below.

the birth of the child in case the marriage took place later.

Points to bear in mind when searching marriage indexes are to look under the less common of the two surnames, or the less common Christian name, to remember to search under surname variants, and to allow for the use of additional Christian names, or variants of the ones which appeared on the birth certificates of their children. For example, Ellen may be substituted for Helen; Herbert Ernest (according to the infant's birth certificate) may be rendered Ernest Herbert or Herbert only at the time of his marriage.

The former name of the mother, as recorded on the child's birth certificate, may not be the name under which she appears on a marriage certificate, for she may have been married before, yet remarried under her maiden name. This is one reason why you may initially fail to locate the expected entry in the index. However, if you think that the index entry of one of the parties is correct, based on the registration district, or the date, or the name itself, it is always worth applying for the marriage certificate to discover the name of the spouse. Other reasons for failing to find the entry are that the parents were not in fact married; or that the union was only a common law one; or that the couple were married abroad (especially if the husband was in the Armed Forces or was engaged in trade overseas). There are separate indexes relating to marriages celebrated at sea and registered at the port of arrival, to those registered with the British Consul, and to those of Army personnel, and the same applies to births and deaths.

A marriage certificate gives the date and place of the ceremony (Church or Register Office), whether it was after banns, by licence, or registrar's certificate, and who performed the marriage. If it was a Church wedding, the denomination is given. The names, ages, current marital status, occupations and residences of groom and bride are supplemented by the names and occupations of their fathers. Finally, the names of at least two witnesses, often relatives, are included. When the bride was a widow you may thus discover both her former married name and her maiden name.

Ages may be inaccurately given on marriage certificates, perhaps out of deference to a much younger spouse, or because one party was still a minor and marrying without parental consent. The bald description 'of full age' merely indicates that a person was over the age of twenty-one. Divorced people could describe their marital status as single, and the

DIED IN HIS CHAIR.

MAN OF 90 WHO REFUSED AID.

Dr. Galpin (the City Coroner) and a jury enquired at the Settling Room, Oxford, on Tuesday afternoon into the circumstances of the death of Henry Francis Harris, aged 91, which occurred at 23, Albert Street, Jericho, on Monday. Deceased, it was stated, had always refused medical attention.

George James Harris, electrician, of 160, Wanstone Park Road, Ilford, Essex, son of the deceased, said he was informed the previous day of the sudden death of his father, whom he last saw in June of this year. Deceased had generally been a healthy man, and had always evinced a strong objection to being medically attended.

Isabella Elizabeth Saxton, widow, of 23, Albert Street, Jericho, Oxford, said deceased had lodged at her house for fifteen months past. He had appeared to be a very healthy man. On Monday he got up about 9.30 a.m. and had a cup of cocoa for breakfast. Then he complained of shortness of breath, that he could not hear, and that he had pains in his stomach. He sat in his chair before the fire the whole of the morning, and died in that position about 2.40 in the afternoon. Witness had several times asked him to see a doctor, but he never would, and he would never take medicine.

Dr. Sankey deposed that he was asked to see the body after death. He had made a post-mortem examination, and found that death resulted from heart failure, due to intestinal obstruction following cancer of the bowels.

A verdict was returned in accordance with the medical evidence.

Henry Harris in retirement in 1907, aged about 79, photographed by Henry Taunt, a famous Oxford photographer. Surviving members of the family were somewhat reticent in talking to Colin Harris about old Henry Harris, and it appears that he was generally regarded as a ne'er-do-well and a bit of a rogue and vagabond. (Photo: The Bryan Brown Collection)

only means of telling whether either party was divorced would be by having a search made of the records of divorce, at Somerset House, in London, dating from 1857. A coincidence of address, far removed from the couple's known place of origin, may suggest that they were in lodgings of convenience to fulfil the four weeks' residence requirements for marriage in the local church. The father of one of the parties might be dead at the time of his child's marriage, but this may not be stated on the certificate. If a person was adopted, the father named on the certificate will not be the true father, and this can complicate the next stage of research.

The information on Irish marriage certificates is similar to the English and Welsh, while the Scottish ones contain the names of both sets of parents; those for 1855 also give the present and usual address of the couple, and details of former marriages and any offspring.

The third category of document is the death certificate. The quarterly indexes of deaths in the General Register Office in London are arranged by surname, Christian names, registration district, district number, and page reference to the certified entry. From 1866 the indexes add the age at death, as given by the informant; this may not be accurate. From 1969 the date of birth, if known, is given.

Death certificates can be very useful, for they give not only the approximate year of birth, but also the occupation, current marital status if a woman, parentage if a minor, and also the name, address and relationship of the informant to the deceased. The date, place and cause of death are given, which will lead to the most likely place of burial, and perhaps to a gravestone which might yield further clues about origins and career. If the death was sudden a coroner's inquest may have been held, and there should be a note to this effect on the certificate. Details of the inquest would have appeared in the current local newspaper. Once you know the date of death it is always a good idea anyway to consult the local newspaper for a death notice and obituary.

Irish death certificates follow the English pattern, but Scottish certificates give not only the names of the deceased's parents, but also that of any spouse. In 1855 data about birthplace, residence, marriage and named issue, with their ages, were also supplied. Australian death certificates add details of burial, and include names, ages, and deaths of offspring, the name of the spouse, length of the marriage, and the place where it was solemnized, the length of the stay in the state, the deceased's birthplace, and names and birthplaces of both parents.

The death of Henry Harris in 1919 at the age of 91 (although his marriage certificate—see above—would indicate that he was only 89). The certificate (right) reports that an inquest was held, and Colin Harris was able to find a report of the inquest in the Oxford Chronicle *for 19 December 1919 (left), which reveals the existence of a son, George James Harris.*

[Printed by authority of the Registrar General.]

CERTIFIED COPY of an ENTRY OF DEATH
Pursuant to the Births and Deaths Registration Act 1953

HB 955492

D. Cert.
S.R.

Registration District				Oxford				
1 919 . Death in the Sub-district of				Oxford	in the	County of Oxford		
Columns:— 1	2	3	4	5	6	7	8	9
No.	When and where died	Name and surname	Sex	Age	Occupation	Cause of death	Signature, description, and residence of informant	When registered	Signature of registrar
445	15th December 1919 23 Albert Street, Saint Thomas Oxford U.D.	Henry Francis Harris	Male	91 years	Tailor (Retired)	Natural causes viz: Heart failure due to intestinal obstruction following cancer of the bowel.	Certificate received from Henry F. Galpin, Coroner for the City of Oxford. Inquest held Sixteenth December 1919	Seventeenth December 1919	Walter Allen Butler *Registrar.*	———

Certified to be a true copy of an entry in a register in my custody.

.... H. Wood ....Superintendent Registrar.

.... 3 0 MAR 1978 ....Date.

CAUTION:—Any person who (1) falsifies any of the particulars on this certificate, or (2) uses a falsified certificate as true, knowing it to be false, is liable to prosecution.

American death certificates similarly give the birthplace not only of the deceased but of both parents. Thus death certificates abroad can be an important source for the genealogist, as they may give an immigrant's place of origin, as well as details about his immediate family. However, there is a wide disparity in commencement of central registration in other states, and adequate systems do not exist throughout the world.

The Census

The next stage is to look at the Census returns for the whole family unit, and as these records often predate central registration or provide information beyond it, they are an extremely important source.

The Census returns reveal the names of everyone who was in a particular house on the night when it was taken, plus each person's occupation, age, birthplace, and relationship to the head of the household. If you know that your ancestors lived in a particular town, village or hamlet round about a Census year (a birth, marriage or death certificate is the most obvious clue), then you may find the entire family unit at that address. By searching the Census of the whole community other members of the family, of a different generation, or its collaterals, may be found. As the Census was taken every ten years you may succeed in finding the family at a later or earlier date than other records have led you to. Next to the records of central registration, the Census returns are the most productive source for family history in the nineteenth century.

What is a Census? It is a complete count of the population of a given country on a certain day, taken by specially appointed enumerators whose duty it is to deliver schedules to each household in their quota for completion by its head. After the night of the Census the schedules are collected up and handed to the District Registrar for enrolment in Census Register Books. Those for England and Wales are forwarded to the Registrar General in London. Microfilm copies of past Censuses can be searched at the Public Record Office in London. Many County Record Offices and libraries have purchased the microfilms of their own area.

In the United Kingdom the Census was first taken in 1801 to discover the total male and female population distribution over town, village and hamlet, the number of inhabited and uninhabited houses, the number of families occupying each house, and lastly the totals of those employed in agriculture, trade, crafts and manufacturing industries. A complete Census has been taken every ten years since then, with the exception of 1941, but only those from 1841 onwards contain names.

In North America the European colonists took population counts for mercantile reasons, for example in Virginia in 1624, and in New France in 1666. Provision for a ten-yearly federal Census was made in the United States of America in 1790, as an aid to a more equitable distribution of taxation and government representation. It was not until 1850 that more than the name of the head of each household in

Right. Part of the 1851 Grasmere Census showing the household of John Green at Pavement End. John Green was a substantial farmer (see also p. 102 below), employing four labourers, and his two sons were in related trades. One son had married a girl from Lancashire, and one would guess from the grandson's name that her maiden name was Elizabeth Smith. A search of the parish registers or of marriage indexes in the General Register Office would in all probability locate a marriage between Daniel Green and Elizabeth Smith at either Revington or Bury some time in the 1840s. The birth entries of all the family could easily be traced in the relevant parish registers.

Below. Old Pavement End. The date of this photograph is not known (except that it was before 1925, when alterations were made), but this view of the back yard is substantially as it must have been at the time of the 1851 Census. The name was originally Padmire End (or 'Paide Mirende' in a document of 1810), but was changed to Pavement End some time in the second quarter of the 19th century. (Photo: property of Mrs Lena Parker, Grasmere)

No. of House	Name of Street, Place, or Road, and Name or No. of House	Name and Surname of each Person who abode in the house, on the Night of the 30th March, 1851	Relation to Head of Family	Condition	Age of Males	Age of Females	Rank, Profession, or Occupation	Where Born	Whether Blind, or Deaf-and-Dumb
6	Kilbarrow	Jane Eliz.th Gibson	Head	Widow		53	Landed proprietor & fund holder	Yorkshire Malton	
		Henrietta Charl.tte D.o	Daur	U		23	Fund holder	D.o Queensmoupark	
		Eliz.th Anne D.o	Daur	U		20		D.o D.o	
		George D.o	Son	U	19			D.o D.o	
		Jane Bowes	Serv	U		56	Cook	Cumberland Cockermouth	
		Jessie Bowdfoot	D.o	U		29	Lady's Maid	Scotland	
		Mary Dixon	D.o	U		25	House Maid	Lancashire Hawkshead	
		Anthony Wilson	D.o	U	16		Helper	Westmorland Grasmere	
	Two Houses uninhabited								
7	Pavement	Thomas Dover	Head	Mar	25		Coachman	Yorkshire Sedbergh	
		Rebecca D.o	Wife	Mar		30	Dressmaker	Westmorland Lupton	
		William D.o	Son		2			D.o Kirby Lonsdale	
		Elizabeth Saw	Apprentice	U		14	Dressmaker	D.o Docker	
8	Pavement End	John Green	Head	Mar	62		Farmer of 226 acres & Labourer	Westmorland Grasmere	
		Betty D.o	Wife	Mar		59	Farmers Wife	D.o D.o	
		John D.o	Son	Mar	36		Land Surveyor	D.o D.o	
		Daniel Green	Son	Unmar	31		Flour Dealer	D.o D.o	
		Elizabeth Green	Daur in law	Mar		28		Lancashire Rivington	
		John Smith D.o	Grandson		2½			D.o Bury	
		Jane Bennett	Serv	U		22	Farm Serv.t	Cumberland Boston	
Total of Houses I.3 U.2 B				Total of Persons ...	8	11		⑤	A B—Esq.

each township was given, with only the totals of males and females in each household within classified age groups being recorded. The Canadians instituted a regular ten-yearly Census in 1851, but 1871 was the first occasion when it extended over the whole dominion. In Australia population musters were frequently taken between 1788 and 1859, and digests of these, arranged alphabetically, can be seen in the Public Record Office at Kew. The first regular Census was taken of New South Wales in 1828 (see below, p. 41), but was not countrywide until 1881. The Census was then taken every ten years until 1921, subsequent ones being intermittent. In South Africa the first official Census was taken in the Cape of Good Hope in 1865, but the first to embrace all four colonies was in 1904. European Censuses begin at different dates. Among the earliest and best returns are those of the Scandinavian countries, Sweden, Finland and Denmark, while Russia was the last major European power to institute the Census, in 1897.

The English and Welsh Census returns can be searched once they are over 100 years old. The date of the first official Census to contain names was 7 June 1841, and the subsequent available Censuses were taken on 30 March 1851, 7 April 1861 and 2 April 1871. Those for 1881, 1891 and 1901 can be searched for you by the Registrar General's office on application and payment of a fee, but you will need to provide the exact address. The Irish Census returns between 1861 and 1891 were almost all destroyed by fire in 1922, but the surviving returns up to 1911 can be examined at the Public Record Office in Dublin. Scottish Census returns to 1891 are available to the public, and can be seen in the New Register House, in Edinburgh.

The means of reference to the microfilms of the English and Welsh Returns are by the place-name indexes for each Census. Additionally there may be a street index if the place was one of the larger towns or cities, and this will pinpoint exactly an address on the microfilm. When you merely know the town or city where an individual lived it might be worth looking at a contemporary directory, which will list many of its inhabitants and their addresses, before attempting the search.

The 1841 Census was organized by town, village or hamlet. Under each household it gave every person's name, age (rounded down to the nearest five years, so that a person of seventy-eight would be described as seventy-five and a person of twenty-nine would be given as twenty-five, except those under fifteen whose ages were precisely stated), occupation, and whether born in the county, and if not, whether born in Scotland (S), Ireland (I), or foreign parts (F). Rarely was the name or number of the house given. From 1851 onwards exact addresses, relationship of each person to the head of the house, marital status, exact age, occupation, and birthplace, including county, were supplied, plus details of any defect of deafness, dumbness, blindness or idiocy. Religious denomination was not indicated.

There are several points to look out for in searching Census returns. If you cannot find the family at a specific address, look at the rest of the street and its neighbourhood, for it may have changed lodgings, or be absent visiting friends nearby. If the village or hamlet is unsuccessfully searched, look at the returns of those adjacent to it, for the family may not have travelled far, or you may find others of the same surname which may indicate that this was the family's home.

Ages may be inaccurate in Census returns, for instance where there was a considerable age gap between the head and his wife, or where he merely estimated the age of an elderly relative. Birthplaces again are not always accurate, and are not necessarily the place of baptism. If you search a sequence of Census returns you may find ages and birthplaces differ from Census to Census. The birthplaces and ages of elderly relatives are a guide to those of the parents of the head of the house. The relationship of each of those in the household was to the head, not the person next above in the list.

When looking at a particular place note down all the other people of the same surname dwelling there, for parents or brothers and sisters could well be living nearby. If you cannot find your known forebears in one Census, a search of the earlier Census of the birthplace of those of the same generation might locate the person you seek. It may be that your antecedent was part of someone else's household, and only a careful search of the Census will ensure that you do not miss this possibility. Apprentices often left home in their early teens. The family itself might have been visiting, perhaps the wife's parents. If you do locate the family itself, look at the contemporary or earlier Census of the head's birthplace to see if his parents still resided there. Note also the variety of occupations in the family, the acreage farmed and employees maintained, and compare them with their neighbours and the rest of the community.

By looking at a sequence of Census returns you can see how a family grew, and contracted as children moved away, or married and set up households of their own. Perhaps elderly relatives moved in to replace them, or the family took in lodgers, or had servants living in. Look at the spacing of the births of their children, some of whom perhaps died in the

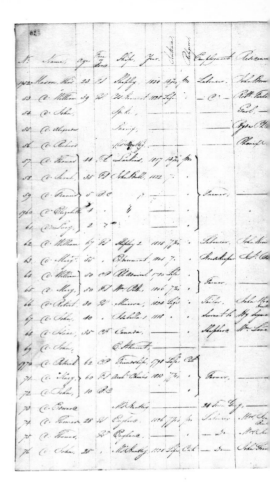

An extract from the 1828 Census of New South Wales in Australia. This Census is most informative, revealing age, status (free or convict), ship, year of arrival, sentence, employment, residence, district, acreage of farms and number of horses, cattle and sheep. From the Census details it is possible to search the ships' musters, which will reveal the date and place of the trial in England. The trial documents can next be looked up, and these will reveal further details about the individual (see below, p. 128). (Kew, Public Record Office, HO 10/24)

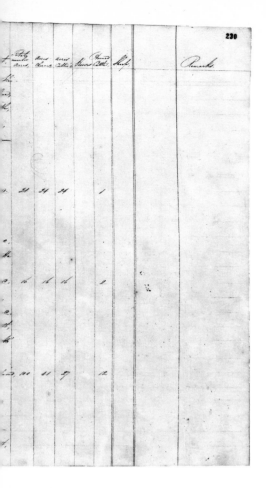

intervening years before the next Census. Did the family move to a more or less salubrious environment? You can tell by the occupations and status of their neighbours. Did the family alter the nature of its business? Try to discover the total population of the community, its chief occupations, and the names of your family's neighbours, who may later be connected by marriage or employment.

The 1828 Census of New South Wales is the most detailed of the colonial Censuses. It records all settlers, convicts and their families, with their ages, occupations, residences, religious denominations, dates of voyage and vessel, and whether they came free, as transportees, or were born in the colony. A copy of this is retained by the Public Record Office at Kew, the originals being in Sydney.

From 1850 the American Census includes the names of everyone in each dwelling in each township. The returns to 1880 are in the National Archives, Washington. They give the age, colour, occupation, state or country of birth and value of real and personal estate of each individual, and also state whether their parents were born abroad, and whether they were married or born during the year of the Census and if so in which month. Details of school attendance during the year, whether literate, whether a male citizen of the United States and if so whether denied the right to vote on other grounds other than rebellion or other crime, are completed by advice as to any disability of hearing, speech, sight or mentality. In 1880 the actual state or country of birth of each person's parents is added.

The Census is a wonderful source for showing the family in its social environment, as well as indicating its composition, mobility, and dates and places of birth. It sets the scene for the next most important class of records, the parish registers.

Parish Registers

The third great resource for genealogists is the local records, the parish registers, and these form the most valuable source prior to July 1837 in England and Wales, for until then it was the incumbent of the parish church who was responsible for the records of baptisms, marriages and burials.

The earliest regular series of parish registers in Europe began in Spain in 1497, and in England and Wales they were introduced in 1538, in Scotland in 1558, and in Ireland in 1634. The vast majority are not extant from the beginning and have gaps, especially during the periods of civil disturbance, such as the Civil War and Commonwealth period, 1645–60. During these years a special official was appointed, known as the Parish Register. He was responsible for recording births, baptisms, deaths and burials, and sometimes was barely literate, or showed little interest in his duties. From 1653 until 1657 only civil marriages were recognized by the state, publication of intention being posted in the church porch or market place for the three weeks prior to the ceremony. Few parish registers contain details of these alliances, but the publications of intent might be recorded. At the restoration of the monarchy in 1660 Commonwealth marriages were officially recognized and occasionally retrospectively entered in the registers. For almost a

generation, between 1645 and 1660, therefore, the registers are likely to be defective. From 1660 they are usually much more complete. In 1831 a Parish Register Abstract was published, listing extant registers and their earliest surviving entries. Additionally, the Institute of Heraldic and Genealogical Studies, at Canterbury, in Kent, has published a useful series of county maps marking off pre-1837 parish boundaries and giving the dates of the earliest known registers.

Many registers up to 1837 have been deposited in Diocesan and County Record Offices, and there is a published handlist to them, issued by Local Population Studies in 1974, with later supplements. A considerable number have been copied and printed, the Society of Genealogists, in London, maintaining a very good collection of these. The Mormons in America have microfilmed numerous parish registers throughout the world, the entries being subsequently typed out and indexed on a county basis in the case of English registers. These are now on the International Genealogical Index microfiches, available in the Mormons' own libraries, and in England at the Society of Genealogists. Many local Record Offices have purchased microfiches for their own counties. Burials are not included. These indexes, and the printed transcripts of registers, should be used cautiously, for they may contain errors of transcription, abbreviated entries, and omissions.

Where the original registers have not been deposited elsewhere, they will be found in the parish church itself. Statutory fees are normally imposed for searching them, and it is a good idea to agree the sum due with the incumbent before embarking on a costly search. It is advisable always to write to or telephone the incumbent to fix a convenient date to scrutinize his registers.

In Ireland almost 1,000 of those parish registers in the custody of the Public Record Office in Dublin were destroyed by fire in 1922, and the remainder are largely still held by the churches themselves. Scottish parish registers can be consulted in the New Register House, Edinburgh, on payment of a search fee. In Australia parish registers are unlikely to extend much more than about sixty years, or two generations, beyond the period of central registration, and the State Archives Departments have collected in many of them. Relatively few parishes in America maintained a regular series of registers because of their inhabitants' unsettled status. The churches and the county courthouses are the places to look for them. Generally, where they exist, parish registers of the Anglican and other churches abroad, such as in South America and the Caribbean, are still in the custody of the incumbent, but there are transcripts of some of them in the Guildhall Library, London.

Top Left. *The baptism certificate of Elizabeth Gardener, born in Norwich. These certificates are copies from the parish register made onto printed forms and given to the parents to keep as their own record of the baptism. Such certificates will be preserved among your family's papers, not in any public collection.*
Right. *The certificate recording Elizabeth Gardener's marriage to Charles Bryan in 1817, extracted from the parish register and kept by the couple as the proof of their marriage. Elizabeth later married William Randall, whose Naval discharge certificate is reproduced on p. 114 below.*

What do the parish registers contain? Baptisms, marriages and burials were usually entered in the same register until 1753, after which the English and Welsh marriages were recorded in separate registers. In 1813 the baptism and burial registers also divided. Prior to 1813 the baptisms usually include date, and name of each child, plus the names of the parents, occasionally adding their place of residence and the father's occupation or status. From 1813 these details were mandatory.

The Book of Common Prayer specifically states that baptism is to take place on either the first or second Sunday after the birth, or on the religious festival nearest to them, or if not then the nearest convenient

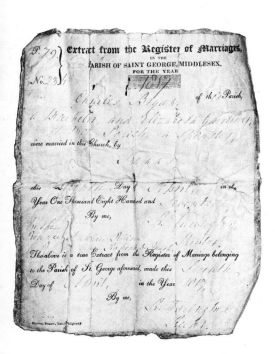

(The Year 1778)　　Page

No
Henry Churchill of [the] Parish of Witney in the County of Oxford and Jane King of [the] Parish were
Married in this [Church] by [Licence] this Seventh Day of May in the Year One Thousand Seven Hundred and Seventy Eight by me Benj. Hallifax [Minister]
This Marriage was solemnized between Us { Henry Churchill / Jane King
In the Presence of { Ja. Turner / Cha. Barry

No
Thomas Kimber of [this] Parish and Elizth Durham of [this] Parish were
Married in this [Church] by [Banns] this Eleventh Day of May in the Year One Thousand Seven Hundred and Seventy Eight by me Geo: Watkin [Min.]
This Marriage was solemnized between Us { Thos Kimber / Eliz Durham
In the Presence of { James Skipton / Hannah Badcock

No
James Appletree of [this] Parish Batchelour and Elizabeth Collier of [this] Parish Widow were
Married in this [Church] by [Licence] this Twenty Fourth Day of May in the Year One Thousand Seven Hundred and Seventy Eight by me Benj. Hallifax [Minister]
This Marriage was solemnized between Us { James Appletree / Eliz Collier
In the Presence of { Eliz. Nichols / Wm Polley

No
Thomas Cooper of [the] Parish of Middleton Cheney Northampton-Shire Butcher and Martha Kirby of [this] Parish were
Married in this [Church] by [Licence] this Twenty third Day of June in the Year One Thousand Seven Hundred and Seventy Eight by me Benj. Hallifax [Minister]
This Marriage was solemnized between Us { Thomas Cooper / Martha Kirby
In the Presence of { Jno Taylor / Christor Eaton

date. The interval between birth and baptism can be much wider than this, and it is a good idea to examine a fifteen-year period around the expected year of birth to allow for this, and to include other brothers and sisters. Occasionally a whole cluster of children was taken by their parents for baptism, and the register may record their individual dates of birth. Sometimes a child may have been privately baptized, later being received into the Church. Both baptisms will be recorded in the register. If you failed to find your forebear in the Census, but located another person of the same surname and generation in the expected place, it is worth looking at the registers of his birthplace, because they may yield the entry of your ancestor. In Scotland the mother's maiden name was retained in the registration of her child's baptism, whose place in her number of offspring might be given.

English and Welsh marriage entries to 1753 often merely give the names of both groom and bride and the date of the ceremony. From 1754 marriages were written up into a special printed book, and include not only their names, but their abodes, marital status, and sometimes occupations. The entry will record whether banns had been read in their two churches on the preceding Sundays, or whether a licence had been purchased. The signatures of both parties, those of at least two witnesses, and of the officiating clergyman complete the data. From 1837 these registers were the basis of the information sent to the Registrar General in London, and if you know the exact place of a couple's marriage you can obtain the same details considerably cheaper from the parish register, and they will bear autographs, which the Registrar General's copies do not.

Often the couple took their first-born child back to the bride's parish for baptism, and it is therefore a good idea to look at the baptism registers too, having located the marriage. Do not forget, also, that the marriage may have been subsequent to one or two baptisms, and the register normally will give the name of the reputed fathers.

Where you find a marriage, but not the baptisms of the couple's offspring, and you cannot find them in the adjacent parishes, or within a five-mile radius, it may indicate that the family was Nonconformist, especially if there had been a licence for the marriage. You will probably find their children's baptisms in the registers of a local Nonconformist chapel. Most of these registers are now in the Public Record office, in London (see also below, p. 54).

The Banns Books from 1754 are useful in cases where you can locate the children, but not their parents' marriage. It may be that the husband previously resided in that parish and banns would therefore have been read in the church. The Banns Books will give you the dates of the three Sundays on which they were read, plus the name and parish of the bride. The marriage register of her church will contain the details of the ceremony, during the week following the third reading.

If you do not know the date of birth of an ancestor, it is best to examine the baptism registers back for at least twenty years, having deducted fourteen years from the year of marriage. Perhaps the burial register, or a gravestone inscription, will supply details of age. Before 1813 burial registers do not generally record age at demise, but merely the date of inhumation, name of the deceased, and occasionally marital status, or parentage, abode, occupation and even the cause of death.

Two pages from the burial register of All Saints church in the City of Oxford. At the top of page 11, three-month-old Henry Tagart has survived the death of his mother for a few weeks only. (Oxford, Bodleian Library, MS. D.D. Par. Oxford, All Saints b. 4, pp. 10–11)

Between 1667 and 1814 all burials were supposed to be in woollen, and a relative was required to make an Affidavit to this effect within eight days of the burial. These are recorded in the registers as 'Aff'. The initial letter 'P' indicates that it was a pauper funeral. Entries describing a person as 'hurled' or 'tumbled' into the ground normally refer to those Nonconformists who were interred without the benefit of the Anglican rites. From 1813 printed burial registers include not only the date of burial and the name of the deceased, but also his age and residence.

In using parish registers it is important not to neglect the burial registers, especially when you have children of identical names, baptized at about the same date, for one may have died an infant and thus solve the problem of identification. Again where the baptism registers describe a father as 'junior' or 'senior', when this adjective ceases it probably coincides with the burial entry of one of them. Burial entries after 1813 tell you the approximate year of birth of an individual and can save a lot of needless searching. You also know which year to start searching for his will. Burial entries can also complement and be complemented by the information on gravestone inscriptions.

It has been reckoned that it was rare for a family to remain in a parish for longer than three generations without a break, but movement is

Page 10.

BURIALS in the Parish of *All Saints in the City & in the County of Oxford* in the Year 18.19-20

Name.	Abode.	When buried.	Age.	By whom the Ceremony was performed.
Mary Whitefoot No. 73.	in the Parish of St Peter le Bailey	July 23rd	51 yrs	Rd. M. Matthews Linc. College
Archibald Windsor Hickman No. 74.	High Street in this Parish	Oct. 17th	4 mnths	Wm. Yeadon Curate
Stephen Richardson No. 75.	High Street in this Parish	Dec. 19th	59 yrs	Wm. Yeadon Curate
Emma Langfitt No. 76.	All Saints Parish	Dec. 19th	2 years 5 months	Hadford Offi. Min
Thomas Knapp No. 77.	Parish of St Peter le Bailey in this City	1820 Jan. 21st	86 yrs	Wm. Yeadon Curate
Charles Hodgkins No. 78.	High Street in this Parish	March 5th	46 yrs	Wm. Yeadon Curate
Elizabeth Hastings No. 79.	Queen Street in the Parish of St Peter le Bailey	March 8th	76 yrs	Wm. Yeadon Curate
Caroline Tagart No. 80.	High Street in this Parish	June 9th	26 yrs	Wm. Yeadon Curate

Page 11.

BURIALS in the Parish of *All Saints in the City & in the County of Oxford* in the Year 1820

Name.	Abode.	When buried.	Age.	By whom the Ceremony was performed.
Henry Budd Tagart No. 81.	High Street in this City	July 21st	3 mths	Wm. Yeadon Curate
Thomas Hanks No. 82.	Swan Court in this Parish	Sept. 5th	69 yrs	R. M. Matthews Linc. College
George Mills No. 83.	Bear Lane in this Parish	Sept. 13	5 days	Wm. Yeadon Curate
Catherine Holman No. 84.	Parish of Shoreditch London	Sept. 27th	7 yrs	Wm. Yeadon Curate
Mary Giles No. 85.	High Street in this Parish	Nov. 28th	39 yrs	Wm. Yeadon Curate
Jane Butler No. 86.	High Street in this Parish	Dec. 3	65 yrs	Wm. Yeadon Curate
Mary Ann Rainsford No. 87.	Radway Warwickshire	Dec. 23	27 yrs	Wm. Yeadon Curate
William Canton No. 88.	High Street in this Parish	1821 March 28	58 yrs	Wm. Yeadon Curate

likely to have been to or from a neighbouring parish. Certainly in the case of towns and cities a move to new lodgings would probably mean a change of parish. If you are unable to find the family before a certain date in a particular parish, then the next approach is to fan out the search to include the registers of adjacent churches, or to try Nonconformist registers. By searching the registers of a cluster of parishes in a county you can also discover the distribution of the family name over it.

If the parish registers are defective or missing, there may be duplicate copies. In 1598 the Anglican Church authorities decreed that not only should all previous baptisms, marriages and burials, especially since 1558, be copied up into a parchment book, but that annual returns of entries from 1598 should be made by the incumbent of each parish to the registrar of the diocese in which it lay. These returns are known as the 'Bishop's Transcripts', and are kept in the Diocesan Record Offices (often now combined with the County Record Offices). As the Transcripts took the form of loose-leaf parchment sheets, they were easily mislaid, and it is unusual for a complete series to date from commence-

John Green's gravestone in Grasmere churchyard. This John was the father of the John Green who was baptized in 1789 (see above, pp. 29 and 39). His burial on 19 July 1839, three days after he died, is recorded in the Bishop's Transcript (below), now in the County Record Office, Kendal.

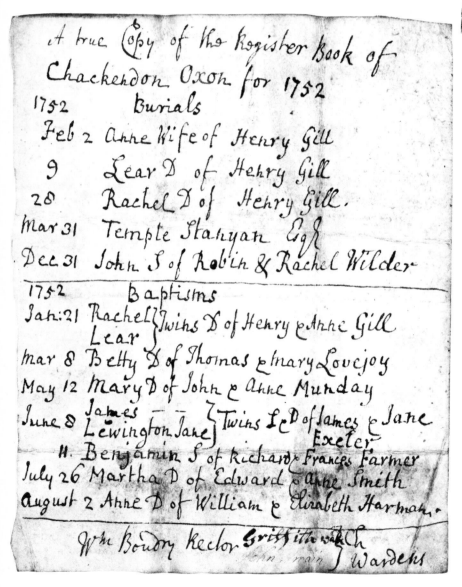

A Bishop's Transcript of the burials and baptisms in the Oxfordshire village of Checkendon in 1752, made by the incumbent and sent to the Diocesan Registrar for his records. It is signed by the Rector and his two churchwardens. (Oxford, Bodleian Library, MS. Oxf. Dioc. papers c. 509)

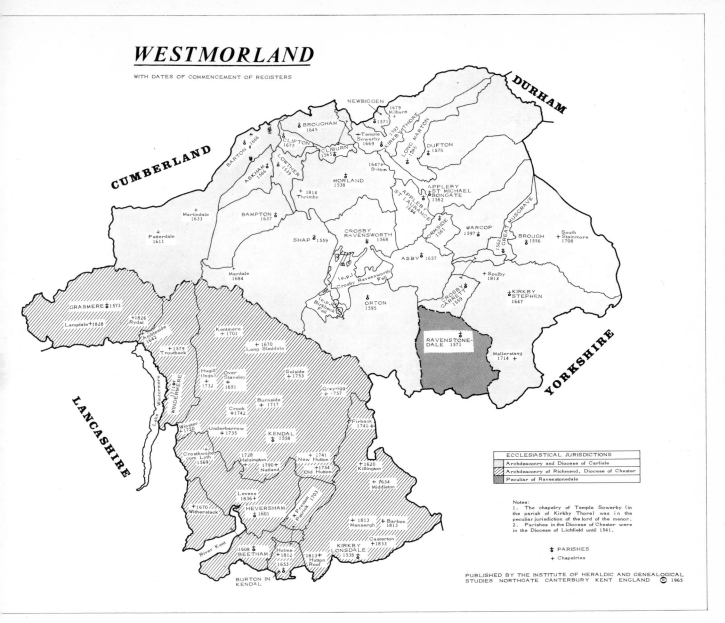

WESTMORLAND

WITH DATES OF COMMENCEMENT OF REGISTERS

ECCLESIASTICAL JURISDICTIONS
Archdeaconry and Diocese of Carlisle
Archdeaconry of Richmond, Diocese of Chester
Peculiar of Ravenstonedale

Notes:
1. The chapelry of Temple Sowerby (in the parish of Kirkby Thore) was in the peculiar jurisdiction of the lord of the manor.
2. Parishes in the Diocese of Chester were in the Diocese of Lichfield until 1541.

☦ PARISHES
+ Chapelries

PUBLISHED BY THE INSTITUTE OF HERALDIC AND GENEALOGICAL STUDIES NORTHGATE CANTERBURY KENT ENGLAND © 1965

The parishes in the County of Westmorland, showing Grasmere, adapted from the map published by The Institute of Heraldic and Genealogical Studies, Canterbury, Kent (see above, p. 42). The dates indicate the earliest surviving registers for each parish. Crosby Ravensworth Fell and Birkbeck Fell are 'extra-parochial', i.e. uninhabited and not claimed by any parish.

ment to the mid-nineteenth century when they were discontinued. In the diocese of London, for instance, only a part of the early seventeenth and early nineteenth centuries are covered. They are generally organized by parish, but some, like those of Norfolk and Suffolk, are arranged yearly by deanery, making the search laborious.

Bishop's Transcripts are not only useful for filling in gaps in the parish registers, but they sometimes correct and amend the originals, and even contain extra entries. They can also introduce errors of transcription, and abbreviations, and so it is advisable not to rely on them alone. If you are searching parish registers deposited in a Record Office, and those of a relevant contiguous parish are still held by the church, the Bishop's Transcripts can effectively be used instead. It normally costs nothing to search the Transcripts.

Parish registers and Bishop's Transcripts constitute the major source about our antecedents potentially from the sixteenth century onwards. They are a means of tracing continuity of residence, size of family, filiations and mobility, and if you are lucky you may be able to trace your ancestors back to the age of the Tudors.

47

The Parish Church and Parish Chest

If you can it is a good idea to visit the church where your antecedents worshipped because the churchyard may contain memorials to them. Families were often buried in their own plots, and a group of tombstones found together will show if this was the case. In my own village churchyard, at Grasmere, there is a line of twelve gravestones erected to four generations of one family and covering less than 100 years. Although these inscriptions are not sufficient to construct a reliable pedigree, reference to the parish registers in the church will clarify the various relationships. Individual stones sometimes contain inscriptions to several generations of a family, recording birthplaces, marriages, parentage, residence, occupations, and outstanding characteristics of the deceased.

Earlier memorial inscriptions were generally confined to the prosperous middle and upper classes, who were often great benefactors to the church. They would have been buried either in family vaults or in the crypt, and commemorated by monumental brasses before the sixteenth century, or later by tablets inserted in the floor or on the walls, or

Left. *The parish church at Cheriton, Gower, West Glamorgan. (Photo: Janet and Colin Bord)*

Below. *A benefactors' board, dated 1779, recording donations to be distributed to the poor, made by M. Lloyd, Morris Jones, Robert Evans, Henry Thomas, Mrs Catherine Morris and Mr Madockes, in Pennant Melangell church, Powys. (Photo: Janet and Colin Bord)*

Left. *Elizabeth Gay's tombstone speaks for itself! It stands in the churchyard of St Clement, Cornwall. (Photo: Janet and Colin Bord)*

Right. *The tomb of Sir John Pole in the church at Colyton, Devon. He died in Middlesex on 16 April, and was buried at Colyton on 13 July 1658, some three months later. (Photo: Janet and Colin Bord)*

even by fine tombs in special niches in the wall or in side aisles. These inscriptions are sometimes our only way of knowing what marriage alliances they made, the number and names of their children, and their public offices, especially if their origins were obscure. Idealized likenesses portrayed in contemporary costume, and the display of the family's coat of arms, make many of these tombs impressive and colourful, where Cromwell's troops did not damage or destroy them.

Later, seventeenth- and eighteenth-century monuments in the churches bear sculpted heads of the deceased and elaborate testimonials to the finer points of their characters.

Look also at the church furniture and ornaments, some of which may have been purchased by the family. There is usually a printed church history available to tell you who bought the various items. Perhaps the family donated money for distribution among the poor. Such benefactions are often listed on a special Benefactors' Board. A pew might have been reserved for the family and labelled accordingly. In my own church at Grasmere there is a curtain embroidered in 1939, incorporating the names of past and present worshippers. If the family was entitled to bear arms there may be a wooden funeral hatchment emblazoning its coat of arms, which had originally been carried in the funeral procession. There are five of these in Grasmere church, relating to the Le Fleming family of Rydal Hall, the patrons of the living.

The parish chest was originally stored in the vestry and contained all the parochial records. Few of these chests now survive and many of their records have passed into the hands of County Record offices. These include the Vestry Minutes, giving insight into the appointment of annual officers like the two churchwardens, and the judicial business and administration of the parish. The vestry could enforce payment of maintenance by reputed fathers, and mete out punishment to moral

offenders. It also reviewed the accounts of the other church officials. Churchwardens' Accounts dealing with payments for repairs and improvements to the church fabric, and the collection of pew rents, afford another useful source at the parochial level. Both these series of records occasionally date from the sixteenth century.

From 1691 the Accounts of the Overseers of the Poor detail the regular payments of maintenance to the poor, and the distribution of clothes or disbursements for the cost of materials for them to work. The cause and length of the need is usually given, and the reason for its cessation. These charitable activities were subject to annual review by the vestry, and the Poor Rate Books record the collection of funds to meet the expenses from the other parishioners, based on the value of the property they occupied. Highway Surveyors' Accounts contain names of those in default of statutory labour before 1834. Other contents of the parish chest to interest the family historian include original wills of benefactors to the church, relating to charities or trusts to help particularly the poor and widowed, census lists compiled before 1841 and apprenticeship indentures of poor boys and girls who were bound out, often as agricultural labourers and domestic servants to parishioners, by the Overseers of the Poor.

Another important group of documents about the poor are the series concerning Settlement and Removal. These papers date from 1691, and were directed at regulating the flow of indigent families into already hard-pressed parishes. Such families or individuals were subject to a searching examination by two Justices of the Peace, to discover their last place of legal settlement, to which they could be returned if they seemed likely to need relief. The records extend to 1834 and give a wealth of information about a person's past history. Settlement was gained through birth, apprenticeship, marriage with a native, employment for over a year, contribution to parish rates, or residence in property worth over ten pounds a year, whichever was the latest. If

A very old oak parish chest still in the church at Lower Peover, Cheshire. It dates from the fifteenth century. (Photo: A. F. Kersting)

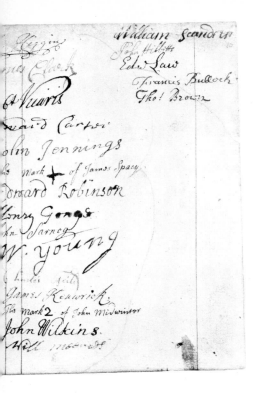

Above. *An extract from the Vestry Minutes of the parish of All Saints in the City of Oxford. It records a decision by the churchwardens and Overseers of the Poor to 'contract with James Pigot for the maintenance of the poor of this parish at the rate of threescore pounds by the year for three years'. It is followed by an interesting variety of parishioners' signatures (including James Spacy's mark). If your ancestors were settled in a parish for some time there is a good chance that their names or signatures may appear on documents such as this. (Oxford, Bodleian Library, MS. D.D. Par. Oxford, All Saints, c. 1, pp. 9–10)*

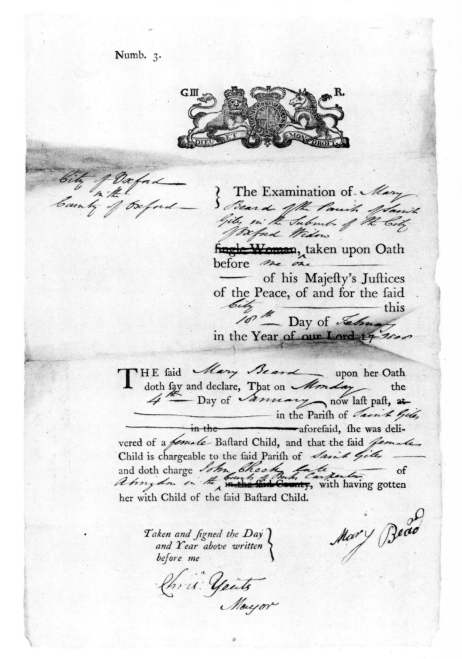

Above right. *A bastardy paper from the parish records of St Giles's church, Oxford. The Examination of Mary Beard took place before a magistrate on 10 February 1800, and the document has found its way into the parish records because the upkeep of the child was a charge upon the parish. It is useful to the genealogist because it not only names the alleged father, but also gives his occupation and former place of residence. (Oxford, Bodleian Library, MS. D.D. Par. Oxford, St Giles, c. 27 (6), fol. 7)*

none of these conditions was fulfilled, examiners had power to order a Removal back to the last legal settlement, under escort by the parish constable. The Settlement papers and Removal Orders were kept for future reference (see below, p. 100).

The parish chest may also contain a tithe map and apportionment, drafted between 1836 and 1842, when the donation to the incumbent of one-tenth of a person's annual produce from his land was commuted to an annual sum based on the price of corn. If you can find your family in the 1841 Census, this map will pinpoint its exact residence, and the apportionment will show the acreage, state of cultivation, title, annual value, and owner's name if different.

Back numbers of parish magazines will contain death notices and obituaries of parishioners, as well as baptisms and marriages.

Other Ecclesiastical Records and Dissenters

There is another group of records dealing with life at the parochial level, which can help to amplify a family's history, and these are stored in the Diocesan Record Offices. They relate to the twice-yearly visitations made by the archdeacon to the parishes in his jurisdiction, and to the triennial visitations conducted by the bishop over the whole diocese. Parsons and vicars had instructions to 'exhibit letters or orders, certificates of subscriptions and dispensations, all preachers, lecturers, curates, readers, schoolmasters and ushers to exhibit licences, all impropriators and farmers of tithes to exhibit endowments and pay pensions, and procurations, all churchmen and sidemen to take their oaths and make presentments, executors to bring in the wills of their testators, all criminals and delinquents to answer articles ...' Quite simply, the visitations were to inquire into faith, morality and administration. The Archdeacon's Court met in one of the larger churches once every six weeks, to handle business reported during the visitation. It granted licences to surgeons, physicians, apothecaries, midwives and schoolmasters who wished to practise in a parish, and applications often include testimonials from relatives, friends and past clients, and can reveal their original parish. Cases of slander, sexual misbehaviour, and applications for marriage annulments were also heard, with statements made by witnesses. Non-payment of tithes, offences against church property, and non-appearance to present wills for probate were also punishable by the Court, the penalties ranging between fines, public penance and excommunication.

The visitations were also directed at discovering and controlling the extent of dissent from the Established Church, especially by Roman Catholics, and visitation reports often include lists of Catholics and their sympathizers. Other occasional lists of communicants and non-attenders at church were made, the surviving ones being held mainly in the Diocesan Record Offices. Individual dioceses, like Carlisle in 1787, and the parishes themselves, sometimes drew up extensive lists, and the places to look for these are the Diocesan Record Offices or the parish chest. The 1563 Census (in the Harleian Manuscripts in the British Library) and the Compton Census of 1676 give totals of numbers, and not normally names.

From 1562 non-attenders were subjected to a shilling fine for each service missed, on a cumulative basis, and the Archdeacon's Court records note the dates of these charges. Between 1592 and 1691 the fine was raised to twenty pounds a month, and Recusants' Rolls listing those persons found liable (chiefly Catholics, although denomination is rarely stated) are in the Public Record Office, in London. They are arranged by year, on a county basis, and give the names, family relationships, places of residence, status and occupations, and details of the fine, its commencement and when discharged. If this was not paid the individual's land could be confiscated and he himself imprisoned. Also in this repository are the Assize Circuit records of minutes of the trials of Recusants, and these may give the denomination to which they belonged. Quarter Sessions records, in the relevant County Record

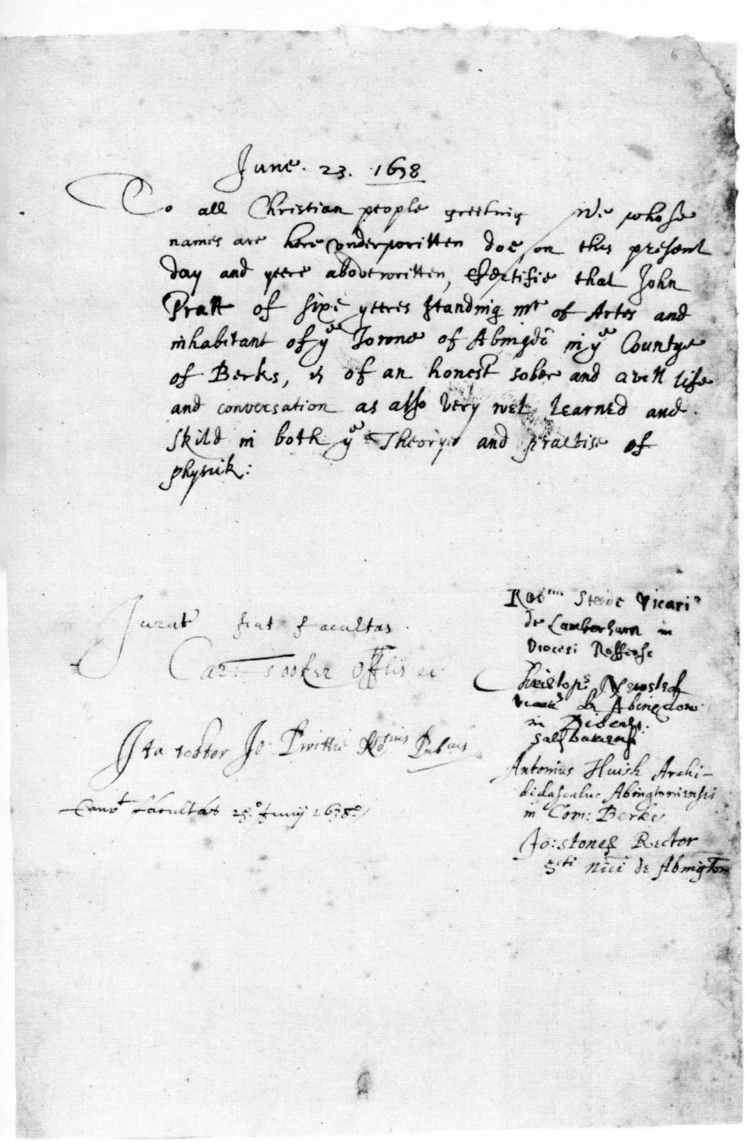

June 23. 1638

To all Christian people greeting wee whose names are here underwritten doe, on this present day and yeere abovewritten, Certifie that John Pratt of five yeeres standing Mr of Artes and inhabitant of ye Towne of Abingdon in ye County of Berks, is of an honest sober and civill life and conversation as also very well learned and skilled in both ye Theorye and practise of physick:

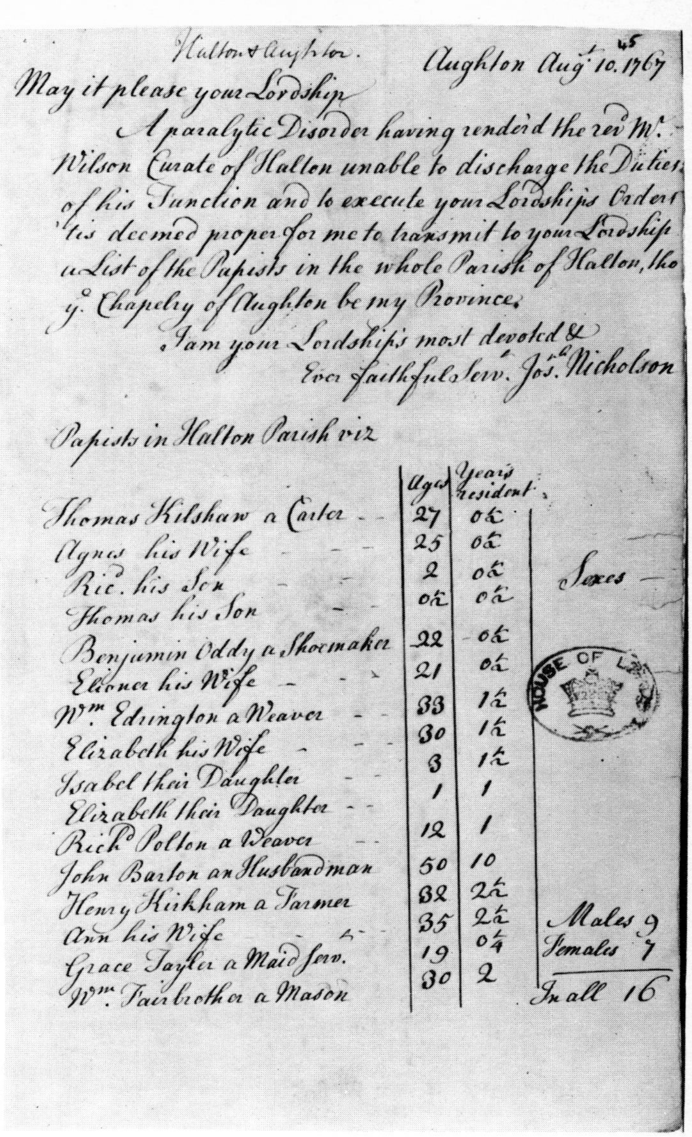

Halton & Aughton. Aughton Augt. 10. 1767 45

May it please your Lordship

A paralytic Disorder having render'd the revd. Mr. Wilson Curate of Halton unable to discharge the Duties of his Function and to execute your Lordships Orders 'tis deemed proper for me to transmit to your Lordship a List of the Papists in the whole Parish of Halton, tho' ye Chapelry of Aughton be my Province.

I am your Lordship's most devoted & Ever faithful Serv. Jos. Nicholson

Papists in Halton Parish viz

	Ages	Years resident	Sexes
Thomas Kilshaw a Carter	27	0½	
Agnes his Wife	25	0½	
Ric. his Son	2	0½	
Thomas his Son	0½	0½	
Benjamin Oddy a Shoemaker	22	0½	
Elloner his Wife	21	0½	
Wm. Edington a Weaver	33	1½	
Elizabeth his Wife	30	1½	
Isabel their Daughter	3	1½	
Elizabeth their Daughter	1	1	
Rich. Polton a Weaver	12	1	
John Barton an Husbandman	50	10	
Henry Kirkham a Farmer	32	2½	
Ann his Wife	35	2½	Males 9
Grace Tayler a Maid Serv.	19	0¼	Females 7
Wm. Fairbrother a Mason	30	2	In all 16

Above. *A certificate granted on 23 June 1638 to John Pratt allowing him to practise 'physick'. Such certificates, which licensed individuals to practise as physicians, surgeons, apothecaries or midwives, were granted by the Archdeacon's Court after an application was received, often supported by ardent testimonies from the applicant's clients and friends. (Oxford, Bodleian Library, MS. Oxf. Arch. papers, Berks. c. 162, no. 6)*

Above right. *A sample from the Papist Returns of 1767, from the parish of Halton, Lancs. The inquiries were instigated by the House of Lords, which instructed the bishops to send a circular letter to the incumbent of every parish. This is one of the replies. The 1767 returns are particularly full. (London, House of Lords Record Office)*

Office, record similar trials for non-payment of fines or tithes, and for refusing to serve in the county militia.

The Protestant Oath Rolls for the year 1641–2 include the names of those persons over eighteen, arranged by town, village and hamlet, who took the oath to uphold the Protestant succession, and these are a useful directory, although they do not survive for all counties. The House of Lords Library in London has the original lists, along with the sacrament certificates of all those taking military or civil office after 1673.

During the period 1645–60 a Parliamentary Committee for Compounding dealt with the confiscation of estates and the imposition of severe fines on known supporters of King Charles I during the Civil War. In this group were many Roman Catholic gentry families, who consequently suffered a severe setback. The papers connected with the investigations are well worth consulting because they give the extent and value of their property, and the names and rents of their tenants. There is a printed calendar of these, and the originals are in the Public Record Office in London.

In 1680, 1705–6, 1767 and 1781 lists of Papists were compiled, and these are in the House of Lords Library, London. After 1715 Catholics were obliged to register their estates with the Clerk of the Peace of the county where they lay. If your antecedents were Catholic both these sources are of great potential value as directories, which is after all what they were supposed to be. The Catholics also had to pay double the assessment for the Land Tax, made on the annual value of their estates, and extant lists from 1692, in the County Record offices, will identify them by the relatively high assessments.

Many Catholics met privately for services, or in chapels attached to Catholic country houses, but few formal registers of baptism, marriage and burial survive earlier than 1778, when the first Catholic Relief Act was passed. After 1754 all except the Quakers and Jews were required to marry in the Established Church, but the Catholics continued to record these events in their own registers. Usually the registers are in Latin, and in the case of baptisms they include the names of godparents and the mother's maiden name. Catholics often had their progeny baptized in the Anglican church as well, so that the registers could be used as proof of age, whereas their own registers could not. Many Catholic registers are still in the churches, but a few North Country ones prior to 1837 were deposited with the Registrar General in 1840 or 1857, and can be seen in the Public Record Office in London. Some of the Lancashire and Hampshire registers have been published by the Catholic Record Society.

The earliest known Protestant Nonconformist register dates from 1644. From the previous year, 1643, until 1660, the Established Church in England was Presbyterian. During the whole Commonwealth period (1645–60) the registration of births, marriages and burials in the parish registers was a civil, not a religious matter, and they included dissenters. The Conventicle Returns of 1669 list dissenters, their denominations and their meetings. They have been printed in G. Lyon Turner's *Records of Nonconformity*.

After the Restoration, it was not until the Declaration of Indulgence in 1672 allowed Protestant Nonconformist 'teachers' to be licensed, and applications to be made for meeting house licences, that their formal records started. Licences were granted either by the Diocesan Courts or Quarter Sessions. Before this the three oldest dissenting groups, the Presbyterians, Baptists, and Independents, may be difficult to trace as a body. The Act of Toleration in 1689 provided for the registration of licensed meeting houses with the same courts, and a crop of chapels quickly sprang up. Their registers of baptism and burial to 1837 were collected up by the Registrar General at the same time as the Catholics', and were examined prior to acceptance as legal documents. They are now in the Public Record Office, but a number of early Nonconformist registers are either still in the hands of the chapels themselves or have been deposited in County Record Offices.

When using Nonconformist registers it is important to note any discrepancy between the chapel's foundation and the date of the earliest deposited register. It is often worth approaching the chapel itself, or the headquarters of the denomination, to see if either holds the earliest records. Many chapels changed denomination several times in their history, and it is a good idea to look at the registers of all the chapels in the area. The family may have followed a favourite minister in order to have its children baptized by him, and so you may have to look at chapels for your own denomination which lie anything up to

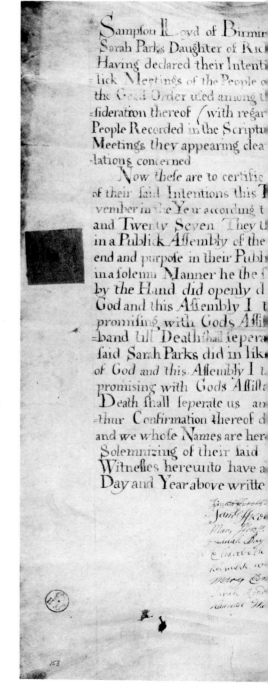

thirty miles away from the family home.

Occasionally ministers took the registers with them when they moved to a new living, so that entries from entirely different localities may be gathered in one volume. The registers contain dates of baptism and possibly of birth, the infant's name and those of his parents, including the mother's maiden name, their abode and the father's occupation. The Baptists registered births of infants and baptisms of adult members. Burial registers generally survive from the eighteenth century, when the chapels had their own burial grounds, the largest in London being that at Bunhill Fields. Parentage may be given in burial registers in addition to abode, and occasionally the age of the deceased.

In the mid-eighteenth century there was a sudden growth of Nonconformity, the Methodists gaining many adherents, particularly in the swift-growing mining and industrial areas like Cornwall, Wales and the Midlands. A lot of families had a passing connection with these dissenters and it is always worth looking at the chapel registers of their home area.

In 1742 Dr Williams founded a library where copies of birth certificates were issued to dissenters on payment of a fee, the originals being entered in registers to keep a permanent record of those births not adequately registered by the chapels themselves. These registers continued to 1837, when central registration was started. Some entries were retrospective, and parents took the opportunity of registering their own as well as their children's births. The indexes to the entries in these registers, and the registers themselves, have been transferred to the Public Record Office.

Members' Rolls of admission to the congregations, and of departures from them, giving the circumstances, minutes of the meetings of chapel officials, and memorial tablets inside the chapels are also worth your attention. Similarly, the official central denominational repository will contain extensive printed and manuscript records of ministers, outstanding members, and local groups.

The Quakers maintained good birth, marriage and burial records from around 1650, each event being reported to the Registrar of the local Monthly Meeting. Digests, one for each county, and dating from the earliest entries to 1837, contain abstracts of about 260,000 births, 40,000 marriages and 310,000 burials, arranged chronologically within each initial letter of the surname. These digests help to trace not only the family's lineage, but also its mobility. After 1837 a digest of Quaker births in Great Britain was continued until 1959, when birthright membership was abolished, a digest of deaths until 1961, and a digest of marriages is still maintained. All of these can be viewed at the Friends' Library in London, while Dublin and Edinburgh are the locations of Irish and Scottish Quaker digests.

The original minutes of the English and Welsh Monthly Meetings, to which the digests refer, are retained in the Public Record Office, in London. The digest will give you the name of the Meeting, the date of registration and the volume and page number in the minutes where the entry will be found. Birth digests detail names of infants and parents, their place of abode and father's occupation. Marriages in the digests do not give the names of those relatives and Friends present at the ceremony, but only the date, the Monthly Meeting, how to locate the

A Quaker marriage certificate recording the marriage of Sampson Lloyd and Sarah Parks in Birmingham on 29 November 1727. It shows the characteristic procedures and forms of words used by the Quakers. The same marriage will be recorded in the minutes of the Monthly Meetings, now in the Public Record Office. (London, Library of the Religious Society of Friends, Lloyd papers)

entry, and the names of both parties and their parents. The Monthly Meeting entry will also bear a list of all the witnesses at the wedding. The burial digests give date, and even age at decease, plus parentage, place of residence and occupation of the deceased, duplicated in the minutes themselves. Ages were included, even in the seventeenth century, so it is possible to know roughly when each person was born.

Other useful sources for tracing Quaker ancestors are the minutes of the Men's and Women's Meetings, which dealt with such matters as the supervision of property and inquiries into the backgrounds of intended spouses to make sure that they were convinced Quakers, were not related, had no other engagement, and were not remarrying in haste; parental consent was also sought and recorded. Character references about newcomers were sent by other Meetings and enrolled in the minutes, as were testimonials of deceased members. The Friends' Library in London has a comprehensive list of the whereabouts of these minutes. Other records relate to the sufferings of Quakers for non-payment of tithes, and refusal to serve in the county militia from circa 1650 onwards, taken from Quarter Sessions and Assize records. Most of those in the seventeenth century, up to 1689, are printed on a county basis in Joseph Besse's *Sufferings of the Quakers*, published in 1753.

Two other important categories of Nonconformists in England are the Huguenots and Jews. Along with other European Protestant refugees of the late sixteenth and seventeenth centuries, the Huguenots were absorbed fairly quickly into the Anglican Church, their own registers recording newcomers over perhaps three generations at the most. The earliest immigrant church register was that of the Walloons at St Julien, Southampton, in 1567, and the main centres where the Huguenots gathered were London, Norwich, Ipswich, Southampton, Canterbury, Bristol and Plymouth. In London, Christ Church, Spitalfields, and St Giles in the Fields contain duplicated marriage entries of the original Huguenot churches. The Huguenot Society has copied

Above left. *A Jewish marriage certificate, known as a* Ketuba. *It is reproduced by kind permission of Mrs C. Z. Pearlman, whose marriage on 21 February 1971 it commemorates. It was written and illustrated by the bride's uncle, Dr M. Munk, of New York.*

Left. The Huguenot church in Soho Square, London.

Right. An old Huguenot street in London, Fournier Street, Spitafields. The large attic windows were designed specially to give the weavers good light for their looms. At the end of the street is an old Huguenot chapel, which was converted into a synagogue and has since been converted into a mosque.

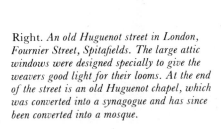

and printed the registers all these foreign Protestant churches. A printed return of aliens in the City and suburbs of London, 1523–1625, taken from taxation returns, is especially useful.

In the Huguenots' country of origin, France, parish registers only commenced in 1579, duplicates being made from 1667. The duplicates are stored at the relevant town halls (mairies) and departmental archives and have been microfilmed. The vestry minutes (Actes du Consistoire) give details of newcomers' birthplaces, and also consents for marriages. In 1796, the parish registers of France and Belgium were nationalized by the French Republic (which annexed Belgium), and since then the basic genealogical source in both countries has been the 'état civil' (birth, marriage and death records) kept by the local municipalities. The Belgian parish registers date from about 1600. The Mormons have microfilmed these, along with the indexes made in 1865, while the originals are in the relevant state archive repositories, the communes, or the parish churches themselves.

There are only twelve synagogues in England more than 100 years old. Many of the Jewish archives are written in Hebrew, and the patronymic and metronymic naming systems add to the problems.

Jews tended to congregate together, usually around the ports of entry, and even had their children baptized in Anglican churches. In London the main ones were St Dionis Backchurch, St Katherine Cree, and St Helen's Bishopsgate. Although Jews were allowed back into the country in 1650 after an official absence of 350 years, and the earliest settlers came from Spain and Portugal, the vast majority of Jewish families in England stem from nineteenth- and twentieth-century immigrants from eastern Europe, so that migration is still within living memory, or is documented in passenger lists, naturalization papers, and registers of aliens, all in the Public Record Office at Kew. The Jewish Museum, in London, also contains much valuable material on Jewish families.

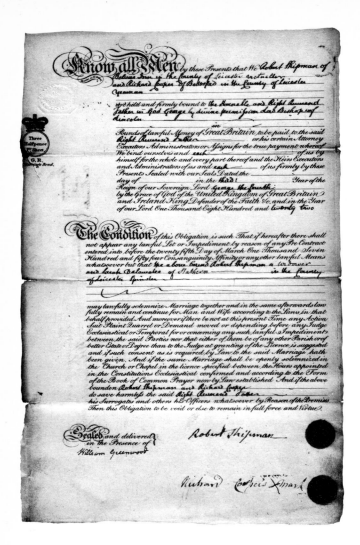

The marriage allegation, dated December 1822, of Robert Shipman, signed as his application to the Bishop of Leicester for a licence to marry Sarah Delawater, a widow. The allegation was made on a standard printed form, and the applying for and granting of licences was a routine matter. Between 1822 and 1824, however, certified baptism entries were attached to the allegations, and that for Robert Shipman showed that he was born in 1751, making him 71 at the time of this marriage. (Leicester, Leicestershire Record Office, 1D41/38, 1822, Shipman/ Delawater; photo courtesy of Leicestershire Museums, Art Galleries and Records Service)

Marriage Licences and Wills

After the Earl of Hardwicke's Marriage Act of 1753, a marriage celebrated in the Established Church was only valid if banns were read in church, or a licence was purchased from the bishop of the diocese or his surrogate. If the bride and groom came from different dioceses then one of the two Vicars General of the two archbishoprics would be approached for a licence, and the Faculty Office of the Archbishop of Canterbury if they resided in different archdioceses. Nearly all the surviving records concerning marriage licences are held by the relevant diocesan repositories, and some have been summarized and printed, or indexed. Many of the records are still in their original bundles, arranged chronologically.

Who obtained a licence? They were confined to no particular group, but had to be paid for. They were private, and more speedy than the reading of banns, and were favoured by the gentry, those wishing a hasty marriage, and Nonconformists. The parish register will record whether a licence had been issued for the marriage.

What the Diocesan repositories hold are the allegations by the groom and his surety that there was no just impediment by way of a former existing marriage, consanguinity, affinity or other lawful hindrance, to prevent the marriage taking place at the specified church or churches,

Right. *The will, dated 28 May 1805, of Mr John Giles, a baker of Caversham in the County of Oxfordshire. One of the witnesses was John Giles's apprentice. (Oxford, Bodleian Library, MS. Wills Oxon. 232, 1805)*

Far right. *The last page of the most famous will in English literature, that of William Shakespeare, made on 25 March 1616. The testator died one month later. The interlinear addition on line 9 contains the only mention of his wife in the whole document and the famous reference by which the 'second best bed with the furniture' was bequeathed to her. The property was left in the main to his daughter Susanna, and there are legacies to his other daughter, his sister and also friends. The will was proved on 27 June 1616, as is recorded below William Shakespeare's signature. (London, Public Record Office, Chancery Lane, Prob. 1/4, p. 3)*

within a prescribed period. These date in a regular series from the reign of Henry VIII and were often accompanied, until 1823, by a bond. The signed allegation contains the groom's name, residence, current marital status, and occupation, and those of his bride, with their ages (often only approximate because it was sufficient just to prove that they were over the age of twenty-one, or if not, to prove that parental consent had been given). The date of the allegation was normally not more than a few days before the marriage. The surety for the truth of the allegation, and the performance of the marriage, was often a friend or relative. The allegation gives considerable detail not available in the marriage register itself, and can point to the parish of marriage if this was not known before.

Another very important source for the family historian is wills. A will is a written instrument providing for the disposition of a person's real estate (land and buildings), while a testament disposes of his personal property (money, pictures, furniture, tools and leasehold land). The two are usually combined and can only take effect on the testator's death. The document, to be valid, must be dated, be described as the last will and testament, must have been made while its author was of sound disposing mind, and was possessed of property worth at least five pounds, and must have been signed by him at the bottom of each page, and at the very end in the presence of two witnesses, who were also able

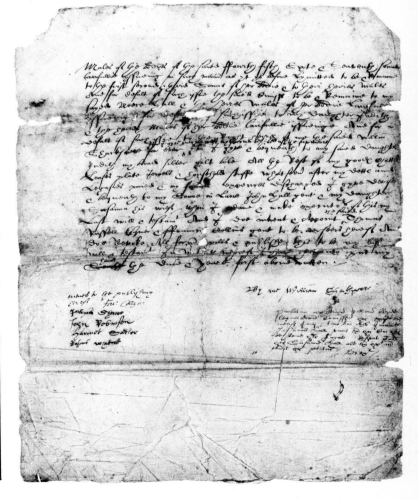

to attest in each other's presence. Additions or modifications, called codicils, can be affixed, dated, signed and witnessed like the will.

Before 1858, after the testator's death, the nominated executors were required to present the will to the appropriate ecclesiastical court, if the estate lay in England or Wales. A person leaving property in one archdeaconry generally had his will proved in that Archdeaconry Court, but a person holding property in two archdeaconries would have had his will proved in the Consistory Court of the bishop of that diocese. The two archbishops, of York and Canterbury, each had their own Prerogative Courts with authority over their constituent bishoprics, and the superior court of all was the Prerogative Court of Canterbury, whose regular series of wills dates from 1383. This court also had jurisdiction over those dying overseas and leaving estates in England or Wales. In addition there were Peculiar Courts belonging to lords of manors and others, with their own probate jurisdiction. The executors were not bound to take the will to the appropriate local court, and it is wise to search the calendars or indexes of wills of all those probate courts serving the area where your antecedents lived. For reasons of prestige, large landowners often had their wills proved in the Prerogative Court of Canterbury, even if their estates were concentrated in one diocese.

The wills of the 300 or more ecclesiastical courts are housed in County Record Offices, Diocesan Record Offices, and occasionally libraries throughout the country, those of the Prerogative Court of York being kept at the Borthwick Institute of Historical Research, at York, and those of the Prerogative Court of Canterbury in the Public Record Office, in London. In the Public Record Office too are the indexes and abstracts of all the wills and administrations recorded in the Estate Duty Office from 1796 to 1857. Anthony Camp's guide to *Wills and their Whereabouts* lists addresses of all the probate repositories in the British Isles, and those calendars and indexes which have been printed or microfilmed. The Society of Genealogists, in London, has a very good series of these microfilms. Prior to 1858, the calendars will usually give the testator's name and abode at the time of making the will, and the date of probate. They also include lists of administration grants, taken out when the deceased died intestate and the family applied to the court for the appointment of his next of kin as administrator.

Since 1858 wills have been proved in civil District Registries, the chief being the Principal Probate Registry, at Somerset House, London, which contains copies of all the local wills and administration grants as well as those proved in London. These can be examined on payment of a small fee. There are annual indexes giving the name of the deceased, his place of residence, date and often the place of death, the names, addresses, occupations and relationship to him of the executors, the date of probate, and the total value of the estate. The indexes also include details of administration grants. There are relatively few wills of women until the Married Women's Property Act of 1882 allowed them to own property of their own.

When looking for the will of an individual it is wise to search for the name in the calendar or index of the appropriate court for at least the ten years subsequent to his death, as probate may not have been immediate. Once found, you will be able to examine either the original

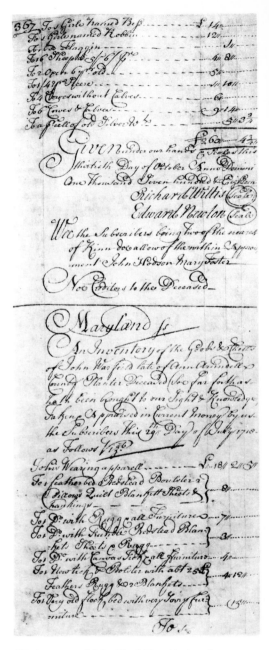

The inventory of John Warfield, a planter of Ann Arundell County, Maryland, dated 29 July 1718. The inventory begins with household goods and continues for a further three full pages, including slaves and livestock. (Two entries belonging to the previous inventory at the top of the page shown here are also slaves.) John Warfield was an antecedent of the Duchess of Windsor. (Annapolis, Maryland, Hall of Records, Prerogative Court (Inventories), Vol. 1, p. 367)

Part of the inventory of the goods of John and Margaret Statham of Packington on Heath, Derbyshire, 1 April 1588. Detailed inventories such as this provide a fascinating insight into the social life of the time, for they often list every object in the house, room by room, along with its saleable value. (Lichfield, Lichfield Joint Record Office)

will, if filed with the court, and thus see your antecedent's signature, or the court's registered copy, enrolled in a book, with the Probate Act added at the bottom (in Latin if before 1732), sometimes many years after the will was composed.

It is very important to read the whole will, however long, because it can be a goldmine of information. Besides the name, abode and occupation of the testator, and the dates when the will was drawn up and proved, you may find reference to his birthplace, the family home, vault or traditional burial place, details of his landholdings both in extent, nature and situation, and perhaps even how he came by them, and who were his tenants, or his landlords. The will may mention the date and terms of his marriage settlement, his most treasured possessions and who he wished to enjoy them, any investments and debts, and bequests to the poor and others. He will usually mention his wife, children, grandchildren, and other kinsfolk, godchildren, friends, neighbours, servants and apprentices.

A series of wills relating to your family over a period of several generations can provide you with much more biographical information than any other source, and because many of the local courts have a continuous run of wills from the sixteenth century at least, you may be able to produce a fairly elaborate pedigree, using wills in conjunction with parish registers. They can supplement gaps left in the registers, sort out problems of identification, prove links with families elsewhere, and show how the family moved and prospered. By examining contemporary wills of families allied with yours, or of friends and fellow parishioners, you can often bridge a gap left where your own family did not make wills. A search of the local will calendars can also show the distribution of the surname in the area if you have failed to locate the family in a particular parish.

Another record of the deceased's possessions which often survives, filed in the same probate court, is an inventory of his goods. Such inventories, usually made within a few days of the person's death, give the approximate saleable value of each item of furniture, tools, furnishings, crops gathered in, cattle and swine, and debts owed to him. They are often listed room by room, so that you can reconstruct the whole house and its furnishings in great detail, and discover minimum value of a person's goods and chattels, and the type of trade in which he was engaged.

This chapter has been concerned with introducing the major basic sources you will meet in tracing your ancestors, with special reference to British archives. Those who need to search abroad will find that nearly all countries follow the same procedures in national and local registration of the vital events in each individual's life. We shall now consider the types of repositories you will encounter, and how to derive the maximum benefit from them.

3 Using the Sources

T his is essentially a practical chapter to advise you on search methods and organization of material, and is based on personal experience. It is addressed primarily to those who are undertaking genealogical research for the first time and who are new to the world of archives and original documents. This world can be a bit daunting at first, for reference systems can be confusing, and documents difficult to read and understand. Some of the advice in this chapter will inevitably seem elementary to the experienced researcher; its aim is to smooth the path for the beginner.

Types of Record Repository

Records of central government dealing with, for example, taxes, the Armed Forces, foreign and colonial affairs, immigration and the Census, will generally be found in the national archive repository of a given country. In the case of England and Wales this is the Public Record Office in London. There are also special government departmental record centres containing files of their more recent activities, for instance the Army Record Centre at Hayes in Middlesex, the Home Office, the Passport Office, dealing with records of migration, and the Registrar General's Office for the Census. They are not normally open to the public.

The next administrative level is that of the county, and each English county has a County Record Office, containing records of local administration and justice. At an even more local level come the Guildhalls and Town Halls of the cities and towns, responsible for their own administrative records.

The central registers of English and Welsh births, marriages and deaths are in the General Register Office in London. The General Register Office is supported by a countrywide network of local registries which record the basic information on births, marriages and deaths, and forward copies of the entries to the central register in London. Thus every district has a local registry which houses the original birth and death certificates, and copies of marriage certificates. These local registries can be used for genealogical research, but it is only the central General Register Office that maintains comprehensive indexes and is properly equipped and staffed for conducting searches. Copies of church marriage certificates are sent to the local registry by the individual incumbents, who retain the originals in their own parish registers.

There are also Archdiocesan and Diocesan Record Offices containing much useful documentation about church administration and justice, and of course wills (up to 1858). In England the Diocesan Record Offices have been combined in many cases with the County Record Offices, although the diocesan boundaries do not always coincide with those of the county. Since 1858 the national repository of wills has been the Principal Probate Registry in Somerset House, London.

Individual religious denominations will generally have their own libraries of printed and original material. There are also special repositories for particular classes of archive, for example regimental museums or trade union headquarters, and most national societies and professional bodies maintain libraries perhaps containing material which appears nowhere in print.

Local museums and public libraries are often well stocked with material of special interest to their own areas, and some have a section specifically devoted to local industries and crafts, and perhaps have a good collection of old local photographs. Public libraries will contain telephone directories, electoral rolls (with back numbers), local and national newspapers (again with back numbers), and they may have microfilm copies of national archives pertaining to the area. They will

Genealogical research a century ago. This print of the new Register of Wills Office at Somerset House, London, was published by the Illustrated London News *on 30 January 1875. Apart from top hats and long dresses, the scene is much the same today. (Photo: The Illustrated London News Picture Library)*

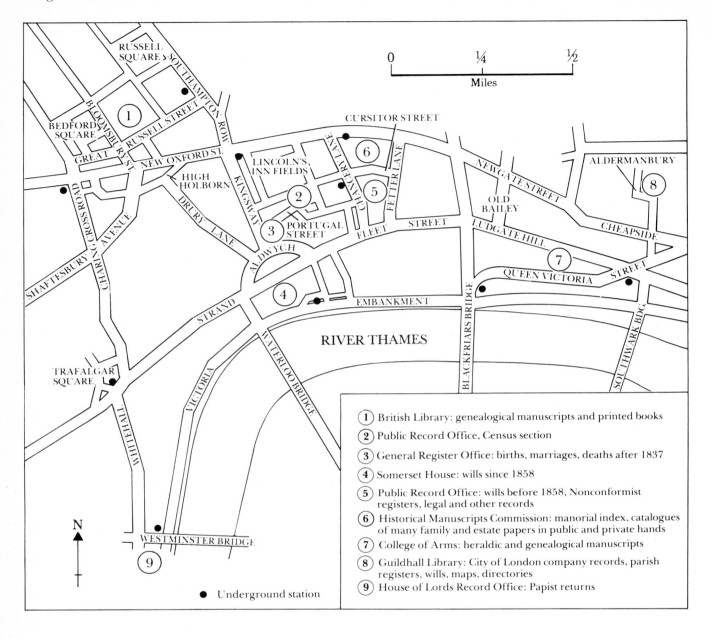

1. British Library: genealogical manuscripts and printed books
2. Public Record Office, Census section
3. General Register Office: births, marriages, deaths after 1837
4. Somerset House: wills since 1858
5. Public Record Office: wills before 1858, Nonconformist registers, legal and other records
6. Historical Manuscripts Commission: manorial index, catalogues of many family and estate papers in public and private hands
7. College of Arms: heraldic and genealogical manuscripts
8. Guildhall Library: City of London company records, parish registers, wills, maps, directories
9. House of Lords Record Office: Papist returns

● Underground station

A map of central London showing the principal record repositories of London. Their full addresses are given in Appendix III.

also have a collection of local guide books, trade and street directories, maps and histories. The inter-library loan service will obtain for you at your branch library many of the books I have listed at the end of the book. The librarian can also advise you as to whether there is a special Local History Library, and if a Local History or Family History Society exists in the vicinity. Major libraries like the British Library in London and the Bodleian Library in Oxford require a reader's ticket to gain access, and while many of the printed books can be consulted elsewhere, their manuscript collections are unique.

In Appendix III I have given the addresses of the principal record repositories in Great Britain, and also a list of printed directories from which the addresses of foreign, local and specialized archives can be found; I have also given the addresses of the main European, Commonwealth and American genealogical societies, to which readers can turn if their researches take them abroad.

Using the Repositories

Before using any repository, particularly if it is any distance from your home, it is advisable to write or telephone first; if you don't you can waste a great deal of time, for opening hours and other conditions vary widely. For instance, some repositories are open in the evening, others close for lunch, and there may be an annual closure for stocktaking. It may be that you will need to reserve a seat. Inquire whether you need to order documents in advance (some are housed away from the repository and may take a few days to produce), and how many you can order at a time. Make sure that it does hold the class of records you wish to see, and for the relevant period; although there may well be a printed guide to the contents of the repository, it may not be sufficiently recent or detailed to meet your needs. Lastly, ask about its exact location, car-parking facilities and public transport.

When you enter the record repository see what reference systems it has to the records. They may be catalogued and indexed, or listed chronologically in class lists, while other records may even have been transcribed and printed. The printed guide should tell you about those

An outline flow chart showing the basic steps for the family history researcher. At the centre of the chart is the key word 'reappraisal'. Strictly speaking a line ought to lead from every stage into the reappraisal box, for it is vital to take stock at every stage of your research, and to add the latest information to your pedigree as you go along.

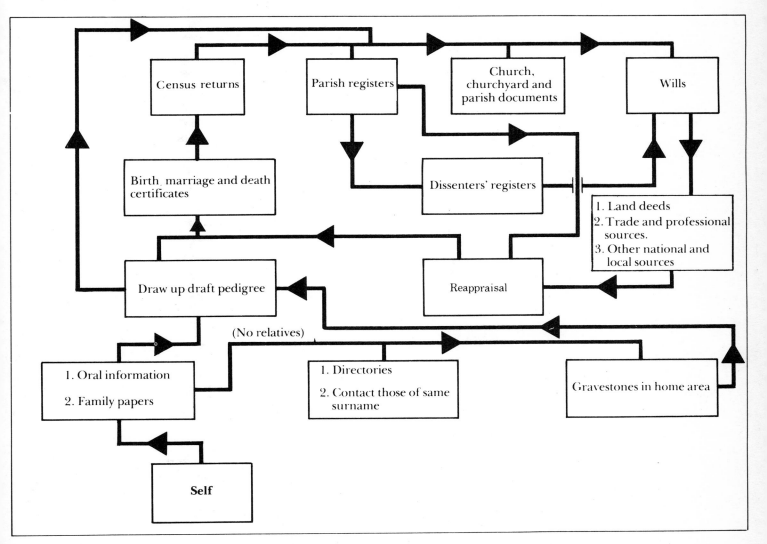

sources in print up to its date of publication. Look at the open shelves and discover what other material there is, like early street directories of the town in which you are interested, local histories and books on specific topics of local significance. If there are any record office publications scan the list of them to see if any would be of special use to you. It is also worth inquiring about photocopying facilities, as this may save time if your visit is to be a brief one and the documents are difficult to read, or you would like to collect your own copies of sources.

If the waiting period for documents to be produced is a long one, it is essential that you order the first batch of them as soon as possible, and have references ready for the next order. It is a common mistake to waste time fiddling about with the card index drawers, or staring at a confusing array of unlabelled catalogues, without understanding how the system of cataloguing and referencing works. Do not hesitate to ask for advice, especially on your first visit, and remember that even the most experienced searcher had to start somewhere.

If you are unable to conduct the research yourself, most repositories have a list of local researchers you might contact, but it is a good idea to discover their charges before asking them to act on your behalf. The Association of Genealogists and Record Agents also maintains a list of its elected members, while the Society of Genealogists in London keeps a list of names of recommended searchers.

Some repositories are not open to the public, and you will have to rely on the good services of their keepers for information. If you do need to contact them, write a clear, concise letter stating exactly what information you seek, give the full names of the person concerned, and at least an approximate date, and do not make vague or involved requests. Always enclose a stamped self-addressed envelope for your reply, and offer to pay for the keeper's help. You could also ask if it might be possible to purchase a photocopy of the material found, but do receive an estimate of the cost first. It is a kind thought to write and thank your helper afterwards.

Note-taking

Most record repositories insist on the use of a pencil only, to protect their documents. It is preferable to use loose-leaf file paper rather than a notebook, as it can be rearranged in a filing system, whereas notes in a notebook cannot. Buy paper of an even size, and with a margin to allow for additional marginal notes. Have a small notebook handy for listing references to documents you wish to examine, for jotting down interesting but irrelevant entries in these documents, and for making memos.

Always take the trouble to make tidy, well-written transcripts or abstracts of documents, for this saves time in the long run and ensures accuracy. If you produce hastily scribbled and abbreviated notes you are more likely to make mistakes, and then to make new mistakes or garble the sense when you come to write the notes up. Do not mark or lean your elbow on the original document, or write notes on top of it. I have often seen this done, and the damage caused to fragile documents can mean their removal from access.

This alphabet shows some of the elaborate letter forms that were developed in official documents. They come mainly from legal and Chancery documents of the sixteenth and seventeenth centuries. The page is taken from A. Wright's Court Hand Restored *(5th edition, 1818), and reproduced in Hilda Grieve's* Examples of English Handwriting 1150–1750, *published by the Essex Record Office, 1954.*

A general Alphabet of the Old Law Hands.

ALPHABETS from A. Wright's *Court Hand Restored* (5th ed., 1818, plates 18, 19), illustrating a variety of forms of letters, mainly but not entirely from 16th and 17th century Legal and Chancery hands.

Any analysis and interpretation of the document's contents should be left until you reach home. Concentrate only on taking complete and accurate notes or copies, and on getting through as much material as possible without being too ambitious or rushing. The notebook will help, especially if you have carefully planned your programme in advance. You can tick off all those sources you have seen and make sure you have looked at the essential documents. Your pedigree chart and county map should accompany you on each visit, so that you can constantly refer to them as you work. The map will advise you about neighbouring parishes and probate courts to consult.

When working I try to record each document on a separate sheet of paper for ease of filing. Otherwise a seemingly useless abstract may be tucked away at the bottom of a page under an even more useless abstract, and forgotten. It may later turn out to have contained a vital clue of only it could have been found. A couple of unrelated abstracts on the same sheet make filing difficult. It is a good idea therefore to develop sound practice in note-taking right from the start.

Always put the name of the repository at the head of each page of notes, the title, date and reference number of each document, and state whether what you read was the original, a transcript, or an extract. It may seem pedantic to insist on all this, but remember that each page of notes will be filed separately, and there is nothing more frustrating than discovering at a later date that you cannot trace the source of a document you copied.

If it is indexes or calendars to records you are searching, note down the period and sources they cover, even if you do not manage to find your surname in them. Note the surname variants you looked for. If there are other entries, but you are only interested in your direct forebears, or a particular place, then note down that this was the case, and which places the other entries related to. Perhaps you searched a limited period—it is essential to specify which. You can thus avoid repeating the search several times over. It is easy, when looking at a wide range of indexes, calendars, directories and so on, to omit to note

This document combines the problems of both language and handwriting. It is the 'Inquisition Post Mortem' carried out by the Crown into the estate of Sir Gerard Salvayn at York, dated 'Tuesday, the eve of St Lawrence, 47th year of Edward III'. Written in Latin, in a 'Court hand', the document is an example of the Crown's practice of inquiring into the estates held by the chief landowners at the date of their death (see below, p. 106). Modern transcriptions of many of these difficult documents can be found in the series Calendar of Inquisitions Post Mortem, *published by HMSO, 1954. This one appears in Vol. XIII, p. 271. (London, Public Record Office, Chancery Lane, C 135/235/24)*

down their titles, authors, and dates of publication. It is just as important to keep a record of those negative sources as it is of the positive ones.

Always read through your notes to make sure you understand exactly what you have written, and that it is unambiguous. This will spare you having to go back and read the document again. Was the document dated? Have you put the date down? Did you look at the back (dorse) of the document to make sure there was nothing else written on it, which might be relevant? I always write the names of people mentioned in a document in block capitals, which makes for ease of reading.

Patience, resourcefulness, common sense, imagination, and perseverance are the hallmarks of a good genealogist.

Problems of Handwriting, Language and Dates

There are three major problems involved in reading original documents: handwriting, language and dating systems.

You will find that old letter forms are initially intimidating and difficult to decipher, and some letters even seem totally alien. Practice is the only way of mastering old handwriting (palaeography), but your eyes do become gradually attuned to reading earlier hands as you trace your ancestry back.

Certain types of official document have a particular handwriting style peculiar to that department, while local sources have a wide variety of styles ranging from a tight, controlled hand to a loose, evilly spelt dialect or a barely literate scrawl. You can learn to predict an individual clerk's way of writing certain letters, but as the clerk changed, so might the writing habits. One good way of practising reading old documents is to compare a variety of facsimiles of them with line-by-line transcripts. There are several books on the market containing such exercises. Some contain alphabets of both capital and small letters, and you should use these when reading original documents. Many official documents were couched in formulaic terms, and when office copies were made, these words were abbreviated, so it is helpful to know the most common abbreviations.

If you are unable to read a particular word, try to identify each letter in turn, by locating them either in the alphabet or elsewhere in the document, and build up the word gradually. If this fails, leave a blank and look to see if the word occurs somewhere else and you can identify it by its context there. Perhaps the missing word can be identified by its own context. If you are still unsure, write out the word exactly as it appears, and by getting the feel of each letter you can often guess what it was intended to be.

In making a transcript (an exact copy) or taking an abstract, always write down all personal and place names exactly as you see them, and interpret later. It can be easy to confuse them with more familiar modern names which may be quite unrelated.

In England the language of legal documents until 1732 was Latin (although English was used during the Commonwealth, 1650–60), so it is an advantage to have a rudimentary knowledge of Latin grammar

comon, condicon = common, condicion (condition); bar indicates letter dropped

e ſ = -s; flourish to indicate plurals

It = item; flourish **'** to indicate letters omitted, e.g. **ovy** = every

p̄, p̄ = pre

p = pro

ſ ſ = per, par

7 z ꝛ = and

ꝯ = con-

ꝯdicōn = condicion

X = Christ

Xian = Christian

wid = widow

Wittm = William

w^t = with

w^{ch} = which

y = th-

y^t = that

y^e = the

t'i = £

ſ = s., shillings

d = d., pence

iij = 3 in Roman numerals (last digit is nearly always long)

iiij^{xx} = iiij^{xx} = 4 × 20 = 80

ꝛxx^{ti} biij^{s} iiij^{d} = cxx^{li} viii^{s} iiii^{d} = £120 8s. 4d.

and vocabulary. Occasionally you will find that Norman French was used. Both languages were heavily Anglicized by the late Middle Ages, and many of the records were formulaic in character, so that you can reasonably easily wade through the preamble to the core of the document. Quite a number of these records have been translated and printed, so that you can see how they were set out and what the formulas mean. Do look at the originals even if the documents have been printed, because occasionally words are omitted or mistranscribed.

What you need to discover are the date and place of composition of the document, the names of those mentioned in it, their residences, status, and relationship to each other, and the circumstances giving rise to the document. A medieval Latin wordlist should help you if you are unsure as to the meaning of individual words, and if in any doubt at all copy out the document word for word, or at least the phrase in which the problem arises, or even have a photo- or other suitable copy made and tussle with it at home. If it is only one or two words causing difficulty the custodian of the records is normally pleased to help identify them. The earlier the Latin document the easier it is to read, but by the fifteenth century the writing and abbreviations had

Some examples of abbreviations you are likely to come across in old documents.

deteriorated considerably. Fortunately the vernacular hand began to emerge around the same period.

Lastly, the problem of dating: different calendars have been observed throughout the world, which creates problems for scholars and travellers. In 1582 Pope Gregory XIII tried to synchronize the dating schemes in the Christian world into a uniform calendar. The trouble is that the Gregorian Calendar was not adopted by all countries at the same time, so that for instance when William of Orange left Holland on 11 November 1688, he reached England on 5 November.

Scotland adopted the calendar as from 1 January 1600, but the rest of Great Britain not until 1 January 1752. Until then the first day of the year was 25 March (Lady Day), and the whole of that month was the first month of the year, February being the twelfth and last. Thus there was a hiatus period between 1 January and 24 March in modern eyes, and dates falling in this period before 1752 are usually rendered as Old or English Style, for example 30 January 1740 would be written as 30 January 1739/40, or 30 January 1739 Old Style. Additionally, in 1752 only, 2 September was followed by 14 September in Great Britain, to allow the solar year to catch up. In looking at documents before 1752 it

This elaborate document, in Latin, is an example of the 'secretary' hand common in legal (and other) documents in the sixteenth century. Dated 1575, it is a record of proceedings at the manorial court called by the Steward of the Lord of the Manor of Moggerhanger in the parish of Blunham in Bedfordshire. The Steward is likely to have been a local lawyer and the writer his clerk. (Bedfordshire, County Record Office AD 1104/11)

is essential to write down the dates exactly as you see them. The actual date (in modern calendar terms) can be worked out later.

The months September, October, November and December take their names from the Latin words for seven to ten, and are hence sometimes abbreviated as 7^{ber}, 8^{ber}, 9^{ber} and 10^{ber}. In the pre-1752 calendar, of course, these were in fact the seventh to tenth months of the year. After 1752, 7^{ber} is still September, although it is now the ninth month of the year. The Quakers always referred to months by their numbers.

You will also encounter regnal years in certain official records, such as taxation returns and Acts of Parliament. The regnal year begins on the date and anniversary of the current monarch's accession, and this has been so since 1272. Thus 12 George III is the twelfth year of George III's reign (25 October 1771–24 October 1772). During the Commonwealth ordinary dating was used, but when Charles II was restored to the throne in 1660, this regnal year was described as 12 Charles II, and began on 30 January, the anniversary of his father's execution, although the Restoration only occurred on 29 May 1660.

Instead of giving the exact day and month, a document may be dated by a religious festival or saint's day, or the number of days or day of the week before or after it. Occasionally there are problems if a document was dated by Easter, and this came twice in the regnal year, as it did in the reign of Charles I. C. R. Cheney's *Handbook of Dates* is indispensable for discovering the actual dates of such documents.

Legal records are organized under the four legal terms: Hilary, Easter, Trinity and Michaelmas, as well as the regnal year. The regnal year or the monarch might alter mid-term, and so the document will reflect this. For example, Trinity 2/3 Henry VII allows for the new regnal year which began on 22 August.

This shows what a parchment roll looked like. It is made of sheets of parchment stitched together, attached to rollers at each end. This example is the Fenwick Roll, a heraldic manuscript of the time of Henry V and VI, in the College of Arms, London. It contains 1,035 painted shields, commencing with the arms of Prester John and ending with contemporary English Earls and Lords.

Other Problems with Original Documents

When you finally come to look at original documents you may find that they are so large and unwieldy that you have difficulty in unfolding them, never mind keeping them flat enough to read. Many older documents were made of vellum, and later folded. Most repositories supply paperweights to keep them flat once you have managed to unfold them. When reading them it is helpful to put a ruler under each line as you read it, so that you do not lose your place while taking notes. It is easy to transpose or omit lines, and thus misconstrue the whole sense of a document because of this.

Sometimes there will be torn edges, stains or faded scripts. It is often possible to discern what the missing words or word endings should be, but stains and fadings out can conceal whole sections. If there is no duplicate copy, it is a good idea to look at the document under ultra-violet light as this brings up the writing underneath. Look under curled-up corners of a document, as there may be a date lurking there, and similarly on the dorse, where a later endorsement may give you more information about the matter discussed.

Some official records are rolled up. These rolls can consist of many

An example of eighteenth-century 'copperplate' handwriting, used in a Foot of Fine. This was a document recording a sale of land, written three times over on the same parchment. The parchment was then cut into three parts, each participant receiving one, and the third, the bottom or 'Foot', was kept by the Crown (see below, p. 104). (London, Public Record Office, Chancery Lane, CP 25/1231/20 Geo. II Mich.)

membranes stitched end to end to make one long document, which can simply be unwound, or else the membranes may all be stitched together at the top. It is sometimes convenient to drape the roll over a special stand, especially if it is bulky, and to examine the full length of each membrane and turn it over to look at the entries written on the dorse. Occasionally these will be upside down. When using rolls it is important to note the number of the first membrane you search, to avoid looking at it again, and to examine the reverse. Rolls of numbered membranes usually have a margin on the left-hand side in which the names of the protagonists are noted, or the places concerned. It is thus relatively simple to pick out the heading you want.

There may be additional problems of convoluted or unfamiliar terminology, and lack of punctuation. Documents were usually formulaic in content, and the gist of the case may often be found in a few words among a mass of stock phrases and legal jargon. Documents are normally dated at the top or bottom, and the names of interested parties listed at the beginning, or close to the beginning. If the document concerns a dispute the names of the defendants should be repeated at the end. Thus you will quickly find out who were the main participants, but you will still need to read and digest the whole document. This will probably be a laborious process at first, but it is essential to understand what the case was about, and once you have studied a few of them your reading speed will increase.

Individual words and phrases may present difficulties of interpretation, for example legal jargon, especially in relation to land law. You will find it useful if you know a little of the social and legal history of the period in which the document was written. The following is a list of some of the most likely terms you will encounter:

fee simple—hereditary freehold land which could be transferred elsewhere by gift, sale or will.

fee tail—hereditary freehold land which could only pass to the descendants of the original holder.

seisin—possession of the land.

demesne—land retained by the lord of the manor for his own use.

messuage—house, outbuildings and yard.

appurtenances—appendages to the land.

moiety—usually a half-portion of an estate.

coparceners—coheirs.

quitclaim—release of all rights, interest and potential legal action by the grantor to the grantee.

tenant in chief—tenant holding land directly from the Crown.

escheator—Crown representative who collected revenues due to it, especially on the death of a tenant in chief.

primogeniture—custom whereby the eldest son inherited to exclusion of other issue.

Borough English—custom whereby the youngest son inherited to exclusion of other issue.

socage—services not necessarily fixed in nature or amount, later commuted to money payments.

toft and croft—house and enclosed arable land or meadow adjacent to it.

close—enclosure from open fields.

curtilage—yard and outbuildings of a house.

pightle—small piece of land in the open fields, or small enclosed plot.

yardland or virgate—about thirty acres.

headland—strips of land at end of a ploughed field on which the plough turned.

hide, ploughland or carucate—the amount of land which could be ploughed in a year and support a family. Varied with the region.

It may be necessary to consult a legal dictionary, but for most of the words which have ceased to be used or have subsequently changed their meaning, the two volumes of the *Shorter Oxford English Dictionary* are usually adequate. Dialect words can often be found in one of the local printed glossaries.

Here are some alternative uses of familiar terms denoting relationships:

natural son—legitimate son, born in marriage.

father, son—stepfather, stepson, father-in-law, son-in-law, spouse's father-in-law, spouse's son-in-law.

nephew—grandchild.

cousin—nephew or niece.

son-in-law—son by spouse's previous marriage.

son of my wife—son born by wife's previous marriage.

my now wife—present wife, indicating a previous marriage.

kinsman—blood relative, relative by marriage, in any degree.

brother-in-law—stepbrother.

A minor was a person under twenty-one but over eight, and a child under that age was an infant. 'Mrs' was often a courtesy title given to an unmarried lady of some social standing, and 'Mr' denotes the same social status. 'Sir' not only denoted a baronet or knight, but also a cleric.

Analysing the Evidence

After each excursion to search source-material you should marshall all the resulting notes, and add onto the pedigree chart those names and dates which you have proved to belong to it. By doing this at every stage you have a clear picture of what still needs to be proved, and what sources you must next seek out. If the evidence you have collected is not substantial enough, there may be other sources to turn to, or perhaps all you can do is weigh up the circumstantial evidence and decide where the balance of probabilities lies.

Evidence should not be contradictory, although occasionally the original clerks did make errors, or you yourself may have misread or misinterpreted the sources, or have missed out an important detail. If you are in doubt, look at the document again. Another possibility is that your ancestor concealed the truth, and deliberately gave false information, or perhaps was under a misapprehension about certain names and dates. A particularly difficult problem to solve is the cause and use of aliases. They were often adopted for a very good reason, and if someone took pains to conceal his origins from his contemporaries, then there may be little hope of your uncovering them.

If you know approximately when an antecedent, say Thomas Thexton, was born, but no baptism entry can be found in the appropriate parish or Nonconformist chapel registers, although a Thomas Thexton appears in the registers five years earlier and later, what do you do? Was your source of the date of birth correct? Can you check other sources to corroborate this? Babies were not necessarily baptized immediately. Did either child have brothers and sisters whose names were perpetuated by your Thomas when he named his children? What happened to these two Thomas Thextons? Look at the burial and marriage registers to see if you can locate them. If the marriage was after the period of central registration, then the father's name should be given. What about the father's abode and occupation—was there any similarity with those of your Thomas Thexton? Perhaps one of the fathers left a will—did it refer to Thomas?

Another possibility is that you may find two Thomas Thextons baptized in the appropriate year, with the same parentage. Look to see if the earlier child was buried, but it is more likely that one entry recorded a private baptism and the other the child's reception into the church.

Thirdly, you may have widened the search to take in the neighbouring parishes, and have found a Thomas Thexton baptized in one of them, close to your Thomas's year of birth. Is this your ancestor or not? Did this parish register indicate the father's abode? Did the father marry there, and if so where did the register say he lived? What happened to the family? Did it remain there, or move on? In the parish where you hoped to locate him was there a couple of the above child's parents' names having issue baptized there earlier or later? Where was the father buried? If it was where Thomas later lived perhaps the burial entry, gravestone inscription, or will might give a clue as to his place of origin. The Census may show his father living with Thomas, and the age tally with that in the burial register.

'Italic' handwriting of the seventeenth century. The letter, dated 9 December 1632, is from Lady Ann Meautys to her sister, Lady Bacon. (Essex Record Office, Braybrooke archives, Cornwallis-Bacon papers, D/DBy C23/2)

Fourthly, maybe you found several entries of Thomas Thexton, the children of different parents. What happened to them? Do the burial and marriage registers help? Look at the names of their siblings for clues as to a pattern, or similarity of parental residence and occupation. The wills of the fathers and sons, or others of the same surname in the area, may help to explain what became of these Thomas Thextons, and thus help to sort out which was your ancestor.

When looking at wills make sure that the names corresponding with entries in parish registers relate to people still alive when the will was drawn up. Where there is much duplication of Christian names among different families of the same surname, it is very easy to confuse them. Make sure also that these individuals are not ascribed impossible ages to fit into the will. Continuity of landholding and occupation are clues in identifying the different family units, and it is also often worth looking at wills of collateral branches, friends and neighbours to clarify the pedigree.

It is important not to accumulate so much evidence that it gets out of hand before you try to analyse it, as you will end up not being sure of what you already know and what you are still looking for. It is infinitely preferable to analyse your material as you go along, and to incorporate it onto the pedigree chart. Constantly refer back to your previous notes during your searches, for clues you may have missed.

What to put in your pedigree. This checklist gives all the basic information that ideally you should try to fill in for all your ancestors. The order is a standard one used by genealogists.

Male

1. Full names of each male, including surname
2. Known places of residence, the earliest first, with dates
3. Occupations, professions, status, titles, military or naval rank
4. Educational and professional qualifications
5. Awards, decorations
6. Landownership details, including dates
7. Exact date and place of birth and/or baptism, including county
8. Where educated
9. Any local or official appointments held (e.g. churchwarden)
10. Details of military service, including dates, campaigns, mentions in despatches, and regiment
11. Details of date of any emigration
12. Whether mentioned in anyone's will, and the date
13. Date and place of death and/or burial, and the county
14. If a gravestone (monumental inscription) was erected to him
15. Date of will, and probate, with the name of the probate court
16. Date of administration grant, and the court
17. Ages as recorded in the Census

Female

The wife's name is normally written on the right of her husband's; the first wife is placed on his left, and the second and succeeding wives on his right. The surnames of females are conventionally not included.

1. Full name
2. Places of residence before marriage and in widowhood, including dates
3. Occupation or profession
4. Educational and professional qualifications
5. Awards and decorations
6. Exact date and place of birth and/or baptism, including county
7. Full name, surname, residence, occupation or profession, qualifications, awards and decorations of her father if she married into your family
8. Exact date and place of marriage or marriages, including county, plus details of her other husband as in 7
9. Exact date of decree absolute of divorce (entered prior to details of any subsequent remarriage)
10. Whether named in anyone's will, and the date
11. As in 13, 14, 15, 16 and 17 under Male

Drafting a Pedigree

The illustrations show several ways in which you can set out your pedigree chart. One system is to place all the males on one side of the chart, in order of seniority of birth, followed by the female issue of the same parents. This is not strictly necessary. What is necessary is that you should have all those people of the same generation, regardless of parentage, on the same line, so that you can see at a glance exactly how they are related to each other. You will need a large sheet of paper to ensure this.

If you are making a circular or birthbrief type of pedigree, these only allow spaces for your direct ancestors, and not their brothers and sisters. If you wish to chart out these individuals as well, then you need to be generous in your allocation of space to each family.

What do you include in the pedigree? Ideally you should aim at all the information listed in the table, the information being slightly different for males and females. In practice, however, you are unlikely to discover as much detail as this for many of your ancestors.

Adopted children are not of the blood, and therefore no descent line joins them to the family of adoption. Illegitimate issue are indicated by a wavy descent line, even if the parents subsequently married. Any dubious descents are indicated by a dotted line until definite proof can be found. If a person had offspring by more than one marriage then the issue should be shown as descended from the relevant union.

Always place the latest generation lowest on the pedigree, but not right at the bottom of the paper as you may want to add later descendants. Allow a depth of about two inches per generation. Each time you discover an earlier generation you add it onto the top. Any persons of the same surname, in the same parish, but so far unconnected to your branch, may be added at the side of the chart as a reminder, on the generation line where you would expect them to be.

Only put factual information onto the pedigree chart, and use a pencil so that you can erase it if you later need to correct or expand a biography as new information comes to light. Thus you have set out in pictorial form what you have achieved so far, and know at a glance which stage you have reached. It is also more readily understood by others who may see it.

What to do with the Information

The chart only contains the briefest summary of your knowledge. It is in your notes that your full information is kept, along with your references and records of searches, and it is essential to maintain your notes in good order. Not only are they the documentation of the work you have already done, but you need to be able to refer to them for clues as to where to look next. It is an excellent idea to file your information in a loose-leaf binder right from the start, as this encourages tidy habits, makes for easy reference, and can be carried on your search travels.

Sooner or later you will have to reorganize your material into sections. Your own notes can be filed with the latest generation at the

M

John Harris
bapt. 11 Oct 1778, St. Giles, Oxford
Carpenter, St Peter le Bailey, Oxford
Freeman 15 Sept. 1800
d. 21 Feb 1843, Oxford

= **Mary Grubb**
bapt. c. 1778/9, St Peter le Bailey, Oxford
m. 8 Nov. 1801, St Peter le Bailey
d. 1848, Oxford

N

John Harris
bapt. 9 Nov. 1803, St Peter le Bailey
Carpenter, St Ebbe's
Freeman 18 Aug 1825
d. ? c.1853

= **?**
m. c. 1825 – 1831,
probably at Kensington,
Middx.

other issue

O

Henry Francis Harris
b. c. 1828-31, Kensington, Middx.
d. Dec. 1919, Oxford.

= **Ann Pavier**
b. 1835, St Ebbe's, Oxford
m. 2 Feb. 1852, Oxford Register Office
Tailoress

?

P

Sarah Ann Harris
b. 1852, Oxford

Henry William Harris
b. 1854, Oxford

George James Harris
b. 1857, Oxford
Electrician

Charles John Harris
b. 11 Oct. 1858,
St. Ebbe's Oxford
d. c.1892-4 ?, Brixton, Surrey

= **Mary Lambert**
b. c. 1857, Oxford
m. 3 Sept. 1887

Q

Millicent Mary Harris
b. 28 March 1889, Brixton, Surrey
Bindery assistant (OUP)
d. 1977.

Hubert Charles Harris
b. 1 Nov. 1890, Brixton, Surrey
d. 20 Feb. 1973, Oxford
Compositor (OUP)

= **Annie Martha Eliza Pimm**
b. 9 Jan 1891, Paddington, Middx.
m. 2 Aug. 1919, N. Hinksey
Berks.

George Henry Harris
b. 21 July 1893,
? Brixton, Surrey
bapt. 13 Sept. 1894, Oxford

R

Doreen Millicent Harris
b. 28 August 1920, Oxford
shop assistant (Webbers)

Hubert George Harris
b. 30 Jan. 1923, Oxford
Bookbinder (OUP.)

= **Audrey Mary Smith**
b. 27 December 1928, Oxford
m. 26 March 1949, Oxford
shop assistant (Elliston + Cavell)

S

Colin George Harris
b. 14 Jan. 1950, Oxford
Library assistant (Bodleian)

Marilyn Joy Harris
b. 5 April 1953, Oxford
Laboratory technician (Radcliffe)

Diane Mary Harris
b. 12 July 1957, Oxford
Secretary / receptionist

An example of a draft pedigree tracing back the paternal line of Colin Harris, several of whose ancestors are documented in this book. The family has long been settled in Oxford; John Harris jnr. moved to Kensington, but his son returned. Note that each generation has a code letter, which can be used as part of a reference system to avoid any confusion between the generations.

front, perhaps with a tag indicating the generation or family unit concerned. You may even wish to devote separate sections to each of your direct forebears, and these should be indicated by individual tags (including name and code number—see below). Irrelevant material should be filed at the back, for later reference, and should be arranged either under topics (such as wills), or periods. What is important is that you should devise a method which best suits you, and stick to it. Copies of original documents, and perhaps original sources themselves, can either be filed separately, perhaps in a scrapbook, or with your own notes. If you insert them in a scrapbook you should label each item, attribute it to its source, and have a pedigree and table of contents at the front. They will probably not form a pedigree on their own. Try to arrange them in a book with polythene leaves so that you can rearrange them, but do check that condensation will not harm them, and that the folios are big enough to house the largest document without damage. It may be helpful to keep a list of repositories visited, and the records consulted.

A card index, containing a card for each person on the pedigree chart, can include parentage, biographical details, sources, speculations and ideas for further research, which you would not put on the chart itself. Thus cards are a summary of each person on the pedigree. The cards should be linked to the chart by a cross-reference system. Each generation on the chart should have a code letter, and each person in that generation should have a number. In this way every individual on your chart has a unique code reference which avoids any confusion between people of the same name in different generations, for example.

Another way of recording your direct ancestors is by the circular birth brief. In the first circle you record the details of your father (F) and your mother (M), and then work outwards, recording each generation in the next concentric circle. It can also be quite amusing to reverse the procedure, placing a pair of ancestors in the centre and then recording their ever-increasing number of descendants in each succeeding circle.

Start with the letter S for yourself, the letter R for the previous generation, and so on. The cards are filed by generation letter, and then alphabetically within each generation, the earliest generation letter being at the front of the file. It is a good idea not to start with a number lower than 100 in each generation, to allow for later discoveries.

Adopt a card index system which is simple and stick to it. I have seen card indexes so complicated that they need another card index to explain how they operate!

Some pedigree charts plot out the years covered by each letter in the generation grid, and relate it to the national and local events during that period. This sets your family in a wider social context.

Writing the Family History

At some stage you may wish to produce a permanent narrative account of your family history. Such an account can be approached in two ways: it can be set out impersonally like a chronicle, beginning with your earliest known ancestors; or it can be a personal story unfolding the history of your researches. Whatever you do, a good pedigree chart is essential. Try to illustrate the account with maps, photographs and copies of documents. The danger in writing a family history is that it can become little more than a list of names; always bear in mind the need for the story you are telling to be an interesting one.

Possibly the ideal informal family history is one that is a combined narrative and scrapbook. However, you may feel more ambitious, and decide to print it; and members of your family may be persuaded to subscribe to the cost of production by buying a copy. The method you choose varies with how much you wish to invest, and how elaborate you want the history to be. You may make roneoed or xeroxed copies, or have a printer use off-set litho from a tidy typescript. Obviously, the fewer pages you have the less the cost, and the less need for a strong and expensive binding. Photographs are not cheap to reproduce and you would be advised to make sure you do not lose money on your venture. Decide realistically what your market will be, and obtain estimates from several printers before embarking on the final stage. The cheapest is not always the best. Unless the family history is of exceptional general appeal, you are unlikely to interest a publisher in footing the bill. It may therefore be better to settle for compiling a single scrapbook, and to write an article on the family's history for the local Family History Society journal. You could always ask for more copies of this, or obtain an off-print.

Registering or Lodging your Pedigree

What should you do with the pedigree chart? No pedigree can ever be said to be complete, as it may well be amplified by someone else at a later stage, and so it is of interest to others to know of its existence, just as you would have been grateful for such a pedigree when you began.

Presumably you have given copies of the pedigree to your relatives. You can approach the local record repository to ask if it would accept a

An example of a personal index card, giving details of the James Tanner who appears in the family Bible on p. 32 and in several other documents in this book (see p. 116). The card was kindly supplied by Mrs P. Norman of Middlesex, James Tanner's descendant.

TANNER JAMES bn. 28.2.1794. bapt. 10 10
father JOHN, fisherman mother ELIZAB
occupation mariner status Master. N
marriage i. 26.3.1817 ANN WILLIAMS sp. P
      ii. 27.6.1842 HANNAH SMITH w
children 6 sons. 2 daus.
Bible entries inclu. notes on ships etc
'Vesper' of Padstow 1841. BT 98/43
1841 census - not in St. Ives 1851 'Back
MN List 1859 - exam requirements
Collected entries- Agreements & crew
'West Briton' Shipping news, extrac

died 5.1.1868 Madron workhouse

A Completed National Pedigree Index card.

Surname: **TANNER**	Period: **1782-1979**	Parish: (Earliest first) County:
Special Features: **MARINERS, OCCUPATIONS OVERSEAS**		**ST. IVES CORNWALL**
		MADRON "
		PERSIA
Published in (Full title, reference & date): **EXTRACTS AS ILLUSTRATIONS 'THE FAMILY HISTORY BOOK' PHAIDON 1980**		**MALDON ESSEX**
Compiler: **MRS. P. NORMAN**		
Date submitted: **12th Dec 1979**		Property of National Pedigree Index c/o Society of Genealogists, London

copy as a gift, but often such places are so full of their own material that any more, of a marginal interest, might not be welcome. A local Historical Society, or, better still, Family History Society, might certainly be interested, or could advise you. National or state genealogical societies often have their own libraries, and again they are often pressed for space, but it is still worth inquiring.

The College of Arms in London has thousands of pedigrees which have been examined against the evidences supporting them, and entered in official registers. If you pay the fee for this to be done your pedigree will be assured of a permanent record. Although these registers are not generally open to the public, searches can be made of the pedigrees in response to specific inquiries about a particular surname.

There is also the National Pedigree Index, which was founded in 1976, with the aim of acting as a central clearing-house to put people working on the same families in touch with each other, and to keep an up-to-date slip index of those pedigrees of British families which have been or are currently being researched. You would be doing a great service by completing one of these slips for inclusion in the Index. The address of the Index is given at the back of this book.

Forming a Family History Society

You may be surprised to discover how many others in your area share your interest in genealogy. If a society does not already exist, why not advertise in the local library or newspaper, to see if others might be willing to join in forming one? Usually such societies meet regularly to discuss topics of mutual interest, invite guest speakers, publish journals for members outside the area but with ancestors emanating from it, and work on projects such as the transcription or indexing of local documents to help with their searches. There are many societies all over the world, organized on a national or local basis, or under a federal structure, such as the Federation of Family History Societies in England, formed in 1974. Any of the national societies or local libraries should be able to advise you about existing societies in your own area, or area of interest, for they normally receive their journals or advertise their events. A small subscription is usually charged, and the pleasure that belonging to such a society brings makes it well worth the effort of organizing one. Do make sure, however, that you have good accounting, or you could end up subsidizing as well as organizing it.

If your name is sufficiently unusual it may even be a good idea to try and form a One Name Society, writing to all those of the same surname whose addresses you have found in current telephone directories to inquire whether they would be interested in becoming founder-members. Then you can trace all occurrences of the surname in the available records, publish a newsletter to circulate the results, and perhaps link many members together through your researches.

The success of a society depends on the organizing ability and enthusiasm of its founder and committee: do not be too ambitious in making promises, and try to maintain a reasonable standard in the content of any journals and lectures. Try to persuade experts to come and speak to your society to prevent a lapse into the blind leading the blind. When you do, make sure that you enclose a stamped self-addressed envelope in your invitation, and look after your lecturers, some of whom may have travelled a distance, and are, after all, doing you a favour, perhaps with little or no remuneration. If you can afford it, pay for their expenses and a decent meal, and don't waste their time at the beginning of the meeting with parochial matters, for it is both discourteous and unnecessary.

It is a wise idea to join the national or state society, for they will have many more facilities than local ones, and often provide a means of meeting family historians from all over the country and abroad, and a chance to learn useful ideas for implementation in your own society.

Summing Up

In this chapter I have concentrated on practical advice on how to approach and use original sources, although I am sure that there will be many points I have missed. The first visit to a record repository can be a daunting experience, but if you are well prepared and have a good idea what you are looking for, this feeling soon passes. Lack of response to written requests can be discouraging, but it may be because you have failed to enclose a stamped self-addressed envelope, or your letter was too tortuous and involved; the important point to remember is that you should not be easily put off. You need to be persistent as well as patient. You will never stop discovering new sources, however long you search, because each stage introduces new problems and clues to be pursued. You can still enjoy the search even if you don't always find that elusive ancestor.

Your Family Record
Charts for Recording Your Own Pedigree

The following pages have been designed for you to fill in the details of your own family history. The final, full pedigree of any person, showing a whole network of relationships, can only be set down pictorially on a large sheet. Within the smaller format of a book, the records of the family can be built up in stages.

1. Your direct ancestors (chart 1). This is called a 'birth-brief', and records your direct ancestors in both lines. Most people will probably be able to fill it in at least as far as their great-grandparents with only a few gaps. Couples wishing to record both the husband's and the wife's ancestors should fill their names in at level 'R'.

2. Your direct ancestors' families, and your own descendants (chart 2). The second section enables you to fill in not only your direct ancestors but also their brothers and sisters. In the first chart (2a) record yourself and your brothers and sisters, then your father and his brothers and sisters, and so on. This will show all the aunts and uncles in your paternal line (for a filled-in example, see p. 78 above). The two lowest levels are for your own descendants. If your family was not a large one, you may find space to fill in some of your aunts' and uncles' marriages and their children.

In the second chart (2b), record your mother's family, her father's family, and so on. And to avoid repetition, the two lower levels can be used for your nephews and nieces. The third and fourth charts (2c, 2d) have been left blank for you to fill in as required, tracing back any other line that did not fit in charts 2a and 2b.

3. Records of marriages (chart 3). On chart 2 there will not be much space to record your aunts' and uncles' marriages and offspring (i.e. your cousins). With most families a large sheet of paper would be needed, so that the next stage here is to replace charts by lists. In the thirty panels of chart 3 you can record details of the marriages and offspring of many of your relatives recorded on charts 1 and 2.

4. Family details. The last chart is left blank for you to fill in with more detailed records of the careers of members of your own family. It can of course be added to as your family grows.

1 Your Direct Ancestors

On this chart you should record your direct ancestors - parents, grandparents, and so on. You should give the full name, and date and place of birth and death of each individual, and the date and place of each marriage. The letters N-S are conventional generation grid letters.

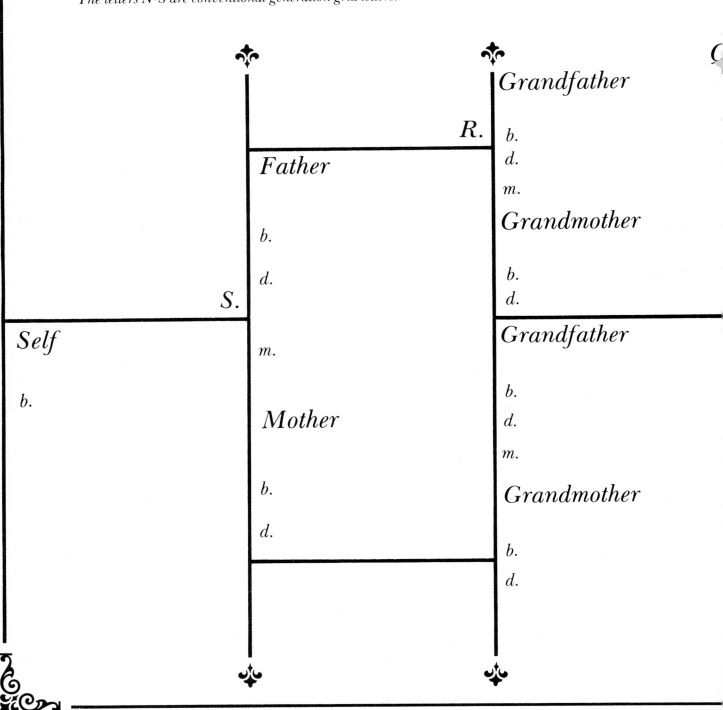

Grandfather

R.

b.

d.

m.

Grandmother

b.

d.

Father

b.

d.

S.

Self

m.

b.

Grandfather

b.

d.

m.

Mother

Grandmother

b.

b.

d.

d.

reat-randparents	P.	Great-great-grandparents	O.	Great-great-great-grandparents N.
p.u.u.		m.		
p.u.		m.		
u.u.		m.		
p.u.		m.		
u.u.		m.		
p.u.		m.		
u.u.		m.		
		m.		

2a Your Father's Family, Your Own Descendants

In this chart you should record your aunts and uncles in your direct male line, beginning with your father's family. The two lowest levels are for your own descendants. If there is space, include also marriages and offspring.

O. *Your paternal great-great-grandfather's family*

P. *Your paternal great-grandfather's family*

Q. *Your paternal grandfather's family*

R. *Your father's family*

S. *Self and family*

T. *Own children*

U. *Own grandchildren*

2b Your Mother's Family, Your Nephews and Nieces

On this chart you should repeat the exercise of chart 2a, this time recording aunts and uncles on your mother's side. Again, you may have space to record marriages and cousins. Use the lower two levels this time for nephews and nieces.

O. *Your maternal great-great-grandfather's family*

P. *Your maternal great-grandfather's family*

Q. *Your maternal grandfather's family*

R. *Your mother's family*

S. *Self and family*

T. *Your nephews and nieces*

U. *Your great-nephews and nieces*

2c Other Ancestors

These two charts have been left blank for you to adapt to your own needs. You may be able to trace one line further back, or you may be particularly well informed about one particular branch of the family for which there was no room on the previous charts.

2d Other Ancestors

3 Records of Marriages

If your family was a large one there will not be room on the preceding lists to record all the marriages and offspring of your aunts, uncles, cousins and descendants. On the following pages these can now be recorded in tabular form. The space marked for children can of course be adapted where appropriate to provide a space for more relevant information. The full names of each couple should be given, with date and place of marriage and date and place of birth (and death) of each child.

Husband:
Wife:
Marriage:
Children:

Husband:
Wife:
Marriage:
Children:

Husband:
Wife:
Marriage:
Children:

Husband:
Wife:
Marriage:
Children:

Husband:
Wife:
Marriage:
Children:

Husband:
Wife:
Marriage:
Children:

Husband:
Wife:
Marriage:
Children:

Husband:
Wife:
Marriage:
Children:

Husband:
Wife:
Marriage:
Children:

Husband:
Wife:
Marriage:
Children:

Husband:
Wife:
Marriage:
Children:

Husband:
Wife:
Marriage:
Children:

Husband:
Wife:
Marriage:
Children:

Husband:
Wife:
Marriage:
Children:

Husband:

Wife:

Marriage:

Children:

Husband:

Wife:

Marriage:

Children:

Husband:

Wife:

Marriage:

Children:

Husband:

Wife:

Marriage:

Children:

Husband:

Wife:

Marriage:

Children:

Husband:

Wife:

Marriage:

Children:

Husband:

Wife:

Marriage:

Children:

Husband:

Wife:

Marriage:

Children:

Husband:
Wife:
Marriage:
Children:

Husband:
Wife:
Marriage:
Children:

Husband:
Wife:
Marriage:
Children:

Husband:
Wife:
Marriage:
Children:

Husband:
Wife:
Marriage:
Children:

Husband:
Wife:
Marriage:
Children:

Husband:
Wife:
Marriage:
Children:

Husband:
Wife:
Marriage:
Children:

4 Family Details

4 How our Ancestors Lived

U p to now the aim has been basically genealogical in the narrow sense—to establish your pedigree as far back as possible, but without elaborating on it in any way. Some of the basic sources already discussed can illustrate the environment in which your ancestors lived, but that is only the start; once you have identified them, there are many other sources to turn to which will tell you more about your ancestors as individuals. As your knowledge increases, you can also begin to ask wider questions. For example, what have you been able to learn about the size of the family, or the intervals between births, or the naming pattern? Was there a high infant mortality rate? Why? Were the wives local? How long did the family remain in any one place? Did it split up? What about continuity of occupation among the family? Did it have to move around to find employment? What was its religious denomination?

These sorts of questions penetrate further into the family's history, and help us to understand its mode of life in a wider social and local background. In this chapter I turn to further sources which should throw new light on the way your ancestors lived. Many archives are organized on a chronological and/or geographical basis, and so you usually need to know names, dates and places before you can use these further records successfully.

Legal Records

Many family historians give legal records a wide berth, because of their sheer variety and volume, and because of their criminal overtones, but actually they are an excellent source of further knowledge about your ancestors of whatever social status, on both sides of the law. People no longer feel much embarrassment at discovering a criminal forebear, who was perhaps transported for a felony we would consider trifling today. In addition to the minutes of criminal trials, there are the lists of those men qualified to serve as jurors, and of those commissioned to keep the peace, which might well have included one of your ancestors.

Civil wrongs, like trespass against a person, his goods or his land, were tried from the early Middle Ages by professional judges in the Court of Common Pleas if the dispute was between two subjects, or the Court of King's Bench if Crown property was involved. I have pre-

Contrasts of time, place and situation, from the aristocracy of Elizabethan England (left) to the slums of 19th-century London (above). One of the fascinations of setting out to investigate your own family history is that you may well find both gentry and paupers among your ancestors. The detail is from a painting of the marriage of Sir Henry Unton in 1596 (artist unknown, National Portrait Gallery, London). The engraving Over London by Rail *(1876), is by Gustave Doré, a French artist who spent much time in the city from the mid-19th century.*

viously referred to the plea rolls of these courts, which contain pedigrees of those persons seeking to establish legal status in order to obtain a hearing (see above, pp. 19–20).

In the fourteenth century the Court of Chancery, headed by the Lord Chancellor, developed to deal with those civil wrongs for which there was no remedy in the other two common law courts, and judgement was based on conscience. This court came to dominate the legal scene to such an extent that by the eighteenth century its legal machinery was almost swamped under the number of claims presented to it, and the wait for a hearing could be almost interminable. The other major court, the Exchequer, dealt with matters relating to debts owed to the Crown, but anyone could claim to be acting on the Crown's behalf. The records of all these courts are deposited in the Public Record Office in London.

Disputes about money, land, goods and contents of wills were presented to the Court of Chancery. The means of reference to the records of the proceedings of the Court is by printed calendars down to the early seventeenth century, and manuscript calendars covering the later Bills and Answers down to the mid-nineteenth century. They are listed under the plaintiff's name, those of the same initial letter being grouped together, and the defendant's name; the nature of the suit and the county where disputed property lay complete the entry. The first

97

A Chancery Master's exhibit of 28 November 1735, relating to a lawsuit between Thomas Noble and William Kemsey. It lists all the relevant papers in the possession of Thomas Noble, who was the defendant in the case. The papers include indentures, accounts and drafts of complaints and answers relating to earlier lawsuits. (London, Public Record Office, Chancery Lane, C 103/184)

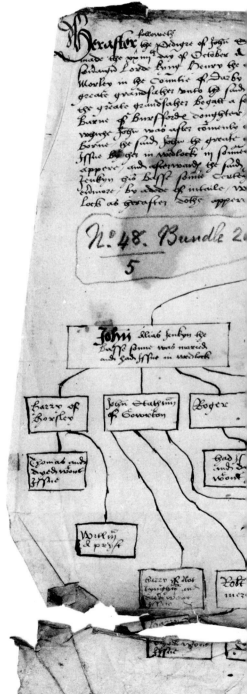

series of calendars to the early seventeenth century do not contain dates, and the only way of finding out the approximate year of a dispute is by matching up the bundle number of the document with the name of the current Lord Chancellor, entered at the front of the calendar. Unfortunately, the names of all the plaintiffs in a case were not always included in the calendars, nor are there cross-reference calendars of defendants. Bills of Complaint might have been filed separately from the Answers sent by defendants, and so you must search the calendars covering the whole of the period in which you are interested. These suits were retrospective, and may relate to events which occurred several generations before, so you should allow a wide period when looking at the calendars.

The Chancery proceedings themselves are made up of the Bills of Complaint, addressed to the Lord Chancellor, the summary (crib) of the charge which was sent to the defendant, his Answer, and perhaps further counter-charges. They are often full of genealogical informations, especially where an inter-family dispute was involved. Details of purchase and descent of property, marriage settlements, wills, mortgages, family migrations and vicissitudes, recorded conversations, and the behaviour of individuals are graphically reproduced in support of the relevant claim or defence.

A list of questions (interrogatories) was drawn up for witnesses to answer for the plaintiff and for the defendant; and their answers (depositions) can be illuminating, not only about the protagonists, but about the witnesses themselves. Their answers include the name, address, age and occupation of each witness, plus his signature at the

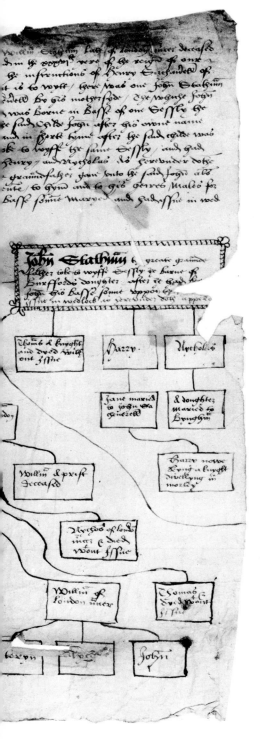

The pedigree of the Statham family among the records of the Court of Requests in the Public Record Office, Chancery Lane (Req. 2/26/48). The pedigree was drawn up on 24 October 1544 for Sir Henry Sacheverell of Morley, Derbyshire, and was produced to the Court of Requests to support John Statham's claim to disputed lands in the same county in 1558.

bottom. Until 1603 and after 1714 they are filed with the Bills and Answers, but during the intervening period the means of reference is by calendars arranged alphabetically by the initial letters of the plaintiff's surname, the defendant and the date. A partial index of these witnesses, listed together with the names of witnesses in the Exchequer Court, plus other sources, was made by Charles Bernau. A microfilm copy of this index is held by the Society of Genealogists in London, and it is invaluable for tracing antecedents who gave evidence in cases of involving their own village, or friends or relatives. The exhibits produced in support of the claim were often left behind with the Masters in Chancery, and these can include original wills, deeds and letters of great interest to the family historian. They are similarly calendared under the name of the plaintiff, defendant and date.

The Court of Requests dealt with land and monetary matters between 1485 and circa 1642, and its records are in the Public Record Office in London. There is a printed surname index to the protagonists, and a place-name index. If you know where your ancestors lived during those years, but cannot discover anything more about them, this source can be very helpful in extending the pedigree further. Even if the surname does not appear in the index, the place of residence might, and as all the papers pertinent to a case were filed together, you may discover that that an ancestor was called as a witness. The information in these records is similar to that in the Court of Chancery.

Perhaps your family has a tradition of 'money in Chancery', unclaimed funds to which it is somehow entitled. Dormant funds of over fifteen years' duration, held by the Supreme Court of Judicature for England and Wales, have been listed and printed annually since 1952. These lists are the only means of discovering if such funds exist, and give the name and number of each account. They can be seen at the Public Record Office, in London, but the Supreme Court, also in London, holds the original papers. In many cases the cost of obtaining sufficient proof of entitlement to these funds would far exceed the totals involved.

There are two classes of criminal records: those of the Assize Courts, and those of the Quarter Sessions, the former held mainly by the Public Record Office, and the latter by the appropriate County Record Office. After 1805 and up to 1892 there are in the Public Record Office at Kew annual criminal registers for England and Wales, arranged by county and then listing the names of persons tried, where and at what date, for what offence, the verdict and sentence. Before this it is a matter of painstakingly searching through the Minute Books of the Assize Circuit concerned, or the Quarter Sessions Rolls.

The English and Welsh counties were divided into seven Assize Circuits, the two judges of each Circuit holding an Assize in all of the constituent counties, twice or three times a year, to try serious offences. These included murder, manslaughter, marital offences, rape, riot, unlawful assembly, vote rigging and impersonation, burglary, trespass, counterfeiting coin, uttering false bills of exchange, treasons and insurrections. The most important sources for the family historian are the Minute Books, each extending over several years and occasionally dating from the sixteenth century, and the Indictments, filed in bundles under each meeting of the Court in a particular county. The Minute Books contain the names, offences and sentences of all those who appeared for trial, while the Indictments, once you have discovered the date of the trial, will give you full details of the offence, the plea, the verdict and the sentence, plus the name, age, occupation and abode of the defendant. Attached to the Indictments there is normally the Gaol Calendar of all defendants awaiting trial, listing names, ages, occupations, abodes, the offence and when and where originally committed and by whom. A list of substantial landowners in the county, liable to be called as the grand jury, to scrutinize the Indictments, and a similar list of lesser landowners entitled to sit as the petty jury to give its verdict, can usually be found in the same bundle.

The role of Quarter Sessions, however, was twofold. Besides dispensing justice, it also dealt with the day-to-day administration of the county. It was composed of not less than three Justices of the Peace, commissioned by Letters Patent from the Crown from among the local substantial landowners, and met four times a year. The Justices of the Peace were responsible for licensing certain traders, alehouses, dissenters' meeting houses, and printing presses, and supervised the administration of the Poor Law, fixed weights, measures and prices, registered Turnpike Trusts, charities, Friendly Societies and Freemasons' Lodges. These records, surviving occasionally from the mid-sixteenth century, can be off-putting because of their bulk and lack of

Below left. A grand jury list from the minute books of the North-Eastern Assize Circuit, 13 July 1771. The grand jury's duty was to examine the indictments to see if there was a case to answer. It consisted of 23 of the major landowners of the county. The Assize records contain many lists of jurors and of prisoners, as well as giving detailed accounts of the offences tried. (London, Public Record Office, Chancery Lane, ASSI 41/6)

Below. A Quarter Sessions decision confirming the removal of James Cooke and his family from St Thomas's to St Giles's parish in Oxford. The St Giles churchwardens and overseers, unwilling to accept this new burden on the parish, appealed against the Removal Order but their appeal was rejected. The document is now among the accounts of the Overseers of the Poor of St Giles's parish. (Oxford, Bodleian Library, MS. D.D. Par. Oxf. St Giles, c. 27 (C), fol. 45)

This old engraving shows the scene at the Crown Court of Hertford, with the prisoners being led in to face the judge. (London, Mansell Collection)

A local paper reports on Saturday 25 February 1843 the Inquest on John Harris, who died, aged 66, after being run over by a cart. This is Colin Harris's ancestor, born in 1778 (see above, p. 78). Oxford Chronicle and Reading Gazette, *in the archives of the British Library, Colindale Newspaper Library, London)*

An inquest was held on Friday last, before G. Cecil, Esq. coroner, at the Hind's Head, St. Peter-le-Bailey parish, in this city, on view of the body of John Harris.—Thomas Lucas deposed—I am City Marshall; on Thursday last, between 3 and 4 o'clock in the afternoon, I was walking up Walton-place, near the Oxford workhouse, when I saw John Harris walking towards me; at the same time a cart was going the same direction as myself; I saw Harris stagger and fall under the wheel of the cart; I hallooed ' woe!' and the horse stopped; the horse was going very slow; the wheel came against Harris's body; no blame was attached to the driver of the cart.—George Robert Wyatt deposed—I am a surgeon and apothecary residing in Oxford; on Thursday last John Harris was brought into the lodge of the workhouse about 4 o'clock; I saw him immediately, and examined him as to the state of his head; he seemed confused, as though he had undergone some shock or suffered under some disease of the head; I saw him twice, and afterwards prescribed for him; he died on Tuesday last; my opinion is that he died from apoplexy hastened by the shock sustained in his fall under the cart; he had a very extensive bruise on the right hip and thigh, which I suppose was occasioned by the wheel of the cart; he was 66 years of age.—Verdict, " Apoplexy, accelerated by accidentally falling under the wheel of a cart, and the wheel injuring his hip and thigh."

detailed cataloguing. But because of the wide variety of matters with which they dealt these are just the type of source which can add much to your family history. The Quarter Sessions also enrolled lists of local people liable for jury service after 1696, and these jurors' lists are a directory of men aged twenty-one and over, qualified by their property, giving their names, ages, rank or occupations, addresses, and the annual value of the property, arranged by parish. Between 1673 and 1828 the names of military and civil officers taking the oaths of supremacy and allegiance were also enrolled, and there are also lists of those people commissioned as Justices of the Peace in the county.

On the judicial side the Quarter Sessions dealt with offences against bye-laws and licensing, non-payment of tithes and taxes, failures to pay maintenance for bastards, apprenticeship and Poor Law offences, and many of the same crimes as the Assize Courts, except treason. In the County Record Office also will be the minutes of the monthly Petty Sessions of the Justices of the Peace, and the occasional Coroner's Inquests.

Local newspapers often contain vivid reports of the proceedings at Quarter Sessions and Coroner's Inquests, and if you find an antecedent's name among these records, the newspaper may well enlarge on the case. Local newspapers, some of which are indexed, can normally be viewed on application to the local reference library, or the newspaper office itself, but there is an almost complete run of these, and national newspapers from 1801, at the Colindale Newspaper Library, London, earlier ones being deposited at the British Library.

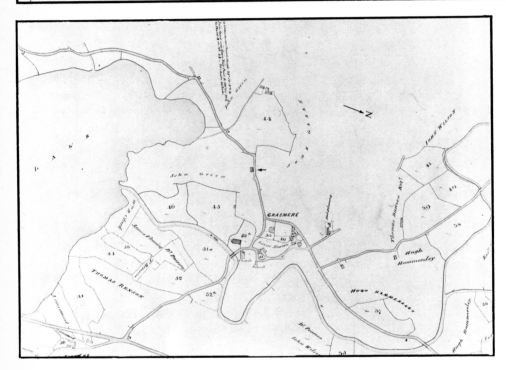

LANDOWNERS.	OCCUPIERS.	Numbers referring to the Plan.	NAME AND DESCRIPTION OF LANDS AND PREMISES.	STATE OF CULTIVATION.	QUANTITIES IN STATUTE MEASURE.			Amount of Rental Rector
					A.	R.	P.	£ s. d.
Fletcher Mary	Herself	7	Kilnhow	Arable	3	2	23	15
Yate William	James Fleming	21	Low Intack	Pasture	1	1	4	9
Yate William	John Green	38	Horsesheads	Arable	3		21	1
Yate John	Himself	44	House field	Arable	6	3	16	
		45	Under Hall	Arable	5	3	20	
		46	Busks	Meadow	3	2	38	
					16	1	34	7
Greenwood James	James Fleming and another	20	Far Close	Arable	4		35	
	Edward Brockelbank	2	Bremmer Meadow	Meadow	2		24	
	Himself	55	Townend Meadow	Meadow	4	2	20	

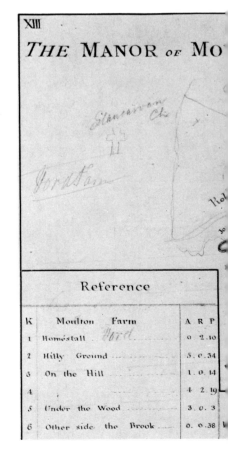

Records of Residence and Landownership

You will have found out where your forebears lived from public and local records, but perhaps may not have succeeded in pinpointing the exact location of a particular dwelling, which may no longer exist. You can discover this information from surviving contemporary maps, some even stating the extent, nature and annual value of the property. Deeds and manorial records will tell you when and for how long the property was occupied, while rates and taxation records show how much they and their contents were worth at a given date.

The most complete series of maps date from the nineteenth century, the chief being those of the 11,800 parishes covered by the Tithe Redemption Commissioners between 1836 and 1842, described else-

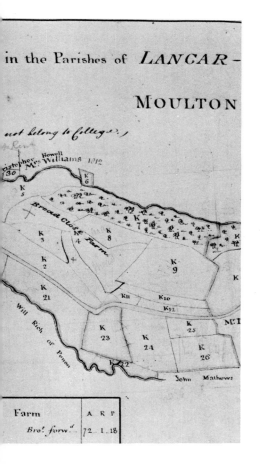

where (see p. 51). Although enclosures took place from the early Tudor period, enclosure maps are particularly voluminous in the nineteenth century, especially after the Enclosure Acts of 1801, 1836 and 1845. From the eighteenth century enclosures were commonly by private Act of Parliament, and the House of Lords Record Office, in London, holds these Acts. The maps and awards to 1836 and from 1845 are deposited in the Public Record Office, those in the intervening period and prior to 1801 being dispersed in the County Record Offices. The awards record the name of the occupier of each plot of land, its extent, nature and annual value, and the size and site of the new allotment made to him based on this information.

The Ordnance Survey maps, based on one inch to a mile, began to appear regularly from 1805; the larger-scale ones did not commence until much later in the century, but even the one-inch maps indicate communications and the terrain of a locality, as well as showing land use and the size of towns and villages.

Before the nineteenth century the County Record Office is the main recourse for other local maps, like those of estates made for private landlords, town plans marking out street names and patterns, or those of public undertakings such as canals and improvements. The British Library has an extremely good collection of older maps, particularly those of whole counties, which may be of marginal interest to the family historian.

While maps may plot out the site of individual homesteads, the manorial court records detail the date of entry to them and the rent that was paid. Many of these are on deposit in County Record Offices, but there is a fairly comprehensive list of the locations of known manorial records at the Historical Manuscripts Commission in London. Some of these records date from the thirteenth century, and may extend to 1925. They are generally in Latin until 1732, written on vellum rolls, or in books. Manorial boundaries did not often coincide with those of the parish, and some of their business overlapped.

The main landownership records of use to the family historian are the minutes of the meetings of the manorial Courts Baron and Leet, the records of rentals, extents and surveys, and the customals outlining the customs observed by the manor, for example in relation to the transfer of property from one tenant to another.

The manorial courts met usually once or twice a year, under the chairmanship of the lord or his steward. The tenants were obliged to appear on pain of a fine, unless a reasonable excuse was given. The minutes of the Court Baron will record the names of non-attenders, as well as the administrative business dealing with surrenders of property to the lord and admission of new tenants. When a tenant died this fact would be enrolled in the court minutes, and before the next heir could be admitted to the land a heriot (like a peppercorn) would have to be paid to the lord. The next heir was determined by the custom of the manor, and might have been the eldest or youngest son, or even a daughter if so specified. These tenants were known as customary tenants. Perhaps the deceased tenant had been a tenant at will: in this case he could have willed his property to whomever he wished, but the will would have to be produced to the court and the relevant part enrolled in the minutes before the new tenant at will could be admitted on payment of a heriot and an entry fine. Collectively these tenants were called copyhold tenants, for they were given a copy of the entry in the court minutes, showing the date of the original tenant's admission, the date and reason for surrender, the extent, nature and annual rent due on the property, and their own admission to it and the sum paid. A tenant might also surrender the property back to the lord during his lifetime, and in this case the new copyhold tenant would pay an entry fine and be given a copy of the enrolment. Each surrender refers back to the tenant's admission, and a sequence of these minutes can extend your pedigree back over several generations and can clarify relationships.

Sub-leases of land for fixed terms by leaseholders from the lord of the manor were also noted in the proceedings of the subsequent court, while the original indentures were kept by the grantor and grantee as their own evidence of title to the land. Many of these have subsequently passed into the custody of County Record Offices, and the earliest may date from the seventeenth century. The indentures give the names of the parties concerned, the date and nature of the agreement with precise details about the property concerned including its annual value and the price to be paid for it, and the length of the lease. Names of current occupiers, and existing longer leaseholders of the property and of the landlord will also be included. There are also leases for specified lives (usually two or three), as well as for fixed periods, mortgages and marriage settlements of the property on the bride and her issue, all affording a very useful source for the genealogist. In the first decade of the eighteenth century attempts were made in Yorkshire, Middlesex and Ireland officially to register leases of over twenty-one years, sales, mortgages and wills bequeathing property, to prevent fraud and to protect purchasers and those seeking mortgages. Copies of the original deeds are enrolled in Registries of Deeds in each of the above areas, and extend to 1938, but they are rather inadequately indexed.

The other manorial court was the Court Leet, which normally met at the same time as the Court Baron, and appointed manorial officials. It heard presentments from jurors sworn from among the more substantial tenants, about neglect of duties, trespass and moral misdemeanours by others in the manor, which were punishable by fine. Rentals, taken twice yearly, record the names of tenants, their holdings and the amount due. Extents and surveys set out the holdings and names of occupiers of property within the manor, but were only made sporadically, for instance on the sale of the manor to a new owner.

Thus the manorial records cover not only a person's property but also his behaviour and conduct as well, and can put flesh on the bones of a pedigree.

Private sales and gifts of freehold property are found in a variety of sources. Rarely do the original deeds survive in family muniments, but copies of them were recorded in monastic cartularies for safe-keeping and future reference, and in official records for statutory or taxation reasons. The earliest regular series of these official enrolments, all of which are now in the Public Record Office in London, are the Feet of Fines, dating from the end of the twelfth century to 1833. There are contemporary calendars to these from 1509 until 1798, under regnal year, county, name and property. The Fine took the form of a fictitious

Rent-day as your ancestors might have experienced it 150 years ago! Distraining for Rent, *painted by the Scottish artist David Wilkie in 1815, is rich in detail of the clothing and typical interior furnishings of the period. Genre and domestic paintings such as this can bring the evidence of documents to life. (Edinburgh, National Gallery of Scotland)*

A page from a Jesus College rent book of 1719, giving the names of tenants and the rents they paid. The page is headed by the rents for Moulton Manor (see previous page). (Oxford, Jesus College Archives)

dispute whereby the defendant agreed to pay the plaintiff a sum for the transfer of the property to him either for a fixed number of years, for specified lives, or for ever. Three copies were made, one for each party and the third enrolled in the Court of Common Pleas, to whom a proportion of the value of the property was paid.

Other sales are recorded in the Recoveries, also in the form of a fictitious legal dispute, dating from the fifteenth century and extending to 1833, whereby it was possible to transfer property previously tied up in the family by fee tail or settlement. These are also in the Common Pleas series, and are inadequately calendared. Sales and creations of private trusts were enrolled on the Close Rolls, especially after 1536, and there are contemporary calendars of both grantors and grantees, arranged by regnal year. Some of these sales and trusts were alternatively recorded on the Quarter Sessions Rolls.

Crown grants of land from an early date appear in Charter Rolls, Patent Rolls, Ancient Deeds, the records of the Exchequer, the Land Revenue Office, and the Augmentations Office (1547 to the seventeenth century), and locating them can be a difficult matter because of the diversity of enrolment. Some, like the Charter Rolls and Patent Rolls, have been printed, but the rest have not, and you can spend many hours vainly searching for a likely entry among the calendars or originals.

When a tenant in chief (direct tenant of the Crown) died, an inquest was held on his possessions in each of the counties where they lay, and these Inquisitions Post Mortem, between the late thirteenth century and 1660, can reveal the exact date of the original grant and details of it without your having to search the above sources. In addition the date and place of death, and the name, age, and relationship to him of the next heir are given. Although written in Latin, the earlier Inquisitions Post Mortem have been printed to the late fourteenth century, and for the reign of Henry VII, so that you can see what they contain before looking at the originals (see above, p. 68).

Taxation Records

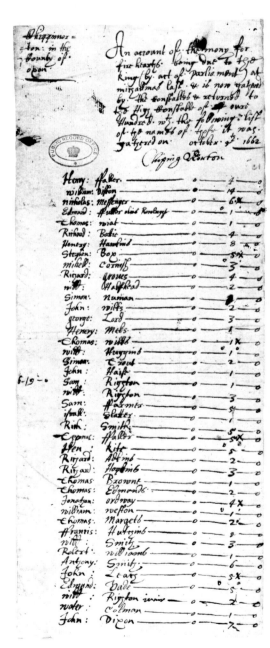

Your forebears, besides paying purchase money or rent, would certainly have contributed to the poor rate of the parish where they lived after 1662, if they were not at the receiving end of poor relief, and I have already referred to these records (p. 50). However, they may also have been subjected to the payment of at least one of the myriad taxes imposed by the Exchequer and Inland Revenue. Some of these assessments, returns, and lists of arrears are filed in the Public Record Office and include Feudal Aids before 1660, the Lay Subsidy from the late thirteenth century until the mid-seventeenth century, the Poll Tax of 1377, 1379, 1381 and 1664 onwards to 1698, the Hearth Tax (1662–89), a few of the Land Tax returns (1798 – 1799), Ship Money 1634–40 (in State Papers Domestic) and the Apprentice Tax (1710–1810).

Feudal Aids were levied for special occasions like the knighting of the King's eldest son, and the marriage of his eldest daughter. Lists of assessments have been printed to 1426, but are restrictive in the people selected to contribute. The Lay Subsidy, voted by Parliament at regular intervals, was based on a person's movables. For the period 1290 to 1332 lists of names of contributors, with their contributions, are arranged county by county, then by Hundred broken down into towns, villages and hamlets. After 1332 the Subsidy continued to be levied, but on a collective basis; personal taxation on goods, wages or lands worth five pounds or more was reintroduced by Henry VIII in 1524. The assessments follow the pattern of the Feudal Aids, and are a useful directory of individuals of a certain status over a wide area. A sequence of the lists can be used to trace the descent of a family in a parish or locality, because widows and sons of individuals were also included. Tradesmen such as shopkeepers would have paid the tax on their stock, and the lists often gave the person's occupation. You will also discover the relative wealth of the inhabitants of a particular place, just as the later Hearth Tax returns list the number of hearths in each house, liable to the two-shilling tax on each. Only those living in dwellings worth less than twenty shillings a year were exempt. The Hearth Tax reached most householders, and can tell you the names of neighbours and serve as a guide to your forebears' location in a street, provided they can be identified as owners of particular houses or land.

The Poll Tax was assessed on everyone over the age of sixteen, and from 1379 was on a graded scale, according to wealth and status. Poll Tax returns are filed with those of the Lay Subsidy and Hearth Tax in the Exchequer series.

The Land Tax was first raised in 1697 and continued to 1832. The returns are arranged by county, Hundred and parish, and from 1782 the owners as well as the occupiers are listed with the tax due. The returns are in the County Record Offices, and copies of those between 1798 and 1799 have found their way into the Inland Revenue series in the Public Record Office, Kew.

Among county records you may also find returns of miscellaneous taxes such as those on windows (1696 to 1851), carriages (1747 to 1782), silverplate (1756 to 1777), servants (1775 to 1852; the earlier returns are in the Public Record Office, and the Society of Genealogists in London has a typescript copy of them), game (1784 to 1807), horses (1784 to 1874), coats of arms (1793 to 1882), dogs (1796 to 1882) and uninhabited houses (1851 to 1924), organized by Hundred and parish and then by name and total due.

Between 1694 and 1704 there was also a tax on births, marriages and deaths, and on childless widowers and bachelors over twenty-five, but relatively few lists are extant. Those for the City of London and its environs have been published, and serve as a census of the parishes they cover.

Electoral Rolls

Only forty-shilling freeholders were entitled to vote until the Act of 1832 extended the franchise. From circa 1695 until 1832 poll books were published for each county after every election, indicating by Hundred and parish those persons qualified by their property to vote, and their residence if elsewhere. The Guildhall Library and the Society of Genealogists, both in London, have an extremely good run of these books. Others may be seen in County Record Offices.

After 1832 the electoral lists of inhabitants of each parish within a Parliamentary division have often been deposited in County Record Offices, and those for the entire country between 1872 and 1876 have been printed. However, it must be remembered that they only relate to those people currently qualified to vote.

What Work did your Family Engage In?

You will probably have discovered the occupations pursued by members of your family from the basic sources, like central registration, the Census, wills and even parish registers. There is still more that can be learned about them from trade, professional, military and naval records.

If your forebear was a tradesman, he may well have been listed in a local trade directory, and may even have advertised in it, or a local newspaper. Trade directories date from the late eighteenth century, and there are two printed guides to directories in London and the provinces before 1856. These will tell you which firms published directories and for what dates. The Guildhall Library has a good series of directories for the whole country. They give the trade, address at the time of publication and the name of the individual, and can be an aid to searching for an address in the Census. Changes of address and descent of a family business can also be traced, but not all tradesmen are found on their pages.

Trade cards and advertisements will tell you something about the scope of the business as well as the current prices of goods. There are good collections of trade cards in the John Johnson collection in the Bodleian Library, in Oxford, and the Guildhall Library, in London.

Above. *These two extracts show how printed directories and voters' lists can help the family historian. From the first list, an 1826 poll book of the freemen of Oxford, Colin Harris discovered that one of his ancestors (see above, p. 78) had moved to Kensington in London (although he was still entitled to vote in Oxford). Using this clue, he can now search the Kensington parish records for further information about John Harris. The second extract is from Lascelles and Co.'s Directory and Gazetteer of the County of Oxford, 1853, and shows John Harris back in Oxford, living in Church Street, St Ebbe's (unhappily now demolished). The right-hand column indicates how each freeman voted in the election.*

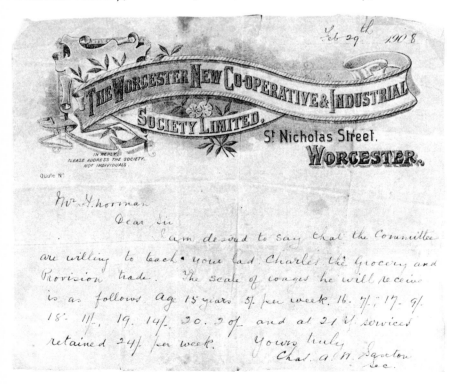

Left. *This apprenticeship letter, 29 February 1908, is interesting for its decorative letterheading as well as for its content. The 'lad' in question, Charles Norman, was awarded the C.B.E. in 1951 and became a Freeman of the City of London two years later. He was knighted in 1965. His freedom of the City and his coat of arms are illustrated below, pp. 110 and 155.*

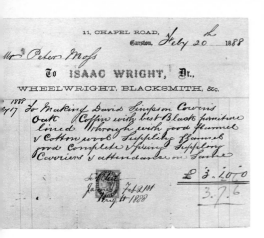

*A late nineteenth-century tradesman's bill.
Documents such as this are among those most
likely to be preserved among family papers.
David Simpson Cowen's marriage is recorded
on p. 35 above.*

*'A new register of the several Termes and
Comencements of the Indentures of
Apprentices bound and presented from the sixt
day of August 1629 by William Manbye
Comon Clarke to the Worshipful Company of
Leathersellers . . .' Documents of the London
Companies can provide a wealth of
information, often giving considerable detail of
apprentices' origins. Several generations of a
family might be apprenticed to freemen of the
same company. (London, archives of the
Worshipful Company of Leathersellers)*

Trade tokens were also a feature of seventeenth- and eighteenth-century life, and there are published catalogues of these.

Certain trades were subject to annual licensing by the Quarter Sessions, for example butchers, corn dealers and victuallers. Any contraventions of local trading regulations or of the licence would be tried before the Sessions (see above. p. 101).

Many trades were controlled from the Middle Ages, and especially after 1563, by guilds and companies, which restricted the number of people engaged in any one trade within the city or borough boundaries, and controlled prices and standards of practice. Most boroughs and cities had their own joint guilds, or individual companies, and many of their records have survived. Those for London are mostly in the Guildhall Library, some dating back to the fifteenth century, while the remainder are still held by the companies themselves. Over the rest of the country either the County Record Office or the borough Guildhall will be the usual repository. Some of their records have been printed. Company records can tell you about the parentage and place of origin of each apprentice, which may lie a long way from the place where he was apprenticed.

Entrance to a trade was controlled by the apprenticeship system, and among the most valuable records for the family historian are the Apprentice Binding Books, containing abstracts of the original indentures. These give the names of the apprentice, and his father or guardian, his place of residence, status or occupation, together with the master's name, address and trade, the length of apprenticeship, and the premium paid for it.

Between 1710 and 1810 there was a tax imposed on apprentices, based on the premiums, and the original registers of these are in the Public Record Office, Kew, arranged chronologically. Up to 1752 details of the father or guardian are included. A printed index of these to

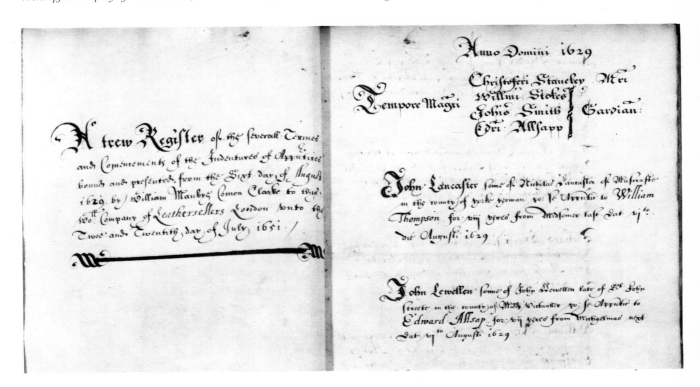

Charles Norman, Citizen and Farmer of London was admitted into the Freedom aforesaid and made the Declaration required by Law in the Mayoralty of Sir Rupert De la Bère, Kt., M.P. — Mayor and Irving Blanchard Gane, Esquire Chamberlain and is entered in the book signed with the Letter V.2 relating to the Purchasing of Freedoms and the Admissions of Freemen (to wit) the 18th day of February in the 2nd Year of the reign of Queen Elizabeth II And in the Year of our Lord 1953 In Witness whereof the Seal of the Office of Chamberlain of the said City is hereunto affixed Dated in the Chamber of the Guildhall of the same City the day and Year abovesaid.

1774 is held by the Society of Genealogists, in London, along with a separate index of masters to 1762, giving the names and dates of their apprenticeships.

The company registers of freemen contain full details of the date of admission, by what qualification (after a term of apprenticeship, by patrimony—the father having previously been a freeman—or by purchase (redemption)), and the current address and name of the new member. Some of these registers are indexed.

Membership of one of the city companies entitled a person to apply for full citizenship (freedom of the City). Records of London admissions date from 1681, and can be consulted in the Chamberlain's Court, Guildhall. They can sometimes be a means of discovering the date of admission to a City company, because applications were usually made within a few weeks of a person's being made free of a company. The address, trade and name of each citizen are given, as are often those of his father.

Also included in company records are minutes of meetings of the council of the company, dealing with the payment made by new members for admission, the enrolment of new apprentices, and reports of failures to pay company dues, or breaches of its regulations. When the other two classes of record are defective these minutes can often help fill the gap.

Where there were no individual companies, permission to trade in a borough might be granted by apprenticeship to one of the burgesses for the normal term of seven or eight years before admission. The Burgess Books are held by the Borough Record Office, the Guildhall, or County Record Office.

Fire policies registered by tradesmen with insurance societies are normally still in the custody of the relevant society. The earliest policies date from the late seventeenth century, and give address, nature of the business, size of the stock and its annual value, plus the premiums paid over a particular period. However, they are generally poorly catalogued, so that you would need to know an approximate date at which to start the search.

If your antecedent discovered a new invention or technique he may have applied to patent it. Before 1852 patents were enrolled on the Patent Rolls, held by the Public Record Office in London. The later ones were filed in the Patent Office, in London. A complete set of printed specifications of patents since 1617 is available there, and printed indexes of the names of patentees.

Records of companies registered after the Companies Acts of 1844 and 1856 are held in the Companies Register, in London, but there are

The freedom of the City of London, granted to Mr Charles Norman on 18 February 1953. Forty-five years earlier Mr Norman had been taken on as an apprentice by the Worcestershire Co-op (see above, p. 108). He was eventually knighted. (see below, p. 155). All three documents are in the possession of Mr Donald Norman, who kindly provided the photographs.

A patent document from the Public Record Office. Benjamin Crosby of Berwick on Tweed had been granted Letters Patent on 25 July 1808 on condition that he produced a specification within one month. The specification was 'inrolled' on 25 August 1808. The photograph shows part of the enrolment and a picture of 'Crosby's Patent Book-stand'. (London, Public Record Office, Chancery Lane, C 73/26/11)

CROSBY's PATENT BOOK-STAND.

printed indexes to them at the Public Record Office, Kew, giving the registration number of the company. The records themselves include the names of directors, the secretary, and the articles of association.

If a business or company went bankrupt then the unfortunate directors would have to appear before the Court of Bankruptcy to have it wound up. The *London Gazette* lists bankruptcies announced since the late seventeenth century. Registers of the court proceedings prior to 1710 are filed in the Court of King's Bench records, which, along with those of the Court of Bankruptcy from 1710, are held by the Public Record Office in London. The latter series is indexed and contains details of the name, and business, the date of the bankruptcy and the name of any person securing his release from jail. The registers of the Fleet Prison (the debtors' prison), from 1685 to 1842, are also held by the Public Record Office.

Friendly Societies were formed by groups of tradesmen as an investment against sickness or inability to work, and by subscribing a regular fixed sum they could ensure relief from the fund in times of hardship. Although individual names of members no longer survive, the rules and regulations of the Societies and the names of their officials were registered with Quarter Sessions after 1793. The rules and regulations of local Freemasonry Lodges did include a list of members when similarly registered. Trade Union records have hardly been touched by family historians, but are likely to contain personal details of members. These only date from the mid-nineteenth century, and although some are still in the custody of the relevant unions many are now at the Modern Records Centre, University of Warwick, Coventry.

Military and Naval Records

If your forebear was engaged in military service then it may be possible to trace his career through attestation and discharge papers, or muster books. British military records to circa 1900 are in the Public Record Office, at Kew, and regimental museums also hold a great deal of material. If you know the regiment to which an ordinary soldier belonged after 1756, and he went to pension, then the dated attestation and discharge papers will reveal details of his military career, his conduct, his medical record, his previous occupation, age at enlistment, and birthplace, together with a physical description. From 1883 the discharge papers are arranged purely alphabetically regardless of regiment, and include the name and relationship of the next of kin.

Those who died on active service, or who did not receive a pension, will be found in the muster books of the regiment. These date from circa 1760 and list under rank, and then alphabetically, the names of all those currently serving, and their dates of enlistment. If you look at the muster of the regiment for the month or quarter covering enlistment the list of recruits will give you his age, while the list of non-effectives when his name disappears from the muster will reveal his birthplace and trade. The attestation and discharge papers and musters can thus reveal much about a soldier's career and background. There are similar records of local militia and volunteers dating from 1780. They are particularly good for the Napoleonic Wars.

If you do not know the name of the regiment but do know where the soldier was stationed at a certain date, the Station Returns will advise as to the regiments which were there at that time, and you can then search the above sources. The Regimental Returns of births, marriages and deaths, held at the General Register Office in London, can also supply this information, and enable you to trace the movements of a soldier and his family throughout the world.

Officers' names, ranks, dates of commission and regiments will appear in the regular series of printed and indexed *Army Lists* after 1756. Earlier officers may be described in printed surveys of the British Army, or sporadic manuscript lists, but it is not until the late eighteenth century that more personal details can be found. After 1793 the Commander-in-Chief's Memoranda include the applications of officers and men for commissions, and these are organized in chronological order. They contain details of family background, supporting letters from relatives, and addresses and current status of the applicant, as well as the reason for the vacant position and the amount paid for the commission.

In 1828 returns were made of all officers retired on full and half pay. Ages at commission, marriages and children's births are recorded, plus details of career, and they are signed by the officer concerned. From 1829 to 1919 similar returns were made of the services of officers still active in the Army, arranged by regiment. Their dates and places of birth and marriage, names of spouses and legitimate offspring, plus details of career and rank provide data which would not be available

Right. Drawing for the Militia, 1849. This painting by John Phillip is a lively evocation of the scene as the eligible local men are drafted into the militia, measured up for their uniforms and examined by a doctor. The setting is the great hall of a country house, whose owner would no doubt be the colonel of the regiment. (Bury St Edmunds, Public Library and Art Gallery)

Below right. An appeal for recruits to join the 113th Birmingham Volunteers, about 1800. This was the time of the Napoleonic Wars when the Army, anxious to keep its numbers up to strength, appealed to patriotic feelings. (London, National Army Museum)

Below. A page from the army pay-book of Pivate William Harman of the Oxfordshire Light Infantry, for the years 1886–7. The pay-book had to be carried at all times, and recorded many personal details. (Oxford, Regimental Museum of the Oxfordshire and Buckinghamshire Light Infantry)

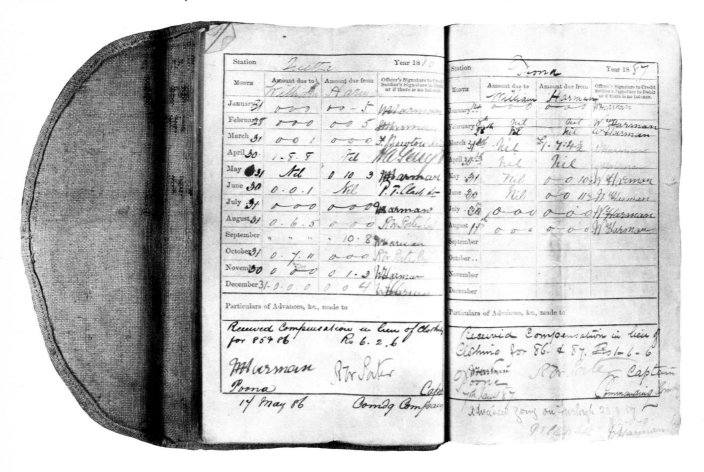

from any other source without a great deal of trouble. There is a fairly comprehensive slip index to these returns.

Pension applications by widows, too, can contain genealogical details about marriage, births of offspring and death of the soldier concerned, and these date from 1755 to 1908.

Earlier records of the local militia are arranged by county, and can be seen either in the Public Record Office (between 1522 and 1640), or in the County Record Offices. They form an almost untapped source, and offer a directory of all those men over the age of sixteen, listed parish by parish, within each Hundred of a county, at a particular date. The Musters of 1569 are particularly good.

In America musters of many militia regiments are held by the Library of Congress, and a large number have been printed. Pension grants made to soldiers serving in the Revolutionary War, the War of 1812, the Mexican and Civil Wars, and to their widows, are retained by the National Archives, in Washington. The applicant had to show proof of his service, and swear an affidavit as to his indigence. Details of birth, parentage, marriage and migration are added, and if the widow was the applicant, then the date and circumstances of her husband's death, and names and ages of children.

Since continuous engagement of ordinary seamen did not commence in Britain until 1853, it is difficult to trace an ancestor's naval career before this, unless you know the name of the vessel and the approximate date he was on board. The Admiralty records, which are all at the Public Record Office at Kew, include ships' musters of crews dating from 1667. These contain names and ranks of the crew, the date and

A naval discharge certificate, 17 August 1814. The document is in the possession of Mr Peter Jones, a descendant of William Randall, by whose kind permission it is reproduced here. William later married Elizabeth Gardener (see above p. 43).

port at which they joined the ship, and the date of the discharge, plus the reason. After circa 1770 they also give age on joining and place of birth. These musters were taken quarterly, and add the names and ranks of Royal Marines conveyed in the ships, and of prisoners captured. The log books of these vessels, from circa 1688, will tell you the daily position of the ship, any sightings of other vessels, the weather conditions and events on board.

If you do not know the name of the ship but do know where a seaman was at a specific date, then the List Books, from 1673, will tell you which ships were there at that time.

Disbursements from the Chatham Chest to wounded seamen (after 1617 and before 1807) are indexed from 1744 to 1797. Bounty papers (1675 to 1822) deal with payments to widows of seamen killed on active service, and contain considerable personal details about them and their families. The Greenwich Hospital registers of pensioners from 1737 yield the date of admission and discharge of inmates, including officers.

After 1853 there are Continuous Service Engagement Books, which are indexed, and which record a seaman's career and his birth. Later records of seamen's services to 1891 give the same information, and these are also indexed.

Commissioned officers in the Royal Navy were listed in Seniority Lists from 1660 onwards, and in the *Navy Lists* according to rank and seniority, from 1782. There is a printed *List of Commissioned Sea Officers, 1660–1815*, and biographies of many of them have been published. Passing certificates of Lieutenants from 1691 to 1902 contain details of previous vessels in which they sailed and their rank in each, and those from the late eighteenth century have baptism certificates attached, but these are not always accurate. There is a manuscript index to the Certificates between 1789 and 1818, the others merely being indexed at the end of each volume, or alphabetically entered in the registers. There are also sporadic returns of officers' services, dating from the late eighteenth century, which include details of birth and death.

Passing certificates of the boatswains, gunners and pursers date from 1731, and the later ones also have baptism certificates attached to them. Additionally, there are records of the qualifications of Masters between 1660 and 1830, with baptism certificates filed alongside; and returns of superannuated warrant officers' services in particular years, such as 1802.

Records of Royal Marines start in 1790 and take the same form as the attestation and discharge papers of the military regiments. These are held in the Public Record Office and are alphabetically arranged under the year of enlistment and discharge.

Before the registration of merchant seamen began in 1835, and after it ceased in 1856, the only recourse for information about antecedents in this service are the Crew Lists of the ships themselves. From 1747 to 1851 the masters or owners of the ships were required to keep muster rolls for each voyage made, including names, abodes, and dates of enlistment of their crews, and the name of the last ship in which each seaman had sailed. Few survive, but those which do are held in the Board of Trade series, in the Public Record Office at Kew. After 1835 agreements about wages, capacity and nature of the voyage, made with the seamen, were added to the muster of men on board. For the period after 1861 only a few of these are in the custody of the Public Record Office, the rest being dispersed. They are arranged chronologically by port, and then by vessel.

Between 1835 and 1856 a system of registering seamen existed, and the early alphabetical registers contain names, dates and places of birth, normal residence, literacy level, previous capacities, age at first going to sea, if they had ever served in the Royal Navy, and the date and place where registered. After 1844 tickets were issued, and the registers

Part of a famous ship's muster, that of the Bounty, 1787. The captain's name heads the list. Note that the ages and birthplaces of some of the crew are given. 'Widow's Man' was a fiction—for every 100 men, provision was made for one extra. Captain Bligh was commander of the men on board, John Fryer was master of the ship. (London, Public Record Office, Chancery Lane, ADM 36/10744)

Bounty Paid	Nº	Entry	Year	Appearance.	Whence and whether Preſt or not.	Place and County where Born.	Age at Time of Entry in this Ship	Nº and Letter of Tickets	MENS NAMES.	Qualities.	D. D.D. or R.	Time of Diſcharge
.	1	16ᵗʰ Augᵗ 1787	Aug 20ᵗʰ	pᵉ Admlᵗ Order 16ᵗʰ					Lieut Wᵐ Bligh Commᵈʳ			
.		20ᵗʰ "	"	pᵉ Wᵗ 20ᵗʰ Dᵒ					Thomas Huggan Surgeon			
.		" "	"	"					Widows Man	Ab		
.		" "	"	pᵉ Wᵗ 20ᵗʰ					John Fryer	Master		
.	5	" "	"	Volr Leicester			23		Willm Brown	Ab		
.		" "	"	" Hackney			20		Thomas Hayward	Ab		
.		27ᵗʰ "	"	" 27 pᵉ Wᵗ 27ᵗʰ					William Cole Boatsᵐ			
.		" "	"	pᵉ Wᵗ Dᵒ					William Purcell Carpʳ			

subsequently were arranged chronologically by ticket number. There are separate indexes to these. There is also a separate indexed series of apprentices from 1835, but only samples of the original registers remain.

Compulsory certificates of competence were also issued to other merchant seamen like Masters and Mates after 1854, to Engineers from 1862, and Skippers and Mates of fishing vessels from 1883. All of these contain details of birth and previous service. Details of ships' comings and goings are to be found in the Port Books of the ports concerned, and also in local newspapers.

The Society of Genealogists, in London, has the files of applications made by indigent merchant seamen and their widows for relief from Trinity House, 1780 to 1854. These petitions include testimonials from the Masters of the ships in which they last sailed, marriage certificates, children's baptism certificates and the seamen's death certificates where appropriate, as well as the applicants' letters.

Below left. The first page of a Trinity House petition submitted on behalf of John Tanner of St Ives, Cornwall, in 1850. John was the eldest brother of James Tanner, master of the Betsey. These petitions give considerable detail about the applicants' careers and circumstances, and may include baptism and marriage certificates, and testimonials from the masters of the ships in which the petitioners served. (London, Society of Genealogists)

To the Honorable the Master, Wardens, and Assistants, of the CORPORATION of TRINITY-HOUSE of Deptford Strond.

The humble Petition

Here state Name, Age, and Residence of the Petitioner.

of John Tanner
aged about Seventy Years,
residing at Saint Ives Cornwall

Sheweth, THAT your Petitioner went to Sea at the Age of Twenty two in the Year 1803 and was employed in the Merchant Sea Service for 30 Years, in the following Ships and others, and in the annexed Stations:

Here state several of the Ships in which Petitioner went to Sea, and particularly the first and last in which he was employed, and the one in which he held the highest Station.

Year.	Ship or Vessel's Name.	Register Tonnage.	Station on board.	From what Place to what Place.
1803	Maria Royal London	150	Apprentice	From Wales to London
1806	Peggy Padstow	100	Seaman	Cornwall to the Baltic
1809	Robert of London	110	Seaman	London to Robin
1812	Ayr of Saint Ives	105	Seaman Mate	Coastwise
1814	do		Mate	"

Here state Time and Cause of leaving off the Sea.

That your Petitioner left off the Sea in the Year 1845, in consequence of Age and infirmity

Here put Wife's Christian Name.

and has a Wife named Bridget Tanner aged 53 Years, and One Children under Twelve

Names and Ages of Children.

Years of Age, viz.

If not any, insert the word "No" in the Blank, or state the Amount, if any.

That your Petitioner has No Annual Income from Real or Personal Property to the Amount of £ Whatever

Here state what Relief he receives, if any, from any other Institution, from Parish, from Labour, and the Nature of it, or from any other Source,

That your Petitioner's present Means of Support are from Charity

which not being sufficient to support himself and Family, he most humbly prays he may be admitted a Pensioner of this Corporation, at the usual Allowance.

Your Petitioner will ever pray, &c.

Petitioner to sign his Name. John Tanner's mark

NOTE.—By the Act 3rd Geo. 4th, Cap. 40, All Persons imposing or endeavouring to impose upon a charitable Institution by any false and fraudulent Representation, either verbally or in writing, with a View to obtain Money or some other Advantage or Benefit, shall be deemed Rogues and Vagabonds, and may be committed to Gaol or House of Correction for three Months, and there kept to hard Labour.

On Saturday last, a cargo of copper ore, raised in Wheal Trenwith mine, and which was sold on the 11th instant, was shipped on board the Pulmanter, Grenfell, master, at St. Ives Pier; and on Wednesday a cargo of the same ore was shipped on board the Betsey, Tanner, master, at the same place. —These, we understand, are the first copper ores ever remembered to have been shipped from that place.

FIRE.—On Monday night, the inhabitants of Helston were roused from their sleep by an alarm of fire, which was discovered in the premises of a Baker named Toy, and which soon after the alarm was given burst out with such fury, that though the town engines were speedily brought to the spot, and were well supplied with water, it was found

❦ The Professions

If your ancestor was a professional man his name should be listed in contemporary directories of the area in which he practised, or of the professional body to which he belonged. *Law Lists*, dating from 1775, *Medical Directories*, from 1845, and *Clergy Lists*, from 1836, vary in the scope of the information contained, but all give the practitioners' dates of qualification and their current addresses. The *Medical Directories* go further in that they include brief biographies, and at the back a list of obituaries of those doctors deceased since the last issue. As these directories were published virtually annually, it is possible to trace a person's career through from start to finish, and they give a date at which to start looking for a death certificate, will, or newspaper obituary.

The professional association or society to which your ancestor belonged may well have an extensive library of material relating to its members, which has not appeared in print. Addresses can be found in the *Directory of British Associations*.

Records of the five-year articles of clerkship entered into by intending lawyers are filed from 1729 in the Public Record Office, in London, and are arranged in three series, under the courts of Common Pleas, King's Bench, and (from 1876) the Supreme Court of Judicature. They are arranged chronologically by date of admission, but there are manuscript indexes to them. The articles contain not only the name of the clerk and that of the attorney and his address, but the name, address, status and occupation of the father or guardian. The attorney to whom the clerk was articled was occasionally a relative, so these records can be very helpful to the family historian in tracing old family connections with a particular legal practice, and they predate the *Law Lists*.

The Royal College of Physicians, of London, founded in 1518, and the Royal College of Surgeons, of England, founded in 1800, retain records about members and fellows, some of which have appeared in print, notably Munk's *Roll of the Royal College of Physicians of London, 1518–1925*, and Plarr's *Lives of the Fellows of the Royal College of Surgeons*. From an early date physicians and surgeons had to be licensed by the bishop of the diocese in which they wished to practise, and I have already referred to these records elsewhere (p. 52). University records, particularly those of Oxford, Cambridge, Edinburgh and Leyden, in Holland, and those of the London Teaching Hospitals, can add substantially to your informations about individual medical men. The Royal College of Surgeons, in London, also maintains a list of bogus practitioners.

The apothecaries were given licences by their own society, and the records of these, filed in the Guildhall Library in London, date from 1670. They afford personal details of birth and parentage about each applicant. Prior to this they will be found in the records of the Grocers' Company, also in the Guildhall Library.

The Anglican Church drew its clergy mostly from the two ancient universities of Oxford and Cambridge until the mid-nineteenth century, when theological colleges began to provide their own training. Foster's *Alumni Oxonienses* to 1886 and the Venns' *Alumni Cantabrigienses*

James Tanner, born at St Ives on 28 February 1794 (see the family Bible, p. 32 above) recorded details of his career on another page of the same Bible, including the fact that he was master of the Betsey *from 1824 to 1831. A search of the shipping reports in the* West Briton, *published in Truro, revealed the attached entry under the date 19 May 1826. St Ives harbour and pier are seen in the photograph above, taken around 1910. The scene and the type of ship would hardly have changed since the 1820s.*

to 1900 give detailed biographies of each of their students, including what subsequently became of them. Sometimes the date and place of birth, and usually the father's name, residence and status or occupation are given, and in the case of clergymen the date of ordination and the diocese. Ordination papers are held by the relevant Diocesan Record Office, and besides giving details of testimonials, and educational references from tutors, they have baptism certificates attached to them, which will tell you where the ordinand came from, and the names of both his parents. *Crockford's Clerical Directory*, published regularly since 1858, records the careers of all the clergy in the Anglican Church throughout the world, with details of their incumbencies and the patron of the living. It may be that the patron was a relative, and it is interesting to discover the dates and names of succeeding incumbents to see if this family influence persisted.

University records and the directories will give the date of institution to a particular living, while the Institution Books themselves, dating from 1558 to 1838, and filed in the Exchequer series in the Public Record Office, give the reason for the vacancy, and the name of the previous incumbent as well as that of the new one, and the patron.

Foreign Office Lists and Dod's *Parliamentary Companion* yield details of diplomatic and political careers. If your ancestors excelled in any field they might even be included in the *Dictionary of National Biography*, which is particularly strong on men of letters, the law and the Church. *Who Was Who* and Boase's *Modern English Biography* are useful for the modern period.

You may be able to discern a pattern in the choice of career—for example a particular school, college, regiment, living or Inn of Court might be favoured by the family. Family influence and patronage were often responsible, and by delving a little into the background you may discover exactly when and how they came about.

A somewhat jaundiced view of academic life. This university document, an early nineteenth-century print, suggests that over-indulgence and a crusty temper were the hallmarks of the Oxford don. The picture is probably a caricature of a Fellow of Jesus College.

Landed and Titled Families

British families of rank have been well catalogued in printed compendia like Debrett's *Peerage and Baronetage*, first published in 1713, Burke's *Peerage, Baronetage and Knightage* (1826 onwards) and Burke's *Landed Gentry* (from 1846). The first merely documents living relatives of each title-holder, while the other two record not only those still alive, but forebears as far back as the family cared to detail. The onus of providing information lay with the families themselves, and thus the pedigrees should be used with caution. All of these works still appear regularly, being brought up to date on each occasion, and they display the arms used by the families.

The succession of title-holders up to early this century was traced and printed in G. E. C.'s *Complete Peerage* and *Complete Baronetage*, where sources are cited for each statement made. The order of precedence of peers both inside and outside the House of Lords was fixed by the House of Lords Precedence Act of 1539, and the list will be found in the back of any edition of *Burke's Peerage*.

European noble families can be traced in the *Almanach de Gotha*, published annually between 1763 and 1944, its successor, *Genealogisches*

Sept. 24º. 1766

I John Jones born in the parish of Eglwysfach in the county of Denbigh in the Diocese of St Asaph was admitted Scholar of Jesus College in the University of Oxford having first taken the Oaths required by the laws of the Realm and the Statutes of the said College.

John Jones.

An extract from the admissions register of Jesus College, Oxford, which gives not only names but places of birth of those newly enrolled in the college. Jesus College, although given its Royal Charter by Queen Elizabeth I, was actually founded by a Welshman who raised funds in cash and kind in Wales specifically to ensure opportunities for scholastic study for Welshmen. The college still owns small parcels of Welsh land given with these original endowments in the sixteenth century. (Oxford, Jesus College Archives)

Handbuch des Adels, published in 1951, Prince Isenburg's *Stammtafeln zur Geschichte der europaischen Staaten*, 1953–7, reissued between 1958 and 1961, and *Royalty, Peerage and Nobility of the World*, published annually since 1843. Many of the European titles were held not only by the head of the family but by each of its members, whereas in Britain the offspring of title-holders are known by the courtesy titles afforded to them.

Titled and landed families are well recorded in other printed sources, especially County Histories. They often include pedigrees of the most notable houses, which may well also be found registered in the official records of the College of Arms, in London. However, many of the recently ennobled families have risen from obscurity just as the more ancient lines have been submerged, so that there is no guarantee that the most likely genealogies will actually be so recorded. Individuals are found on the pages of Kelly's *Handbook to the Titled, Landed and Official Classes* (from 1874). Substantial landowners will be found in printed directories from the late eighteenth century, and in 1873 a Return of Freeholders was published, listing each owner's residence and freehold property.

The sons of titled gentry families were often sent to Public Schools and the registers of these schools often contain details of the students' backgrounds and subsequent careers. The foremost ones have been printed. The University *Alumni* similarly contain biographies.

Summing Up

I have only been able to mention a fraction of the sources which you will find useful as a family historian. Some of these will be less accessible or unwieldy to search, and others will contain much that is of no use at all because the purposes that they served yield genealogical information only as a by-product. The important thing is to leave no stone unturned and to seek for clues to other sources in the information you already have. You will never stop discovering new leads, and new sources to be explored, so that you can never say that the pedigree is complete.

5 Emigration and Travel

Most people probably have at least one emigrant forebear or distant relative, and it can be rewarding to discover the place of origin and ancestry of the former, or the living descendants of the latter. Emigration and travel is an important and specialized branch of family history, and brings its own problems. For a start, there are usually two separate sets of records involved: those of the country of origin and those of the country of adoption. Unless you know approximately when and where migration took place, the problems are almost insuperable. For instance, there is no regular series of passenger lists of the people sailing to and from British and American ports before the nineteenth century, yet many people can trace their ancestors back to emigrants in the eighteenth century or earlier. Although emigrants might have been attracted by the promise of land grants in the relevant colony, records of these are tantalizingly scanty in detailing the grantee's place of origin. Soldiers and sailors discharged abroad can be traced only with difficulty, because many of the papers were lost or destroyed. Probably the best recorded emigrants of all were the indentured servants sent to help work the plantations, and the convicts.

Ships' Passenger Lists

A number of ships' passenger lists of people leaving British ports for America can be seen in the Public Record Office at Kew. The originals are filed in the Colonial Office series, and form the major part of J. C. Hotten's work, *Lists of Persons Emigrating to America 1600–1700*. Ships' masters contracted with the Government, local authorities or groups of individuals to convey passengers to America, and their memorials of application are filed in the same series. Passenger lists give the name of each ship, her master, date of sailing, the port of departure, and destination. The list indicates each traveller's name, age, occupation, family grouping, and sometimes parish of origin. From 1634 emigrants to New England were obliged to take the oath of allegiance and conformity, and the list will be endorsed to this effect. There may even be a separate list of those under fourteen, and therefore too young to subscribe.

Then there is a gap until 1890, when a regular series of ships' passenger lists of outgoing vessels from British ports was retained. They

The Breakfast Bell, *A scene on board an emigrant ship, 1884. From an engraving in the Mansell Collection, London.*

Names and Descriptions of Passengers.

N.B.—Cabin passengers must also be included in this Schedule, after the other Passengers. Sec. 6 of 26 and 27 Vict., Cap. 51.

Port of Embarkation.	Names of Passengers.	Profession, Occupation or Calling of Passengers.	English.						Scotch.						Irish.						Foreigners.						Port at which Passengers have contracted to Land.
			Married M	Married F	Single M	Single F	Child	Inf	Married M	Married F	Single M	Single F	Child	Inf	Married M	Married F	Single M	Single F	Child	Inf	Married M	Married F	Single M	Single F	Child	Inf	
	Sanders	Edwd				23																						Sydney
	Peachey	John	Baker			22																						Melbourne
	Merritt	Wm	Farmer			38																						Sydney
	Tucker	William	Carrier			50																						
	McCarthy	Michl	Sailor															36										
	Forrest	Hans	Labr															19										
	Neilson	J	Sailor			32																						Sydney
	Roberts	Wm	Farmer	23												28												Melbourne
		Bessie			26																							
	Rain	Michl	Labr															23										
	Babbage	Mary	Nurse		22																						Sydney

Above. Part of the passenger list of the ship Austral, taking emigrants from Plymouth to Australia, 16 February 1890. The list gives the name, profession, age and destination of the passengers, but not their place of origin. (Kew, Public Record Office, BT 27/32)

are in the Board of Trade series in the Public Record Office, Kew, and are organized annually, by port and then chronologically by date of sailing. You must have some idea of the date of departure, or the name of the vessel; otherwise searches of these lists can be laborious. The lists reveal the name and line of the ship, her master, date of voyage and the ticket numbers of each passenger arranged numerically by class. Foreigners are listed separately. Name, age, occupation, native

country, and place of destination are entered on the lists.

Lists of passengers arriving in American ports survive from 1819, and are held in the National Archives in Washington. The information they contain follows the British pattern. In 1892, the Bureau of Immigration was set up on Ellis Island, off New York, to investigate the status and medical backgrounds of new arrivals intending to settle. Lists of manifests of aliens arriving there after 1907 give considerable detail about the date of sailing, and ports of call during the voyage, as well as the passengers' ages, occupations, literacy level, nationality, last permanent address, and name and location of the nearest living relatives in the country of origin. The Library of Congress holds these archives.

The Mormons did much recruiting work in Europe during the mid-nineteenth century and maintained their own shipping lists of converts. These date between 1850 and 1862, and yield place of origin and occupation of each passenger. The lists are in the custody of the Mormons, in Salt Lake City, Utah.

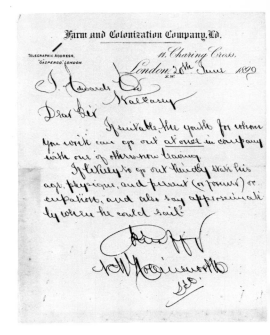

This letter, dated 20 June 1899, reveals the activity of a commercial emigration agency. Many such agencies were set up, and numerous advertising magazines with titles such as The British Emigrant cashed in on the emigration boom in the late nineteenth century. (Oxford, Bodleian Library, John Johnson Collection, Emigration Folder)

Assisted Passages and Land Grants

Privy Council records, in the Public Record Office, which are printed from 1613, and Quarter Sessions papers held by the respective County Record Offices contain spasmodic lists of people sent to the colonies on assisted passages. Some went as voluntarily indentured servants to settlers already there, others were transported under the 1662 Act for the Relief of the Poor. This Act aimed at reducing the totals of those receiving poor relief, and under it the parishes could submit lists of paupers recommended for transportation. The Guildhall Corporation Library, in London, has an extensive series of memoranda of agreements to serve as servants in America or the West Indies between 1718 and 1760. They supply details of name, age, trade, native town, the term of service and the destination. The Public Record Office Treasury papers have a comprehensive run of similar indentures between 1773 and 1776 (Scottish ones for 1774 to 1775 only). The English indentures have a slip index giving name, age, residence, occupation, reason for

WANTED,

By a Gentlemen settled near Philadelphia, in North America,

Some Tradesmen, such as

BRICKlayers, Carpenters, Joiners, Sawyers, Stone-masons, Tilers, Slaters, Plaisterers, Surgeons, School-masters, Book-keepers, Hair-dressers, Wheel and Mill-wrights, Coopers, Black White and Copper-smiths, Linen-weavers, Shoe-makers, Taylors, Gardeners, and those of no Trade, likewise a Number of Farmers who understand the Country Business. Those who are willing to engage are desir'd to apply at No. 5, Cook's-Court, Cammomile-street, near Bishopsgate: or to Mr. *Thomas Miller*, at the City of Bristol, Irongate, near the Tower. Observe these Bills, at the Window. No Apprentices will be taken, without the Consent of their Friends and Masters. The Ship will sail with all Expedition.

Merchants and Captains may be spoke with at the above Office every Day, Sundays excepted. Any Tradesmen or others, that are inclinable to go abroad, will meet with great Encouragement by applying at the above Office. Some Boys wanted, from 12 Years old to 14, 16, 18 or upwards,

An eighteenth-century advertisement for tradesmen and farmers to try their luck in North America. (Oxford, Bodleian Library, John Johnson Collection, Emigration Folder)

'Climbing into the Land of Promise', Ellis Island, 1905. (Photographed by Lewis W. Hine, reproduced by permission of Aperture Inc., New York)

departure, destination, date of voyage, port and vessel.

If your ancestor was an indentured servant but you do not know where he came from, then his master's place of origin is often a clue. A settler in the seventeenth century could obtain grants of land on the headright system whereby he paid for the passage of other emigrants in return for his free transfer of property. Often he would recruit from his own native locality, and his will or the wills of members of the family who remained behind may refer to this place or the kinsman overseas. Early substantial settlers have been reasonably well researched and appear in printed works on colonial history, and can thus point to the likely place of origin of their servants.

In the early and mid-nineteenth century assisted passages helped to colonize new settlements in South Africa, New Zealand, Australia and Canada, and records of these emigrants, and unassisted ones, survive in the relevant state archives. They may be organized under the name of the ship, and the name of a person organizing or paying the cost of the journey, and generally include name, age, occupation, others in the

WHAT A FARMER SAYS
in the
Alberta District.

Name *W. W. Cooper* Address *Leavitt. Cardston Alta.*
S. E. *quato* of Section **6** Township **2** Range **26**

Nationality *English*

Name the several nationalities in your township?
English American Swede Danish.

What is the predominating nationality? *American's I think*

When did you settle in your present location? *about September 1893*

Have you been successful? *Yes so far*

Would you object to stating what capital or outfit you started with?

I started with eight Head of Cattle & Horse Wagon and good health

How much land have you under cultivation in —	Number of —		Value of —	
Wheat — *25 acres*	Horses — *8*		House — *$100*	
Oats — *15"*	Cattle — *12*		Stable — *150*	
	Swine — *6*		Implements *400*	

Alberta runs an advertising campaign (above left). This filled-in form, which incidentally has some genealogical interest, was circulated in England and America to persuade people to emigrate to Canada. In the lower part of the form (not reproduced), Mr Cooper recommends Alberta to his friends, if they want good homes, and continues: 'If coming from United States bring wagons, horses, cattle and what household effects they can put in a wagon. If from England or other foreign country, bring their bedding and warm underclothes.' The idealized picture of farm life in Canada (above) comes from one of the many emigration magazines set up in the late nineteenth century. (Oxford, Bodleian Library, John Johnson Collection, Emigration Folder)

family, plus date of arrival in the colony. If the date is not known this can sometimes be gained from the death certificate, which will state length of stay in the colony.

In 1834 the Poor Law (Amendment) Act provided for the passage of poor families to the colonies at the expense of the Poor Law Unions. This continued until 1890, and the records, arranged by county, Union and parish, are in the Public Record Office, Kew. Arranged alphabetically by surname, they give the occupation and destination of each individual. It is always worth having a search made for further information in the immigration records in the colony itself if you discover that an antecedent emigrated under this Act.

Earlier settlers in America can sometimes be traced through applications for land grants from the Crown. The grants themselves, made on the headright system, or to individual settlers by the Crown, or, from the late seventeenth century, by the colonial governors and Councils, are enrolled in the county courthouses. Copies and indexes to many of them can be consulted in the Library of Congress. A few lists, giving date, location, county, extent and annual quitrent and the name of the grantee, are in the Public Record Office, Kew, in the Colonial Office series, while petitions for grants may be found, along with letters and reports from the colonies, in the same series, and also among the State Papers Colonial (extending from 1574).

Petitions for land grants in Australia from 1784, Cape Colony after 1814, New Zealand from 1820, and Canada from 1830 are also filed in the Colonial Office series, the grants themselves being contained in the respective state archives. Besides telling you the date of the grant, and the value and location of the property, these records indicate the latest date at which the emigrant had arrived in the colony, and serve as a guide to searching other emigration records.

Records of Immigrants

Once they have arrived at their destination, emigrants of course become immigrants, and begin to appear as such in the records of their adopted country. The place of origin and the date of arrival of immigrants can often be learnt from their death certificates, for these usually mention birthplace as well as age at death and the length of stay in the country. Naturalization and denization papers, granting full or partial citizenship, also yield details of birth and date of arrival. In England indexes to these records have been printed from 1509 up to the twentieth century, and the original applications and papers are filed in the Patent Rolls to 1788, and then as part of the Home Office series in the Public Record Office. The Library of Congress holds the American counterparts, plus the earlier oaths of allegiance taken by foreign nationals before secession from the British Crown.

Below. *The emigration business had its ugly side right from the beginning, and pamphleteers were not slow to expose the activities of the shady operators. Readers of Dickens will be reminded of Martin Chuzzlewit's experiences in 'Eden'. (Oxford, Bodleian Library, John Johnson Collection, Emigration Folder)*

Below right. *An immigration document from South Africa. This permit to land was issued by the Permit Office in London, 23 June 1902. Edward Copland of Aberdeen sailed from London as a third-class passenger on the Union Castle line on 26 July 1902. The document gives useful detail, notably the emigrant's home town. (Johannesburg, Africana Museum)*

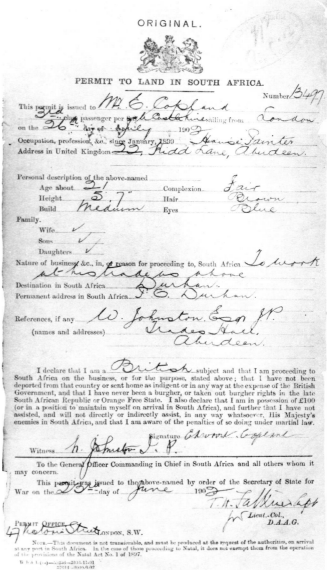

From 1792 in England aliens were required to register their names, address of lodgings or dwelling, and occupation to the county Quarter Sessions, and additionally the Aliens Act of 1836 provided for the filing of certificates of arrival under the relevant port, giving name, nationality, profession and date of arrival. These certificates, to 1852, form part of the Home Office series in the Public Record Office. The registers of the denominational church of groups of immigrants often contain references to their place of origin, and the Huguenot Society has published all those of foreign Protestant churches in England. Wills of immigrants may also mention relatives still overseas, and these can be a very useful clue as to the birthplace of the immigrant too. Lastly, the passenger lists of incoming vessels from elsewhere than Europe and the Mediterranean survive from 1878, and give information as to age, and country of origin. These are held with the lists of outgoing vessels, in the Public Record Office, Kew.

Records relating to financial assistance sought by or meted out to political refugees sometimes include details of origin. In the Public Record Office, Kew, the Treasury Records and Bouillon Papers mark

The main immigrant towns of England. Liverpool has a large concentration of Irish immigrants, but in fact both the Irish and Chinese are widely distributed. Macclesfield should perhaps be included among the Huguenot towns, and Manchester is also a Jewish centre. There are old-established Italian communities in the big industrial towns of England, South Wales and Scotland.

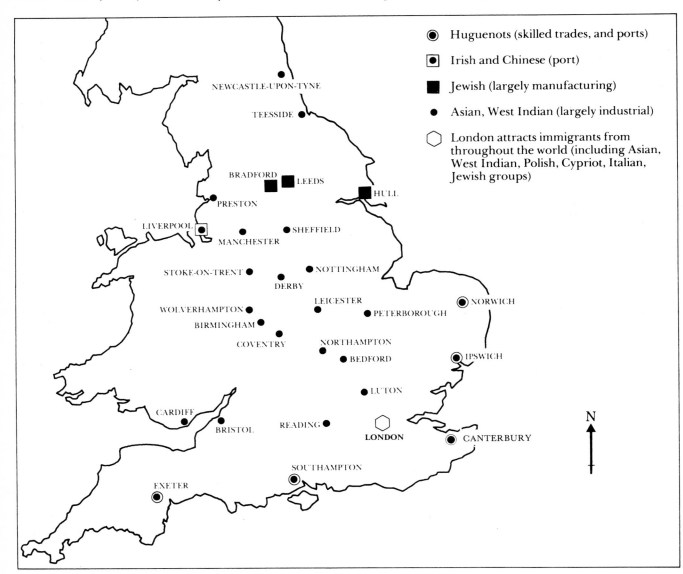

The registration of an alien in Middlesex, 4 May 1797. Monsieur Lemire was probably a refugee from the French Revolution, having arrived in England on 11 September 1792. (London, Greater London Record Office, GLRO MR/A/33)

Hadley 4 may 1797

County of *Middlesex*

Nom, et Qualité ou l'Etat que vous aviez dans votre Païs.
Mon nom est Lemire Je Suis prêtre J'étois Vicaire en France

Lieu de Naissance, et de Residence dans votre Païs.
Je Suis né et Je Residois a Lisieux Ville De normandie apresent Calvados

Age.
mon Je Suis agé de 47 ans

Residence principale pendant six Mois devant votre arrivée dans ce Païs ci.
Ma Residence principale pendant 6 mois avant mon arrivée en angleterre Etoit a Lisieux

Depuis quand etes vous en Angleterre.
Je Suis En angleterre Depuis L'onze Septembre 1792

La Rue, & le Numero de la Maison de votre Residence actuelle.
Je Demeure a hadley chez mr Jumel prés L'Eglize

Vos Occupations presentes, où autres moyens de Subsistance.
Je Donne quelques Leçons de François Et Reçois une partie Des Secours Du gouvernement
SIGNEZ VOTRE NOM. *N Lemire*

An Irish Emigrant Landing at Liverpool. Oil painting by Erskine Nicol, 1871. (Edinburgh, National Galleries of Scotland)

out disbursements made after 1685 and between 1792 and 1828 to the large number of French Protestant refugees arriving at English ports. The Public Record Office also has custody, in the Audit Office series, of the memorials produced by applicants in support of their claim to compensation from the British Crown, as loyalists who lost their estates and property during the American Revolutionary War. They date between 1776 and 1835 and afford considerable detail about their families and impoverished circumstances.

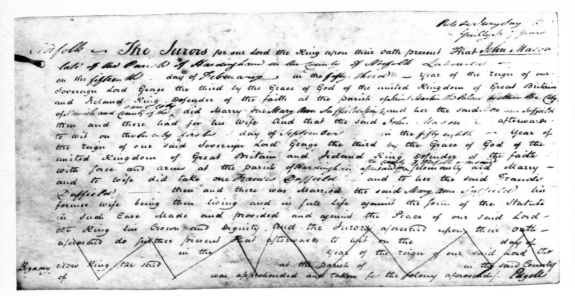

Soldiers, Convicts and Slaves

Other British emigrants found their way to America and other colonies as soldiers. After service they were given pensions and allowed to remain or to emigrate as settlers. Records of the pensions are held in the War Office series in the Public Record Office, Kew, and give dates, amounts, to whom paid and when, and the reason for cessation of payment. There are also pensions records in the state archives of former colonies, dating from 1815 in Canada, and 1846 in New South Wales and New Zealand.

British and Hessian troops who fought in the American Revolutionary War can be found in regimental musters, but you must know the regiment to which an individual belonged, unless he was a commissioned officer, whose name would therefore have appeared in a printed *Army List*. The British military records are retained by the Public Record office, Kew.

The monthly or quarterly muster contained in order of rank, and then alphabetically, all those persons on active service in the regiment, with a separate list of new recruits, casualties, and non-effectives. Some soldiers left to join American regiments, and similar muster records are held in the Library of Congress, in Washington.

Another class of emigrant was the convict. A list of felons transported from the English Home Counties to America during the period 1719 to 1744 has been printed from the Treasury Papers in the Public Record Office. Their origins can be traced through the records of the criminal courts (see above, pp. 96–101). After the Revolutionary War convicts were transported to Australia between 1787 and 1868. From 1788 until 1859 a series of censuses was taken of New South Wales, and occasionally Tasmania, listing alphabetically the convicts and their families. The best of these dates from 1828, and copies of all of them are in the Home Office records in the Public Record Office, and in the Mitchell Library, Sydney (see also above, pp. 39, 41). Apart from personal details the census will tell you the date of the voyage and the name of the ship, while the convict ships' musters will reveal the date and place of trial. These musters contain the names of the crew as well as the

Above. *'Crime is always with us.' This old engraving shows criminals under sentence of transportation being marched from Newgate Jail to Blackfriars for embarkation onto a convict ship. Transportation was begun in the seventeenth century and continued until the mid-nineteenth century. (London, Mansell Collection)*

passengers, and are held by the Public Record Office. Records of pardons report the date of the conviction, the court, the date of transportation and the vessel, the date of the pardon, and also any subsequent change of name. Often Australian certificates are registered under the assumed name, and these pardons are invaluable in discovering the original. The Mitchell Library in Sydney holds records of pardons, and with the Society of Australian Genealogists, based in the same city, specializes in material relating to convict settlers.

The transporting of slaves constituted another form of compulsory emigration. Many hundreds of thousands were sent to America and the West Indies between the mid-seventeenth and early nineteenth centuries. The names and origins of individual slaves are poorly documented, and the records in the Public Record Office at Kew merely contain details of vessels and their ports of call and dates, with the totals of captured natives and their destination. Once in the colonies slaves were sold at auctions or privately, and surviving bills of sale may indicate their place of origin. They were mentioned as property in their

A list of slaves belonging to Hannah Brown of Kingston, Jamaica, 28 June 1820, drawn up according to the requirements for 'Slave Registration and Compensation' after the passing of the Act of Parliament in 1809 abolishing slavery in British territories. (Kew, Public Record Office, T/1/81)

masters' wills, and featured in newspaper advertisements for sale, or as reported missing, in records of trials for offences against their master or his property, and in plantation and estate records. As whole families were broken up and several generations since transportation elapsed before the abolition of slavery in 1833, it is an almost impossible task to trace tribal origins, unless dialect words or place-names are strong enough clues. The tribal name of the original slave forebear might have been transmitted in the folklore of the family, but generally the native culture was quickly submerged. The subject is a difficult one and as yet little work has been done in trying to trace individual slaves back to their original settlements.

Traders and Travellers

Voyages overseas were not always intended to be permanent, and strong links were often maintained with families and business associates left at home. Applications for passports from 1795 to 1898 contain names, intended destinations, and recommendations, the later registers of applications being indexed. They are in the Foreign Office series in the Public Record Office, but only a sample of the originals have been kept.

Traders and merchant seamen abroad, especially in America, the West and East Indies and the Levant, may also be recorded in letters and petitions bound in the State Papers Colonial, and those of the Board of Trade, the Colonial Office, and the Foreign Office, all deposited in the Public Record Office. The Virginia Company and other Merchant Companies trading overseas kept their own records, and the Historical Manuscripts Commission, in London, has a catalogue of these and their whereabouts.

Burgess Books of ports like Bristol and Southampton contain details of the apprenticeship indentures of merchants and their sons, giving the father's name, abode and occupation, which can be very useful in showing the overseas connection, as well as the origins of the planter himself if he was similarly apprenticed. These records are held in the County or Borough Record Offices, and some have been printed. Traders can also be traced through records of litigation in the Court of Chancery, dealing with disputes between associates, or clients, and a wealth of biographical data can be gleaned from them about the nature and extent of the business and its viability. The Public Record Office is the custodian of the suits brought to Chancery.

Births, marriages, and deaths of British citizens abroad can be found either in the records of the countries themselves, or in the British Consular Returns deposited in the General Register Office, or among the ecclesiastical returns, dating between 1706 and 1939, in the tenure of the Guildhall Library, in London. If foreign estates were purchased and the owner died abroad the probate court of the country concerned should have a copy of his will, while the estate papers should be in the regional or state archives office. It is also worth enquiring of the incumbent of the relevant parish where a planter or trader died, as to the possibility of a gravestone inscription to him.

Kerman. The Family Group.
Habib (footman) Ibrahim (cook)   boy
Mother   Daddy
      Baji (nurse) Mollie. Baji-dollie.
Oil was disappearing mysteriously, eventually the "boy" divulged the cook was the thief. For the safety of the boy's life, the boy was discharged.

An English couple marry abroad in 1887, in the British Embassy at Therapia, about ten miles north of Istanbul. John Williams Tanner jnr. (born 11 May 1863) was the son of John Williams Tanner (born 2 May 1831; see the family Bible, p. 32 above), and was the grandfather of Mrs Peggy Norman. This certificate has been kept in the family. Official entries of such marriages abroad are to be found among the Consular Returns in the General Register Office. John Tanner is seen again in the photograph below, with his second wife, servants and youngest daughter, in Isfahan, Iran, where his work as a telegraphist had taken him.

The British in India

A special group of emigrants were the British in India, who can be traced back to the founding of the Honourable East India Company in 1600. Until 1834 no British subject could enter India without the Company's consent, and applications for permission to enter and licences to trade are filed with the Company Court Minutes, in the India Office Library, in London. Those employed by the Company were similarly recorded until 1794, after which the applications of candidates for service are recorded in the form of Writers' Petitions, incorporating details of family background, birth and educational attainments. After 1805 these were superseded by the Committee of College References, recruitment for Company service being from Haileybury College.

Indexed cadet papers of military officers in the Company's own regiments date from 1789 to 1860, and contain similar information to the Civil Service Petitions. Together with the embarkation lists between 1753 and 1860, these sources account for almost every person travelling from Britain to India. The embarkation lists detail the name of the ship, those of the passengers, and their ages, places of origin and destination, and status. Additionally there are the regular printed editions of *Directories*, *Almanacs* and *East India Register and Army Lists* from 1803 to 1860, which contain a wealth of data about European inhabitants, their official positions, residences, and any births, marriages and deaths reported since the previous publication. Details of births, marriages and deaths taken from printed Indian sources are held by the Society of Genealogists, in London.

The India Office Library holds the registers of ecclesiastical returns of baptism, marriage and burial from the three Presidencies of Madras (from 1698), Bombay (1709), and Bengal (1713), though those of the Roman Catholics were not formally registered until 1836. Also there are returns for Sumatra (Fort Marlborough), St Helena, Macao, Whampoa, and Penang for limited periods of the eighteenth and nineteenth centuries.

Wills of Europeans holding property in India can also be examined in the India Office Library, dating from 1704 for the Presidency of Bengal, and from 1728 and 1753 for Bombay and Madras. Native wives and mothers, as well as details of a person's estates are mentioned in these ecclesiastical records. Monuments to those who died there also add to your knowledge about the family, and many of these inscriptions have been transcribed and printed.

6 The Study of Names

There were fourteen entries in the birth columns of *The Times* for 9 January 1980. One of the surnames was occupational in origin (Baker), two were derived from personal names (Baldwin, Selwyn), two were patronyms (Edmondson, Hodgkinson), three probably originated as place-names (Caithness, Hamilton, Sandbach) and four as nicknames, either descriptive (Bell, Moir), or associated with some event in which the original bearer participated, like a pageant (King, Nunn). One surname was hyphenated (Barty-King) and two were of totally foreign origin (Dadak, Grauwin).

This list illustrates five of the ways in which surnames have evolved, and a further study would reveal their possible linguistic and racial origins and their first traceable appearance. For example, Baldwin is a Norse name, and Selwyn Flemish.

What the genealogist seeks to know is the history of his family, traceable through the continuity of surname over many generations. Each family, however dispersed, will be linked by a surname common to all its male and unmarried female members. Names are literally the key to genealogy, but they can present all sorts of problems and pitfalls to the unwary; in some cases they can also provide valuable clues about family origins, and it is very useful for the genealogist to have some awareness of the history of names and naming systems.

This chapter is intended to give a general survey of the history and development of surnames and personal names, and to offer practical advice about how to tackle special problems associated with them.

How People are Named

In Western cultures everyone is given a personal name by his or her parents, soon after birth. This precedes the surname of the parents and both names are normally retained by males throughout life. Females of the family use the surname until marriage, when it is substituted by that of the husband into whose family she has married. She will normally be addressed in correspondence as 'Mrs Thomas Thexton' or whatever her husband's personal and surnames happen to be. After the husband's death his widow still uses her married name unless she marries again and takes her new husband's surname. Sometimes a wife's maiden name is joined to that of her husband by a hyphen, usually coming before his surname. In Scotland a woman also retains her maiden name for legal purposes after marriage.

Hereditary surnames probably developed because of the need to identify individuals, their descendants and families. This was principally because of the hereditary nature of landownership, title and office, which required proof of affinity before transfer to the next heir. When these rights were committed to writing a fixed surname was used to refer to subsequent holders in a particular family. The tax system also required the regulation of surnames to identify families assessed to pay certain dues.

The earliest surnames were not hereditary, but died with the individual or were replaced several times during his or her lifetime. They often derived from personal nicknames based on physical appearance, occupation or events in which the person had been involved. Secondly, the locality of place where the person dwelt might have been added as a tag onto a personal name, changing when he removed elsewhere, or remaining as a reminder of his native abode. Another source was the personal name of the father—John, son of William would be called 'John, William's son'; his son in turn would be

A collage of signatures. The Brownes were the owners of Townend, Troutbeck, Cumbria, and this collection of signatures, dating back to the sixteenth century, is now on display in the house. It provides an interesting study in handwriting styles. (Photo: National Trust)

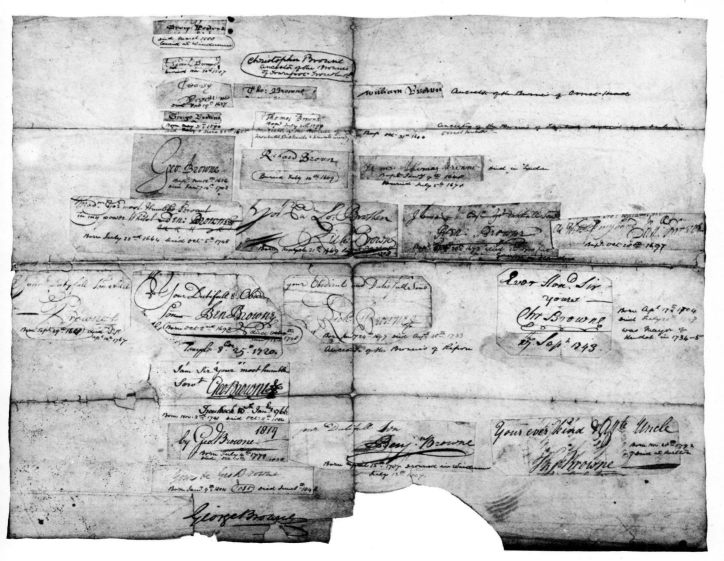

Name	Origin and/or meaning	Name	Origin and/or meaning
Aaron	Old Testament, brother of Moses; name possibly of Egyptian origin.	**Edgar**	Eadgar (944–75), King of Wessex; name revived by Sir Walter Scott's *Bride of Lammermoor*.
Abigail	Old Testament, wife of David; meaning 'the father rejoiced'.	**Elizabeth**	Biblical, from Hebrew *Elisheba*, meaning 'My God is satisfaction'.
Albert	Of Old German origin, meaning noble and bright; became popular because Queen Victoria's husband was Prince Albert.	**Felix**	An East Anglian Saint; from the Latin, meaning 'happy'.
Amabel	From the Latin *amabilis*, lovable; also gave rise to Mabel, Annabel, Arabella.	**Fiona**	Coined by William Sharp for *Fiona Macleod*, probably from Gaelic *fionn*, fair.
Beatrice	Fourth-century Roman saint; from the Latin, meaning 'bringer of joy'; popularity enhanced by use in Dante and Shakespeare.	**Gladys**	Welsh Gwladys, may be a form of the Latin Claudia.
		Hector	Greek hero of the *Iliad*; a popular name in Scotland.
Beverley	A place-name in Yorkshire, England; it became first a surname, then a male Christian name in 19th-century England, and finally a female Christian name in 20th-century America.	**Imogen**	Heroine of Shakespeare's *Cymbeline*; name apparently coined by Shakespeare.
		Jacob	Biblical; the name became transformed into the now very popular James.
Bridget	Originally a Celtic fire goddess, also a Christian saint; the word means 'the high one'.	**Leonard**	From Old German Leonhard, meaning 'bold lion'; Saint Leonard was the patron of captives.
Cedric	Name invented for Cedric the Saxon in Sir Walter Scott's *Ivanhoe*; popularized as Christian name of Little Lord Fauntleroy.	**Margaret**	Margaret of Antioch, patron saint of women in childbirth; from the Latin *margarita*, a pearl.
Charles	Old German *carl*, meaning a man; the name has become very popular only since the 19th century.	**Patrick**	Patron saint of Ireland; from the Latin *patricius*, noble.
Derek	Derived from Theodoric, derived in turn from Old German *theuda*, people, and *ric*, ruler: ruler of the people.	**Ralph**	From Old English Raedwulf, meaning 'a wolf (i.e. cunning) in counsel'; in use before the Norman Conquest in England.
		Sharon	Biblical place-name adopted by the Puritans and transplanted to America.
Douglas	Gaelic, meaning 'dark-blue'.	**Thelma**	Coined by Marie Corelli in *Thelma: A Society Novel* (1887).

called 'David, John's son'. In this system the father's name (the patronymic) originally changed each generation, but many patronymics have subsequently become hereditary surnames (Williamson, Johnson).

Personal names originated as a means of identifying an individual. All sorts of sources have been used for personal names—the Bible, mythology, classical names, saints' names, nicknames, words indicating admired or desired qualities, or virtues which it was hoped would be displayed by their owner. Other personal names have been used as invocations, or as punishment for misdeeds by the parents. Diminutives, pet-names and derivatives of foreign names have also been used, and some are pure invention. The date of birth, the child's place in the order of birth, and the mother's maiden name are other sources.

The custom of giving a child one personal name was common in Western Europe until the late Middle Ages; names were taken mainly from those of saints or martyrs whose names appeared in the Christian Church calendar, hence the term 'Christian name'. As most of the days of the year celebrate a saint or martyr, there was a wide range of choice. In late medieval France, and in sixteenth-century England, two or more personal names were given to infants of the gentry, only one being taken from the Church calendar, but this custom did not become

Some examples of personal names, showing a wide range of sources and meanings, mainly taken from E. G. Withycombe's Oxford Dictionary of English Christian Names.

common until the late eighteenth century, although the Puritans used compound hyphenated religious invocations as Christian names in the seventeenth century in England and America.

One of the personal names may have been taken from a parent, godparent, relative or friend. Occasionally you will find that several children of the same parents were given identical personal names, although this custom appears to have declined in England by the eighteenth century. Each child was identified by order of seniority as 'senior', 'younger', 'youngest'. It is not certain why this practice was adopted, but it has been suggested that where the succession to land provided for named individuals it was a security measure to ensure that the land passed to such a named child.

Where a son is named after his father he is normally referred to as 'junior'. In America, if this custom is perpetuated over several generations, all of whom are still alive, each will be distinguished by a number enumerating the generations from the original bearer.

The parents' whim and taste are important factors in the naming of

Another family souvenir from Townend, Troutbeck, beautifully sewn by twelve-year-old Eleanor Thompson in 1831. Such genealogical samplers were popular in the eighteenth and nineteenth centuries. (Photo: National Trust)

Edmund . Thompson Born March 20 A.D......1790
Eleanor . Thompson Born August 16 A.D......1789
The Names of their Children
Esther . Thompson Born January 11 A.D......1810
William . Thompson Born August 16 A.D......1811
Edmund . Thompson Born March 20 A.D......1813
Ann . Thompson Born February 7 A.D......1815
John . Thompson Born March 7 A.D......1817
Eleanor Thompson Born May 5 A.D......1819
George . Thompson Born July 11 A.D......1821
Thomas . Thompson Born July 16 A.D......1823
Jane . Thompson Born April 2 A.D......1825

Eleanor . Thompson A.D MDCCCXXXI

their progeny. For example, some personal names are given to either male or female children. An unusual distinctive personal name may be given to a child bearing a common surname, while a public or historical personality, or a literary hero or heroine may lend their names for adoption. A national or local event might also be the source. Contemporary taste is replaced by new trends, and names come and go in and out of fashion. For instance, in the sixteenth and early seventeenth centuries classical Greek and Roman names taken from history and literature were used by the gentry in England, while by the eighteenth century there was a revival of interest in Anglo-Saxon and medieval personal names. Religious and biblical names selected by families portray current religious thinking, the Puritans and Nonconformists being prime examples, the former constructing compound names and the latter choosing often obscure scriptural names. Initial letters as personal names are favoured by Americans, but are normally preceded by a more conventional personal name.

In Scotland it was until recently the custom to name the first son after his paternal grandfather, the second after his maternal grandfather and the third after his father. Daughters were named first after the maternal grandmother, second after the paternal grandmother and third after the mother herself. Thus a person's place in the family can be ascertained, and the fixed pattern of names can give a clue as to parentage and remoter antecedents if you are researching a Scottish family.

Naming Patterns in Other Cultures

Surnames have evolved throughout the world and tend to be derived from the same sources: nicknames, place-names, occupation, patronyms or mother's names, or from a miscellaneous class derived from nature, literature, events, diminutives of personal names, anagrams or artificial concoctions. Not all have become hereditary, especially in the Middle Eastern countries.

The shifting patronymic system was still in use in parts of Scandinavia, among European Jews, and even in Wales as late as the nineteenth century. Sometimes a man would be identified not just by his father but by a whole string of antecedents, for example Richard Ap Evan Ap Thomas Ap Howell (Richard son of Evan, grandson of Thomas and great-grandson of Howell). These personal genealogies can be of great value to the family historian where the family stayed in a particular community over several generations. In Denmark, Norway and Sweden, fixed surnames were enforced by statute by 1901; however, there can be confusion in the records, for the same person might be known in his village as Peder Hansen (son of Hans Jensen), but by the authorities as Peder Jensen. Scandinavian immigrants to America continued to use patronymics into the twentieth century.

Cultures where the patronymic system was particularly strong have relatively few surnames once these became fixed and hereditary. The original preposition, prefix, or suffix becomes indelibly attached, and even corrupted so that new surnames evolve, for example Bevan from Ap Evan, Bowen from Ap Owen and Powell from Ap Howell.

A Welsh pedigree of the early eighteenth century, showing the descendants of Yryen Rheged, the progeny of Coel Godelsog (Old King Cole), and illustrating the shifting patronymic system of naming. Yryen's son is Owen ap Yryen, a Knight of the Round Table. Later the sequence is Einon Vawr, Grono ap Einon, and Rhys ap Grono and his brothers. The note in the bottom right-hand corner gives an alternative ancestry of Einon Vawr in the form of a string of patronymics. (London, College of Arms, MS. Protheroe VIII, p. 69)

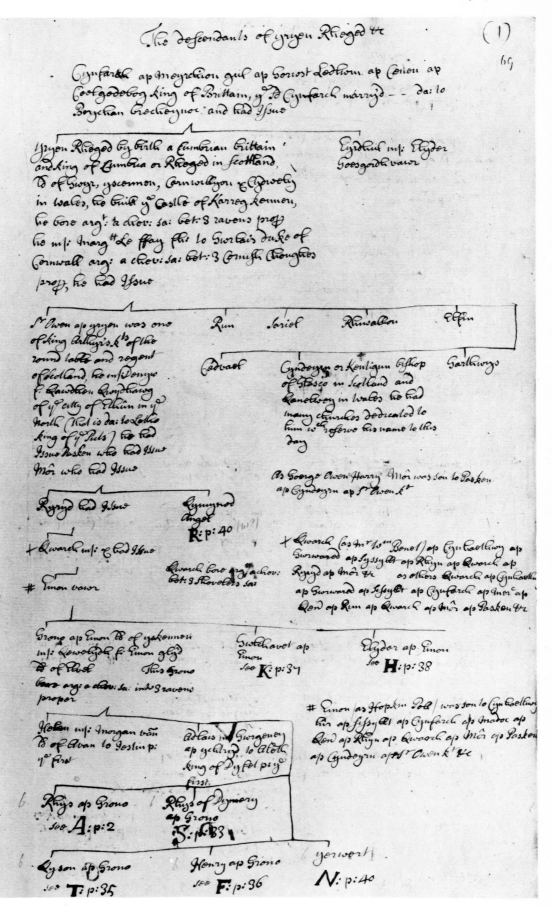

In contrast, Muslim fathers take the name of the first-born son in addition to their own, so that for instance Abu Abdullah Muhammed ibn Ismail ibn Ibrahim ibn Mughirah al Ju'fi al Bukhari is the name of Muhammed, father of Abdullah, son of Ismail, grandson of Ibrahim, great-grandson of Mughirah, of the Tribe of Ju'fi, and born at Bukhara.

Clan and tribal names can be traced back into antiquity, and we know that in the second millennium BC each Chinese family was ordered to take a family name. Tradition asserts that there are about 500 of these ancient family (or clan) names. As junior branches proliferated new clans emerged, each living in their own villages. In 1965 there were still only 1,185 clan names in a population of 700 million people. The clan name is followed by the generation name and then the personal name, women retaining their maiden names after marriage. The generation name is taken from a family poem perhaps compiled hundreds of years ago, which contains 20–30 characters, each representing an entire generation. Each member thus knows the generation names of his forebears and successors. Adoption of a child from a junior branch, or of a prospective son-in-law to ensure continuity of a clan name otherwise endangered, complicates Chinese genealogy, especially as once a son is born to the adopted son-in-law he reverts back to his original clan name. Foreigners taking Chinese names generally used characters of one syllable, or a new character not previously adopted.

Clan names are also central to the naming systems of countries such as Korea, Japan, Tibet, India, Poland, Hungary, Scotland and Ireland. In Scotland the MacDonalds are said to descend from Donald, the MacLochlans from a man of Norway, the MacDougalls from a Dane. In the Scottish highlands only the chief and his immediate family used the clan name originally, as the senior descendants of the founder of the line. The other dependants used genealogical strings of personal names, which eventually were dropped in favour of a hereditary surname, sometimes in fact the clan name.

Migrant groups like the Jews employed the naming schemes of their adopted countries. Until the late eighteenth century, when hereditary surnames became obligatory in eastern and central Europe, Jewish families there used combinations of personal names, those of offices, or places of origin or their derivatives, with each person's father's personal name preceded by 'Ben' or 'Bar' or ending with the suffix -s. Metronyms were common, using the personal name of the mother. Jewish families sometimes translated their own surnames into their adopted language, or used aliases, which obscured their real origins. With the growth of Zionism in the twentieth century some of these were rendered back into Hebrew, and non-Hebrew names were similarly translated, for example Eshkol from Shkolnik, Meir from Myerson and Ben-Gurion from Gruen.

Another stateless group, slaves, were normally given only personal names. When they were freed, they tended to adopt the surname or place of origin of their masters, combined with their own nicknames, or the name of the estate or plantation on which they had laboured, or even the vessels in which they had sailed or the port of arrival. Religious and literary sources were also used. Their true origins therefore often lie unsuspected unless records state their previous servile status.

Patronymics

Preposition
Ap, Ab, Mab (Wales)
Ben, Bar (Jewish)
Ibn (Arab)

Prefix
Mac- (Scotland)
Mc-, O' (Ireland)
C- (Isle of Man)
Fitz- (Ireland and England)
Kara- (Turkey)

Suffix
-son, -s (Jewish)
-oglo (Turkey)
-sson, -dottir (Scandinavia)
-ez (Spain)
-ena, -ana (Basque)
-pulo, -idi, -odi, -adi, -is, -aki (Greece)
-svili, -dze (Soviet Georgia)
-ov, -ev, -in (male), -a, -ina (female) (Soviet Russia)
-enko, -uk, -juk (Ukraine)
-jan, -ian (Armenia)
-ovic, -evic, -skij/ckij, -skoj/ckoj, -owicz/ewicz, (Poland)
-u, -escu (Rumania)

Some common patronymics.

Name	Earliest Use	Meaning
Ackermann	c. 1233	Old English *æcermann*; a farmer, husbandman, ploughman
Alabaster	c. 1198	Old French *arbalestier*; a soldier armed with a crossbow; a maker of crossbows
Batchelor	c. 1165	Middle English, Old French *bacheler*; a young knight
Becket	c. 1155	Old French *bec*, diminutive *beket*; little beak or mouth
Bosanquet	1685	French name introduced by the Huguenots; probably from Languedoc, *bouzanquet*—dwarf
Chambers	1219	A room in a house, reception room in a palace; name given to an official, compare Chamberlain
Doyle		Old Irish, Ó Dubhgaill, descendant of Dubhghaill (black stranger, a Dane)
Drinkwater	c. 1300	Middle English; a person too poor to afford ale; sometimes ironically applied to a taverner
Ewer	1185	Old French *ewer*; a servant who served guests at table water to wash their hands
Faber	1066	Latin *faber*; a smith
Galbraith	1280	Old Gaelic *Gall-Bhreathnach*; stranger-Briton, a Briton settling among the Gaels
Godfrey	1086	Old German *Godefrid*; God-peace
Jenner	12th cent.	Medieval Latin *ingeniator*; a master-mason or architect
Keat(s)	1166	Old English *cyte*, a shed or outhouse for cattle or sheep; could denote a herdsman
Kennedy	c. 1180	Irish Ó Cinnéide; ugly head
Magnus	c. 1114	Latin *magnus*, great; given as a personal name to a king of Norway, after Charlemagne; better known in the form Magnusson, Manson
Neal	1086	Norwegian/Icelandic *njall*, champion; brought to England by the Normans
Pettigrew	1227	Probably old French *petit cru*, little growth; a person of small stature
Roth(man)	1346	Old English; a dweller in a clearing
Simmonds	1066	Two distinct origins: (1) from Old Norse and Danish, 'victory protector'; (2) from Hebrew, 'snub-nosed'
Vincent	c. 1200	Latin *Vincentinus*, from *vincens*, conquering

A selection of English surnames, showing the wide variety of sources involved. Taken from P. H. Reaney's Dictionary of British Surnames.

The English System and its Development

The Normans probably introduced hereditary surnames to England, although some surnames had existed before 1066. They were probably adopted at different rates in different localities and levels of society, although a systematic national survey has yet to be made. Tentative conclusions have been drawn from studies of taxation lists, land-ownership records, and manorial court rolls for particular counties over a long period from their commencement. It would seem that counties closest to central government, like Oxfordshire, used hereditary surnames from the early thirteenth century. Those lying farthest away, like Yorkshire and East Anglia, probably did not use them on a wide scale until as late as the fifteenth century. This is important for the family historian to understand, because it will severely restrict his search for medieval forebears, unless the family continuously occupied or owned a particular piece of land over several generations, and this was well recorded. Even then filiations may not be made entirely clear.

It would seem that people of the same status co-existed, some using hereditary surnames, and others not. People of higher rank seem to have assumed hereditary surnames first, probably because they regularly figured in official documents and because of the hereditary nature of office, title and landownership. These records were systematically kept from the late twelfth century, and their precision in identification of individuals was essential to effective government, especially as the numbers of offices, titles and lands increased. It was convenient to identify an heir by his father's surname or estate.

Persons of unfree status probably assumed hereditary surnames last, though evidence is scanty. Even as late as 1461 an outlaw was mentioned in an official pardon under eleven different nicknames. Servants and apprentices often took the surname of their masters, which may have altered with their changes of employment, and this makes for difficulty in tracing their antecedents.

The appearance of the same surname in one vicinity over a long period does not necessarily indicate that it belonged to the same family, especially where the name derives from a place-name or a common occupation. You may purely by coincidence find two or three individuals of the same surname, at the same place, separated by roughly generation intervals. This in itself does not necessarily mean that the name was hereditary and that they were related.

Here are some examples of common types of English surnames:

Occupational and Status. Steward, Butler, Franklin, Yeoman, Smith, Taylor, Sawyer, Bowyer, Baker, Butcher, Wheeler, Wright. (A servant or apprentice might take his master's name or occupation as his own surname, for example, Roberts, Edwards, Parsons, Masters.)

Personal Names. Baldwin, Selwyn, Richard, Thomas.

Patronymics. Williamson, Thompson, Davidson, Davis, Johnson, Jackson, Jones, Edwardson, Edwards.

Nicknames
  Physical characteristics: Little, Redhead, Gray.
  Character: Younghusband, Loveday.
  Roles in plays or pageants: Bishop, Pope.
  Literature: Alexander, Caesar.
  Nature: Partridge, Pigeon, Rabbit, Rose, Flower, Fish, Bird, Sweetapple.
  Anagrams: Norweb from Browne.
  Invented: Yorkoope from York and Cooper.

Place-Names. Helm, Holm, Thackeray, Thexton, Thorpe, Braithwaite, Hetherington, Ormerod, Gaitskell, Asquith, Billington, Kirby.
  The location of a dwelling is illustrated by Att Hill, Att Wood, Att Well, Yewbank, Tree, Greenwood, Grove, Lee, Longstone.
  Strangers were identified by their place of origin or race: Newcomb, Cornwall, London, Lombard, Fleming, Breton, Dennis (Danish),

Deciphering signatures is not always easy, even if the handwriting is relatively modern, as in this case. The signatures are those of the Jesus College buttery servants, signing for their wages on 17 February 1921. Mrs Pavier (ninth from the bottom) could possibly prove to be related to the Ann Pavier who married Henry Harris in 1852 (see above, p. 36). (Oxford, Jesus College Archives)

Norman and Norris (both Norway).

Foundling children were often given the name of the parish, street or building where they were found, for example Marylebone, Church-yard.

The prepositions 'le' and 'de' do not necessarily indicate the person owned the property, but merely that he lived there.

Problems with Names

The chief problem that the genealogist encounters with names is variability of spelling. When you look through public records you will very likely find that there are variations of your surname, some obvious, and others perhaps surprising and not easy to detect. These may result from dialect differences between regions, from idiosyncratic spellings based on phonetics before standard spelling and widespread education were introduced, or from confusion when spelling does not tally with pronunciation. Some variants may be Anglicizations or derivatives of foreign surnames, and sometimes apparent variants may turn out to be quite distinct surnames after all. Knowledge and experience of surname variations is quickly acquired when one begins to use the indexes of centrally registered records. It is essential to write down a name exactly as you see it spelled in the original, so that you do not misinterpret two distinct surnames as one, and so that you see the likely variants which you may find elsewhere, and approximately at which date they were in circulation. The variation may also tell you how the name was pronounced at a particular date and area. Be careful, however, not to introduce new variants by errors in your transcription of individual letters, particularly u and n, m and w, and f for l and s. When searching indexes, keep a note of every variant that you look under. This can save reduplicated effort later.

Some variations in dialect can be difficult to trace when they drop or substitute initial letters. For example Tuddenham becomes Tudman and then Studman in Norfolk; Ffardon Vardon in Oxfordshire; Holroyd Oldroyd in Lancashire, and Hetherington Etherington.

Spelling can vary within a single document, especially when there was no established spelling; examples are Jefferies, Jeffries, Jefferys, Jeffreys, Geoffries; Lee, Leigh, Lea; Pierce, Pearce, Pearse. A clerk might tussle with an acceptable way of rendering a name he has just heard and write Dodgson as Dodshon; or he might misread it and transcribe Risley for Risby. Where names were pronounced differently from how they were spelled, like Botham, Cholmondley, Beauchamp, confusion was especially likely, as clerks were liable to substitute a phonetic version to represent the sound.

Foreign names present special problems as they become assimilated into another language, and if any of your ancestors were immigrants you should look out for clues as to how an original foreign name may have been changed. Assimilation can occur in several ways. Firstly, the sound can be retained but the spelling changed: thus Pertuis—Pertwee; Coqueril—Cockerill; Garrique—Garrick. Secondly, a similar-sounding name may be substituted. This happened particularly with Scandinavian and Slav names with their 'bj' 'kj' and 'sv' combinations which are not found in English. Thus Bjorn, Kjerret and Svensson become Burns, Cherry and Swanson in America. Sometimes these sorts of changes are less obvious, for example Burke from Berg, or Butler from Botolvson. Thirdly, a similar-looking word may be substituted, although pronounced differently: thus Moulins—Mullins; Huyghens—Huggens or Higgins; Brasseur—Brassey. Name endings may also be dropped or names shortened for the sake of simplicity, particularly in the case of immigrants from eastern Europe. Fourthly, a name may be translated directly into another language: L'Oiseau to Bird, de Bosco or Dubois to Wood; le Jeune to Young, Norskos to Norwood, Østerhuis to Easthouse, Fuksa to Fox. Finally, a name may be abandoned altogether and a more conventional name taken. It may be difficult to trace the origin of an immigrant family using its name alone.

Not only immigrants change their names, however. Anyone can assume a new surname, provided that it is not used to perpetrate a fraud. A wife customarily takes her husband's surname on marriage, but she may still use her maiden name if she prefers. Mere change by common repute, or advertisement in the national or local press are sufficient indications, but there may be difficulties in proving identity for a passport, or welfare benefits. More formal methods exist, which vary in each country. In England, for instance, there are four possibilities: a Statutory Declaration sworn before a Justice of the Peace or Commissioner for Oaths; a Deed Poll; a Royal Licence; or a private Act of Parliament. Many of the Deeds Poll are enrolled on the Close Rolls to 1902, and in the records of the Supreme Court of Judicature after this. They are held in the Public Record Office in London, and are indexed up to 1904 by the former name of the applicant, and subsequently by cross-referencing. Before 1914 it was not necessary for the Deeds Poll to be advertised in the *London Gazette* before enrolment, and it is still not obligatory to enrol them officially. Royal Licences were normally granted to persons changing their names in order to receive a bequest, armorial bearings, or money. Since 1939 aliens wishing to change their names must apply to the Home Secretary for consent, unless it is by Royal Licence.

An alias, as a second name is called, may have been assumed for several reasons, the most common being to ensure its perpetuation. Often the husband of an heiress to a superior estate would adopt his wife's name, especially if it was a distinguished one, or a man inheriting his maternal estates would take his mother's family name. An adopted child might additionally take his adoptive parents' name. Sometimes the alias was hyphenated with the former name, thus creating a double-barrelled surname. A less formal way of perpetuating a family name is to use it as an additional personal name.

Alternatively, an alias might have been given by others as an easy means of identification, especially where there were several people of the same name living in the same community. This would derive from occupation, residence or personal nickname, and die with the person concerned. An alias might also differentiate between different branches of a family.

Other reasons for taking an alias were to conceal identity, to avoid associations with past scandals or scandalous relatives, to Anglicize a

A Deed Poll of 19 July 1907, in which Thomas Martin Fullalove changed his surname to Fuller. (London, Public Record Office, Chancery Lane, J 18/73)

foreign name, or to drop a depreciatory surname. Each alias must therefore be studied on its own merits, but it may be very difficult to trace the circumstances under which it was assumed, while an unrecorded change of name can mean an early end to your search for ancestors.

Tracing the Origin and Distribution of Names

Surnames are the working tool of the family historian in tracing his forebears, but they can also assist in discovering the family's place of origin and its geographical distribution. If your surname is an occupational or personal derivative then this makes for problems because there will be many similarly named families bearing no relationship with yours, but if the surname is derived from a dialect word for an occupation or locality, or from a recognizable foreign name, then a rough idea as to its origin can be adduced. Place-name derivatives are easier to be certain of, unless there are several places of the same name scattered in quite distinct areas, or the place no longer exists or has changed its name. Clans were territorial, and so the problem of discovering where a clan name originated is relatively straightforward. Some of the Scottish clans have their own societies and gatherings to which dispersed and overseas members can belong and so keep in touch with the homeland.

As well as trying to trace a name's geographical origin, it can also be fascinating to study its distribution; indeed, in some cases, the distribution of a name may provide a valuable clue to its origin. The best sources for tracing current distribution are telephone directories, arranged by county or state, and listing names and addresses of subscribers. You will discover how uneven the distribution of the surname can be, and if you plot its incidence on a map, you will see where the majority of entries relate to. This may not necessarily be the original locality, because families may have moved away entirely and have bred large numbers of offspring in one district and not in another. Similarly, occupational, personal, and residential derivatives will not relate necessarily to the same original district. What you will see is the current distribution of the name and its frequency.

Central registration records of birth, marriage and death serve to show the incidence of a surname in a particular region, county, or

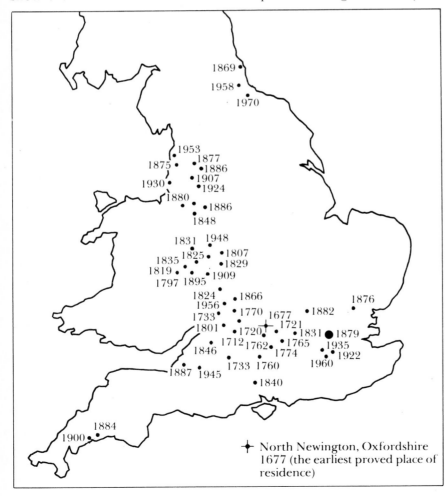

The origin and distribution of the name Fardon. This map, based on the author's searches for the name in the Census, central registration, taxation and Quaker sources, shows the earliest occurrence of the name in different parts of the country, emanating from North Newington in Oxfordshire from at least the early sixteenth century. Every known Fardon in this country can be linked back to this family.

✛ North Newington, Oxfordshire
1677 (the earliest proved place of residence)

The geographical origin of Scottish names is relatively easy to trace, since each clan was originally a tribal unit occupying a certain territory. This map shows the Highlands clans in the 16th century, taken from Fitzroy Maclean's Concise History of Scotland *(revised edn., 1970), p. 68. As the population grew and offshoots settled in new places, the pattern of clan settlement became much more complex. Clan names still predominate in many areas.*

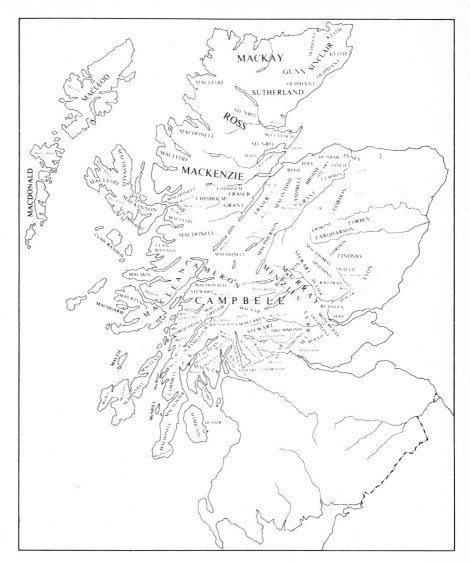

smaller locality over a long period of years. Migrations and alterations of distribution can be traced and can again usefully be plotted on a map. Indexes to wills and, where indexed, the Census returns are also good sources for surname distribution.

Telephone directories will reveal the current distribution of a surname, central registration and Census records will take you into the nineteenth century or even beyond, while indexes of wills could extend the survey back over several hundred years. If your surname is an unusual one it may be possible to trace its total incidence over the whole country, using the same sources. You may even be able to break it down into family groups and speculate as to the place of origin.

Names are our first clue to our family background, and connect us with the other past and present members of the same group in an obvious way. In themselves they can provide an interesting study in origin, meaning and distribution patterns, as well as serving as territorial clues to the family's original location. It is fascinating, too, to discover the meaning—not always flattering—of the name given to its first hereditary bearer.

7 Heraldry

Heraldry is a branch of family history that is often associated with a snobbish pretension to nobility. However, it originally served a very practical purpose in easy identification of individuals, their families and dependants. Because of the flexibility of English society the ranks of armigers (those entitled to bear arms) expanded from the titled nobility to include those whose wealth was based not solely on the land or royal service, but on commerce or the professions. Conversely, as a result of social vicissitudes, it is possible to discover coats of arms granted to families which have subsequently faded into obscurity. The number of families with coats of arms is therefore greater than one might think.

The Origins and Development of Heraldry

The term 'heraldry' applies to the system of personal and family devices portrayed on shields, which evolved throughout Western Europe, probably during the twelfth century, to meet military and civil purposes of identification. It became hereditary and was masculine in character. Certain conventions were observed in the establishment of a coat of arms personal to the holder and his family, and regulations for their use and display were devised and supervised by the heralds, who had early specialized in the recognition of arms.

Heralds existed before heraldry, serving as emissaries for their noble masters, issuing proclamations on their behalf, and officiating at pageants and tournaments. They took their titles from those of their lords. Part of their duties lay in recognizing knights in their lords' retinues, so that they could accurately and swiftly report casualties in battle. The knights, too, needed to be able to recognize one another easily under their armour and chain mail, both at a distance and in battle. Distinctive surcoats, shields and pennons fitted to lances provided the answer. They were brightly painted with devices peculiar to their carrier, and perhaps alluded to family estates, a particular event, or punned the family name. Originally these were simple geometric designs or symbols of valour drawn from the animal or bird kingdoms. At the battle of Agincourt in 1415 the French and English heralds were able to list casualties among their own knights purely by identifying their arms. During the Crusades, when knights of different European countries united against the Infidel, it was important for them to recognize others of their own nationality and group. It became convenient for fathers and sons, and others of close kinship, to bear the

A detail from the Warwick or Rous Roll, the illustrated chronicle roll of the Earls of Warwick. It comprised 66 coloured drawings of figures representing the Kings of Britain, royal and other beneficiaries to Warwick, and the Earls of Warwick, plus narrative histories of their lives written in Latin underneath them, and shields or banners of their arms above. It was prepared by John Rous, a Chantry Priest, of Guys Cliffe, Warwickshire, between 1477 and 1491. (London, College of Arms)

The Grant of Arms to Robert White of South Warnborough, Hants., and his descendants, 14 February 1513/14. The document is written in French, and although English was spoken at Court, legal documents were normally couched in French or Latin. The blazon of the arms is Argent a Chevron gules between three Poppinjays vert beaked and membered purpure collared Or a bordure purpure bezanty. Crest: between two Wings the dexter Or the Sinister Argent a demi-Poppinjay vert volent holding in the beak a slip of Eglantine purpure leaved vert. The two seals are those of Thomas Wriothesley, Garter King of Arms, and Thomas Benolt, Clarenceux King of Arms. (London, College of Arms, Muniment Room, MS. 11/2)

same devices on their shields and surcoats.

In peacetime tournaments provided a means of constant training for war. They were also an excuse for indulging in the medieval love of display, and the heralds recognized the helmeted and vizored combatants and their horses by their brightly coloured heraldic trappings. The convention of superimposing a colour on a metal or fur background meant that the design could more readily be picked out at a distance.

As the numbers of knights using arms proliferated the need arose for a proper register to be kept of the devices used by each, for easy reference and to avoid duplication. These lists were made on long parchment rolls and are of six types. The Rous Roll, from the fifteenth century, displaying the arms of the Kings of Britain down to the Earls of Warwick, is an illustrative record of arms. The Caerlaverock Roll, showing the names and arms of those knights who fought in that battle in 1300, is an occasional record. General rolls detail the arms of world

sovereigns, or take the form of directories of noble or knightly families and their arms. Local rolls relate to families in a particular vicinity, the Dering Roll being concerned with Kent and Sussex. Family historical rolls incorporate arms onto a pedigree showing intermarriage with other heraldic families. Rolls of Ordinaries, the sixth type, are peculiar to England. They display the different basic devices and the charges arranged on and around them on the shield, and then identify their holders. If you cannot identify the family to which a coat of arms belonged, the Ordinaries provide the answer (unless the arms are bogus).

The heralds developed an expertise which was increasingly necessary. Strict regulations for the granting and usage of arms were overdue, and somewhere was needed to house their records. The French heralds were allowed a building of their own in 1407, but the English heralds, although they had adopted a common seal in 1420 and met regularly, did not succeed in obtaining a Charter of Incorporation until 1484, when they were given premises in London. By this date their functions had become formal and ceremonial. Originally arms had been granted by lords to their own adherents, but the Crown gradually asserted its supremacy as a grant-making body, until 1467, when the sheer volume of grants forced it to delegate its authority to the Kings of Arms, under the control of the Earl Marshal. Their successors comprise the modern College of Arms, with its premises in Queen Victoria Street, London.

The College of Arms is the repository of the registered grants and confirmations of arms for England, Wales, Northern Ireland, the Commonwealth, and for Americans of British descent, or settlement prior to 1783. It also houses the Court of Chivalry to try disputes concerning the fraudulent display of arms. Each officer of the College is created by Letters Patent from the Crown, and the six heralds and four pursuivants act as agents for their clients in petitioning the Earl Marshal to allow a grant to be made. Scottish arms are matriculated at the Lyon Court, in Edinburgh, while Irish registers of arms are held by the Genealogical Office, in Dublin.

The first explicit measure of control was attempted in 1416 when armigers were categorized into three groups—those with ancestral

Above. *John Smert, Garter King of Arms from 1450 to 1478, depicted on the grant of arms to the Tallow Chandlers' Company, 24 September 1456. A portrait of the granting Garter King of Arms in his ceremonial uniform was frequently incorporated into the initial letter of grants of arms, and this is still sometimes done today. John Smert was the son-in-law of William Bruges, the first Garter King of Arms. (London, Tallow Chandlers' Company)*

Right. *A heraldic manuscript of the Rhyce family showing the intermarriage of heraldic families and the descent of arms. It was made by Ralph Brooke, York Herald of Arms, in 1600. (Cardiff, Welsh Folk Museum, 70. 109/225, donated to the Museum by Lord Dynevor of Dynevor Castle, Llandeilo)*

Left. *Heraldic banners and shields can be seen in this engraving of the funeral of Sir Philip Sydney, engraved by Thomas Lamb in 1587. As the legend records, the corpse was covered in velvet and carried by fourteen of his yeomen, and the banners were carried by four near kinsmen.*

Below right. *The guidon and tabard displaying the deceased's arms and quarterings, his crest, and the arms of his widow, all of which were carried in the funeral procession of Robert Brooke, sometime Alderman and Sheriff of London, who died on 28 March 1601. York Herald and Rouge Dragon Pursuivant served the funeral. This page is from a volume of funeral certificates in the College of Arms, London (I 16, p. 112), recording the various funeral achievements carried in the funeral processions within the Province of William Camden, Clarenceux King of Arms, 1597–1623.*

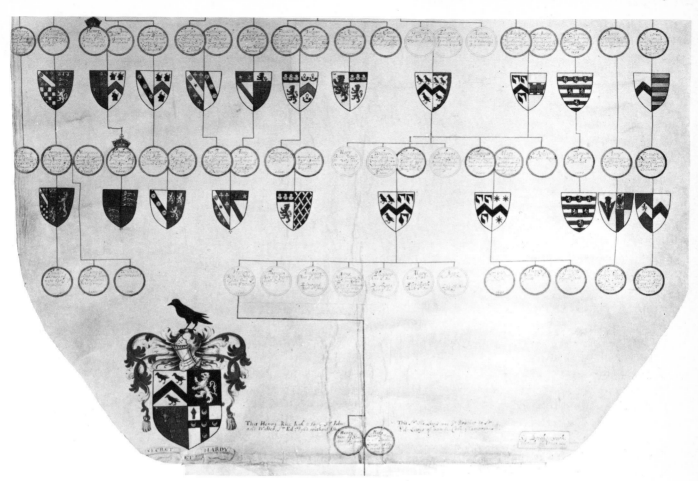

rights to bear arms, those with a grant from an authorized person, and those who had fought at Agincourt. At the end of the fifteenth century an attempt at a countrywide survey of armigers was made, but it was not until 1530 that detailed examinations (Visitations) began to be made, county by county, of the arms and evidences of entitlement of the gentry. Even then some families held themselves aloof from the Visitations, although quite obviously entitled to bear arms. The Sheriff of each county. was required to compile a list of knights, esquires and gentlemen arranged by Hundred, which was used by the Bailiffs to summon them individually to appear, with their arms, pedigrees and other relevant family muniments, before the two visiting heralds. The heralds tricked the arms (sketched them, identifying the tinctures by their initial letters), and noted whether sufficient proof had been given by the family to show it should continue to use them. If not, the family was given six months to supply it. The coats of arms reflect contemporary taste. After the early simple and pleasing designs, sixteenth- and seventeenth-century arms become increasingly crowded and flamboyant, incorporating creatures from fantasy. The arms were also quartered with those of the heraldic families into which they had been married and whose wives were coheiresses. In this way it is possible to trace alliances from previous generations which took place earlier than the recorded pedigrees.

In the sixteenth and seventeenth centuries the heralds attended and supervised heraldic funerals, and ensured that the form and scale of mourning and display were in keeping with the deceased person's rank. Funeral certificates, illustrating the trappings used, are filed in the College of Arms, and also give details about the dead person's immediate forebears and descendants, as well as the date and place of death and burial.

After the Visitations ceased in 1688, pedigrees of the titled, gentry and other families continued to be recorded on payment of a fee, and these were often registered simultaneously when a grant of arms was made. A separate series of the enrolled grants of arms has been maintained from the late fifteenth century, and these can often be matched up with pedigrees of the grantees. The later grants betray a tendency towards landscape and Gothic styles, but by the late nineteenth century the trend reverted to the original freshness and simplicity of the earliest coats. By and large this is still the case, in spite of the huge numbers of grants being made, each of which has to be unique.

Heraldry remains a living force. Grants are now made not only to individuals, but to corporations, schools, universities, commercial firms and societies. It is a distinctive way of identifying them, and just the display of the arms themselves is often enough to identify their holder.

As a reflection of the continuing general interest in heraldry for its aesthetic, historical and genealogical interest, Heraldry Societies flourish in many countries in the world, the first being founded only in 1947, by John Brooke-Little, then aged twenty.

The Language of Heraldry

The language used in heraldry can be very confusing to the newcomer. Here are some of the most common terms you will encounter, and I have also illustrated some of the ways in which you will see arms displayed:

Augmentation—a mark added to an existing coat of arms to commemorate a notable achievement.

Base—the lower half of the shield.

Blazon—a verbal description of the arms, following conventional rules of the order in which the charges are described.

Cadency—marks of difference used by cadets of the family to differentiate them from the head of the family.

Canton—a small square inset in the dexter chief.

Charge—anything displayed on the shield. Charges are grouped into beasts, birds, fishes, reptiles, monsters, flowers, etc.

Chief—the upper half of the shield.

Colours—the conventional colours are red (gules), blue (azure), black (sable), green (vert), and purple (purpure), rendered in French or abbreviated by the first two letters. No two colours are displayed on top of each other.

Dexter—the left side of the shield as you view it.

Escutcheon of pretence—a small shield showing a heraldic heiress's arms, and displayed in the centre of the husband's shield.

Field—the surface of the shield on which the charges are displayed.

Some marks of cadency.

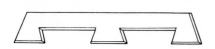

Label, eldest son

Crescent, 2nd son

Mullet, 3rd son

Martlet, 4th son

Annulet, 5th son

Fleur de Lys, 6th son

The Royal Arms

Lion rampant

Lion couchant

Lion passant

Lion statant

Lion rampant reguardant

Lion sejant

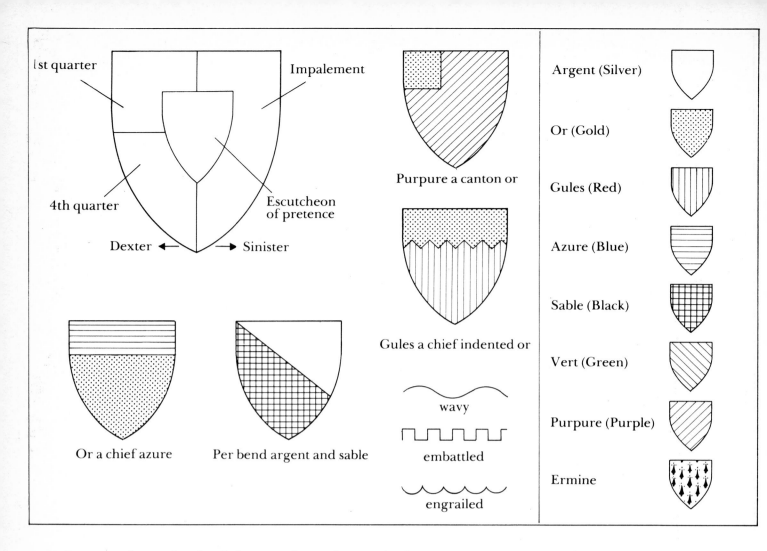

Labels in diagram:
1st quarter · Impalement · 4th quarter · Escutcheon of pretence · Dexter ← → Sinister

Purpure a canton or

Gules a chief indented or

wavy
embattled
engrailed

Or a chief azure · Per bend argent and sable

Argent (Silver)
Or (Gold)
Gules (Red)
Azure (Blue)
Sable (Black)
Vert (Green)
Purpure (Purple)
Ermine

Some of the more common charges on heraldic shields.

Furs—ermine and vair. Colours and metals may be imposed upon them, and vice versa.

Impalement—the display of a wife's arms on the sinister side of the shield, the husband's on the dexter side. Holders of certain offices, like Bishops and Kings of Arms, can similarly display their arms of office.

Metals—Gold (or) and silver (argent).

Ordinaries—the basic geometric charges (see diagram).

Proper—when the charge is displayed in its natural colours.

Quartering—the display of arms of a heraldic heiress ancestor quartered two and three with those of the family in one and four.

Semy—scattered or strewn with the same small charges.

Shield—the vehicle for the display of arms. There is no set rule as to shape.

Sinister—the right side of the shield as you view it.

Tincture—all the colours, metals and furs.

Trick—the method of describing the tinctures using abbreviations.

Charges can be rendered in many ways. The permutations of colour and charges are almost limitless, and new charges (particularly of inanimate objects and from the world of science) are appearing all the time.

Crests and supporters are accessories to coats of arms and are not

The full achievement of arms of H.R.H. the Prince of Wales. It shows his coat of arms, bearing the label for difference, surrounded by his insignia as Knight of the Garter, surmounted by his crest, and supported by a lion and a unicorn. Beneath the arms are shown the royal motto, the arms of the Duchy of Cornwall, and the badges of the heir apparent and Prince of Wales.

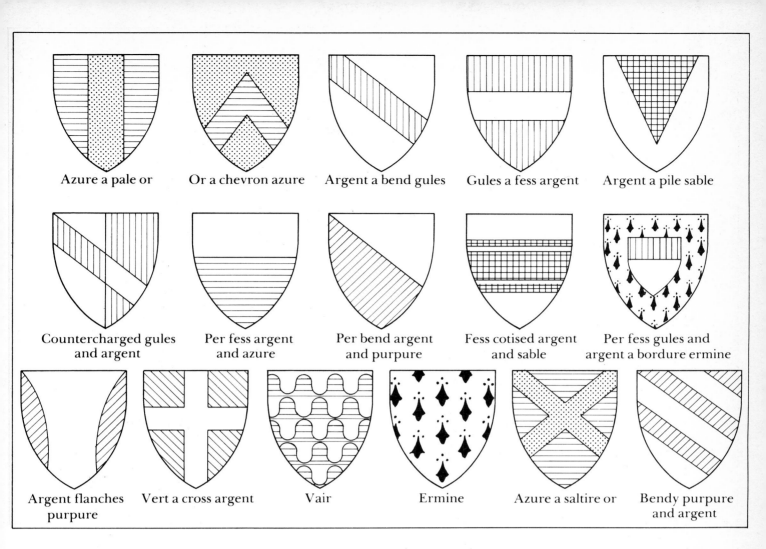

Azure a pale or | Or a chevron azure | Argent a bend gules | Gules a fess argent | Argent a pile sable

Countercharged gules and argent | Per fess argent and azure | Per bend argent and purpure | Fess cotised argent and sable | Per fess gules and argent a bordure ermine

Argent flanches purpure | Vert a cross argent | Vair | Ermine | Azure a saltire or | Bendy purpure and argent

unique to the holder. A crest was originally worn on the helmet and should always be displayed like this, the helmet resting on a twisted band of the chief colour and metal in the coat of arms, out of which the mantling flows (see the diagram). Crests were regarded as a mark of great dignity, and many of the oldest coats do not bear them. The helmet is depicted in one of several ways, depending on the status of the armiger.

Supporters probably originated as margin-fillers in seals incorporating the arms of the parties to deeds, and evolved before the fourteenth century. From the late seventeenth century their usage was restricted to Peers and Knights of the first class of the several Orders, unless by special permission of the Sovereign. Only the supporters used by Peers descend to their successors.

A motto is either an aphorism or an invocation, usually depicted on a scroll beneath the arms, but not included in the grant itself. Mottoes did not generally appear until the seventeenth century; they are not unique to any family, and can be changed at will.

A full achievement of arms will be the shield, crest, supporters and motto, where applicable.

Badges are probably older than any other heraldic device, and are emblems unconnected with the shield or crest, being a distinctive mark used by the family and even its retainers, as a form of livery.

Pennons and standards can incorporate the arms of the holder, but

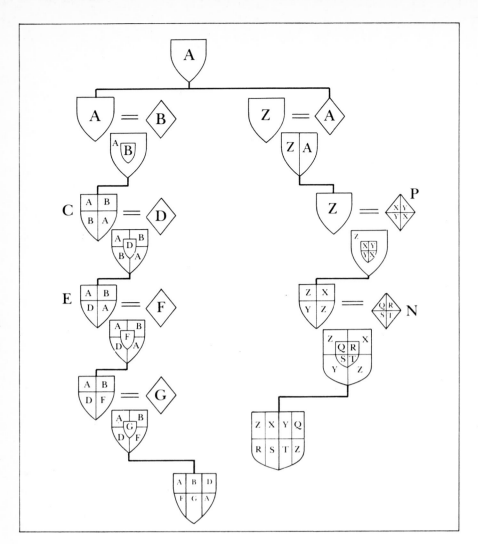

The descent of arms, showing the rules governing their display through inheritance and intermarriage.

more usually contain his badge and motto. They taper to a point, the pennon being much smaller than the standard. Banners display the owner's arms.

The Rules of Heraldry

The grant of arms states who is entitled to bear the specified device. It may be retrospective to as far back as the grantee has applied for, and may extend to collaterals, and to his own descendants. The arms of daughters are displayed in lozenge-shaped shields. They can use them for their own lifetimes, their husbands impaling the arms with their own. If the female is a heraldic heiress then her arms will be displayed in an escutcheon of pretence in the centre of the shield of her husband's arms, and her issue will subsequently quarter them with those of their father. Only if her husband was armigerous could her arms be used by him and their offspring.

Sons bearing their father's arms show their position in the family by conventional cadency marks, but in Scotland younger sons have to matriculate arms for themselves with special cadencies. Illegitimate issue of an armigerous father are indicated either by a bordure wavy around the inside of the shield, or a baton sinister (the ends of which do not extend to the sides of the shield).

Right. *The heraldic tomb of Thomas Chaucer and his wife, Matilda, daughter and coheiress of Sir John Burghersh, in Ewelme church, Oxfordshire. Thomas died on 14 March 1434, and was probably the elder son of Geoffrey Chaucer, by his wife Philippa, daughter of Sir Paon Roet, Guienne King of Arms, and sister of Katharine Swinford, who married John of Gaunt. There is no evidence that Geoffrey Chaucer used the arms himself, and they were probably foisted on him by his father-in-law.*

*A modern coat of arms, taken from the grant
of arms to Sir Charles Norman, K.B.,
1 September 1965.*

Does your Family Have a Coat of Arms?

There are printed Armories giving blazons of the devices borne by arms-bearing families, arranged alphabetically by surname. When you find an entry for your surname you should check with the grant-making body concerned that it is authentic, and that it relates to your own particular family. I have already described the Ordinaries which can help identify the family bearing a particular coat of arms. None of these is fully comprehensive. The College of Arms in London, the Lyon Court in Edinburgh, and the Genealogical Office in Dublin are the only authoritative sources for British heraldry.

Perhaps you have seen the pedigree of your family which includes a coat of arms. Although they may prove to be bogus it is not illegal to use the arms, but they will have no status. Similarly, if you see an early printed pedigree of a family of your surname, which was armigerous, you would need to be sure that you descend from it before satisfying yourself that you are armigerous yourself. In the eighteenth and nineteenth centuries there was a fashion for families to assume the arms of illustrious ancient families of the same name, without any proof of a connection, or even to have an official grant made to them of arms closely resembling the ancient coat.

Where can you see heraldry? Churches and cathedrals will often contain heraldic tombs and inscriptions to deceased local worthies, and even funeral hatchments. Heraldry may also form an integral part of the interior design, in the form of roof bosses and stained glass windows. One of the richest displays of heraldry is to be found in St George's Chapel, Windsor, where the banners, helmets and crests of the current Knights of the Garter are placed over their stalls. The stalls themselves bear brass plates incised and painted with the arms of past and present Knights. The dining hall of the Middle Temple, in London, contains paintings of the arms of past Readers, just as university colleges portray those of distinguished founders and benefactors. Public buildings such as almshouses and Guildhalls may well display the arms of benefactors and masters, and certainly any grant of arms made to the guild or company concerned.

Larger private houses built in the Tudor, Stuart and Georgian periods included the carved arms of the original owners in architraves above the main entrance, and in the wood panelling, fireplaces, furniture, soft furnishings and windows. Embroideries, porcelain and china often incorporate the family arms or crest. Their books more than likely contained bookplates of the arms on the flyleaf, while they used ring-seals of their arms when sending letters. Local collections of deeds still have many of the original seals attached to them which identify the arms of the parties concerned.

In addition to its official records the College of Arms houses many of the private working papers of the heralds, often containing sketches of seals, and church monuments no longer in existence. Other large repositories like the British Library, the Bodleian Library at Oxford, and the Library of Congress in Washington hold much material of a heraldic nature, the British Library, in particular, having a vast collection of armorial seals.

Orders of Chivalry and Awards

The origins of orders and decorations must be sought in the organization of the religious orders in the Middle Ages. The term 'order' derives from the Latin 'ordo', meaning an association of a limited group of people who took upon themselves certain duties and obligations, and followed fixed rules.

Religious orders of chivalry originated at the time of the Crusades, when bands of knights joined together under common religious rules to care for pilgrims and the sick, and chiefly to fight for the Christian faith. They were international in character, subject to a Grand Master, who himself was subordinate to the Pope. These exclusive orders wielded great influence and political power, and became the object of suspicion. Ultimately, the sovereign states where they were based forced the dissolution of the most powerful, the Knights Templar, in 1312, but for almost 200 years they had dominated the international scene.

The two other ancient orders of chivalry were founded as hospital orders, their military functions being subordinate. These were the Order of Malta, founded in the late eleventh century, and the Teutonic Order, and entry to them was based on noble ancestry. Again these were subject to the Holy See, but rival temporal orders were soon founded, with the same aims, under the Grand Mastership of the monarch. Membership was inherited. Among the oldest of these are the Order of Alcantara, founded in 1156, and the Order of Sant' Iago, founded in 1170, both of which still survive.

Royal knighthoods were first granted in the fourteenth century to rival and suppress the power of the religious orders of chivalry and to strengthen the power and prestige of the monarchs. The orders of knighthood met in Chapters, held in chapels in the same way as the religious orders, and the number of members was restricted, admission being conditional on noble birth. Knights were required to wear their insignia at all times, lead blameless lives, do charitable works and support the Sovereign, their Grand Master. The Most Noble Order of the Garter was founded in 1348, and its number of Knights Companion is limited to twenty-five. They wear distinctive robes and insignia at their annual service to renew their pledges and to install new knights.

The Garter stall plate of Ralph Basset, Lord Basset of Drayton, created Knight of the Garter 1368, died 10 May 1390, and buried in Lichfield Cathedral. He served in the Wars in France, and journeyed to the Holy Land and to Spain. His arms are Or three piles their points meeting in base gules a quarter Ermine. Crest: out of a Ducal coronet Gold a Boars Head azure dented tusked and the eyelid Or the mantling cappeline sable. (Windsor, St George's Chapel)

The Knights of the Most Noble Order of the Garter in procession on the occasion of the annual Garter Service at St George's Chapel, Windsor, 1977. The Knights are wearing their robes and insignia. (Photo: Central Press Photos Ltd)

The banners of the present Knights of the Garter hanging above their stalls in St George's Chapel, Windsor. Plates bearing the arms of previous and current Knights are affixed to the backs of the stalls, which are surmounted by the crests of the living Knights. (Photo: A. F. Kersting)

Admission is in the power of the Sovereign as Grand Master, who acts on the advice of the Chapter.

By about 1800 orders of merit, based not on lineage but on personal achievement, were awarded by the Crown. Existing orders were divided into classes to integrate them. The French Legion of Honour was thus instituted in 1802. Other orders of a purely military nature, like the German Iron Cross founded in 1813, or of a purely civilian character, such as the Swedish Order of the Northern Star, founded in 1748, were awarded, as well as hybrid ones like the British Most Honourable Order of the Bath, founded in 1725. This last even maintains its own genealogist to record the pedigrees of the recipients, in the same way as the ancient orders of chivalry had done. The highest order in the United Kingdom is The Victoria Cross, instituted in 1856.

Personal royal orders, like the Royal Victorian Order (1896), are the personal gift of the Monarch. Even in the Communist countries orders are given for meritorious service to the state, for example the Order of Lenin, founded in the USSR in 1930. Some of the old orders have even been retained in Poland and Czechoslovakia.

Each order has its rules and regulations, and its own governing body. In Britain recommendations for military orders go to the Secretary of State for Defence, and for civilian orders to the Prime Minister, each of whom sends a final list to the Queen. Honours Lists are compiled for each New Year's Day, and the official birthday of the monarch, but dissolution lists are drawn up by the outgoing Prime Minister, and occasional military lists may appear. Each is published in the *London Gazette*. The initials of the order follow the name of the bearer, in order of seniority if there are several orders, and can be used before receiving the royal accolade. Subsequent awards in a particular order will always be of a higher class, and the insignia of the lower class are then discarded. The insignia are worn according to the regulations of a particular order, and normally take the form of a badge worn on the left breast, while the higher ranks of the order (Commander and above) wear the badge pendant from a neck-ribbon; Knights Grand Cross wear a sash diagonally from shoulder to waist.

Summing Up

Although a specialized side of family history, heraldry can be seen to extend further into our lives than we perhaps imagine. Its original practical purpose may have changed from the purely military to the civilian, but it was a very useful and colourful way of illustrating a family's connections, as well as alluding to past achievements. If it had not been so flexible in its application, it would have become obsolete long ago, but the situation is quite the reverse.

A panel containing the coat of arms of John Pell of Dersingham, Norfolk, from his tomb in St Nicholas' church, Dersingham. His arms are impaled with those of his wife Margaret, only daughter of William Overend, to whom he was married for 61 years. He himself died on 5 February 1607, aged 80. (Photo: National Monuments Record)

Appendix I
Calendar of Dates

If your ancestors came from or travelled overseas the reason was in all possibility political, mercantile or religious. The date of such a migration might have been influenced by major events or legislation in their country of origin, or by the opening up of opportunities in colonies abroad. I have set out a world calendar illustrating some of the most important dates from the point of view of mobility, starting with the invasion of England by the Normans in 1066, and ending with the exit of the Boat People from Cambodia and Vietnam in 1979.

Besides military conflicts I have included discoveries of new territories and their subsequent history, because of their colonial and trade implications, the attitudes of European countries to their religious minorities, and important dates in the history of slavery.

For the family historian, a calendar of dates can serve to show the historical and social background in which his ancestors moved and set the family unit in a much wider social context.

1066 14 October, Battle of Hastings: Normans conquer England
1073 Ecclesiastical courts established in England
1086 Domesday survey in England
1096–9 First Crusade
1147–9 Second Crusade
1189–93 Third Crusade
1202–4 Fourth Crusade
1215 19 June, Magna Carta signed by King John
1217–21 Crusade against Egypt
1240 Crusade to Jaffa
1258 Provisions of Oxford: aliens expelled from office
1268–72 Fifth Crusade
1290 Jews expelled from England
1306 Jews expelled from France
1337–1453 Hundred Years Anglo/French War
1347–51 Black Death in Europe
1351 Statute of Labourers regulated wages
1361 Black Death in England
1383 Regular series of wills starts in Prerogative Court of Canterbury
1391 Severe persecution of Jews in Spain
1407 Owen Glendower invades England and threatens Worcester
1415 25 October, Battle of Agincourt

1430–1832 Forty-shilling freehold qualification to vote
1453 Fall of Constantinople to the Turks
1455–84 Wars of the Roses in England
1465 Irish living near English settlements made to take English surnames
1484 College of Arms incorporated by Royal Charter
1492 Jews expelled from Spain; Columbus sails to New World
1493 Columbus finds Jamaica; New World divided by Pope Alexander VI between Spain and Portugal; Flemings banished from England
1497 Parish registers instituted in Spain by Cardinal Ximenes
1498 Columbus finds Trinidad and South American mainland; John Cabot finds Labrador and east coast of North America
1501 Anglo/Portuguese voyage to Newfoundland
1505 Portuguese Jews' children under 14 to be given up by their parents and educated as Christians
1505–7 Portuguese establish factories on African east coast
1509 Naturalization papers start in England
1519–21 Cortez conquers Mexico
1530 English merchants form company in Spain; first Heraldic Visitation

1531 Henry VIII becomes Supreme Head of the English Church
1532–4 Pizarro conquers Peru
1535 Landownership restricted by Statute of Uses
1536–9 Dissolution of the monasteries
1536 Unification of English and Welsh governments
1538 English and Welsh parish registers start
1540 Statute of Wills allows freehold land to be bequeathed
1541 Henry VIII becomes King of Ireland and Head of the Irish Church
1546 English Navy Board established
c. 1550 First Walloon refugees arrive in England
1554–8 Roman Catholicism restored in England
1558 Scottish parish registers start
1559 Act of Supremacy passed in England
1561 Scottish Church constitution established by John Knox
1562 John Hawkins starts slave trade between Africa and America
1563 Edict of St Germain recognizes French Protestants; Test Act excludes Roman Catholics from office
1563–1814 Statute of Artificers regulates apprenticeships
1567–8 Hawkins in Guinea and West Indies; English factory set up in Hamburg; Walloons flee the Low Countries; Nonconformists meet secretly in London
1572 St Bartholomew's Day Massacre of French Protestants
1557 Drake claims California for Queen Elizabeth I
c. 1580 Brownists (Congregationalists) founded in Norwich
1581 English Levant Company formed
1582 Gregorian calendar introduced in Spain and Portugal, France, Low Countries, part of Italy, Denmark
1584 Raleigh finds Virginia
1588 The Spanish Armada; English Guinea Company chartered
1591 First English voyage to East Indies
1594 Portuguese monopoly in India broken by English
1595 Dutch start to colonize East Indies
1597 Poor Law Act for erection of parish workhouses for the poor; Poor Rate collection allowed
1598 Bishop's transcripts of English and Welsh parish registers start; Edict of Nantes gives Huguenots toleration in France
1600 Honourable East India Company founded by English; first English in Japan; Scotland adopts Gregorian calendar
1601 Poor Law Act gives powers to parish Overseers of the Poor
1602 Dutch East India Company founded; persecution of Bohemian and Hungarian Protestants
1606 London, and Plymouth Virginia Companies chartered
1609 Baptists founded in Amsterdam
1618 English West Africa Company founded and occupies Gambia and Gold Coast
1618–48 Thirty Years War in Europe

1619 First American Parliament, in Jamestown; first slaves in Virginia, from Spanish West Indies
1620 17 September, *Mayflower* leaves Plymouth for New England
1621 Dutch West Indies Company founded; Scots in Nova Scotia
1624 First English settlement in East India; Dutch found New Amsterdam (New York); Census in Virginia
1625 English Colonial Office established
1628 John Endicott founds Massachusetts Bay Colony; Dutch conquer Java and Malacca
1633 English factory established in Bengal
1634 Oath of allegiance to British Crown to be taken by emigrants to New England; Lord Baltimore founds Maryland for Catholics; Irish parish registers start
1636 Dutch occupy Ceylon; English settlements in Rhode Island and Connecticut
1637 English factory founded at Canton
1638 Swedes settle in Delaware (New Sweden)
1639 English factory founded at Madras
1641 Massacre of Protestants in Ulster
1642 Tasman discovers Tasmania and New Zealand; English Civil War starts
1643 Presbyterian declared Established Church in England; Confederation of United Colonies of New England (until 1698)
1644 Earliest Presbyterian and Independent registers; 20,000 Scots enter England to help Parliamentarians fight the King
1646 English occupy Bahamas
1649 England declared a Free Commonwealth
1650 Jews allowed back into England; English and Dutch colonial frontiers defined in North America
1652 Dutch found Cape Town; Rhode Island enacts first North American anti-slavery law
1653 French occupy Montreal; Cromwell's transplantation into Northern Ireland, and Roman Catholics dispossessed.
1655 English occupy Jamaica; Dutch annex Delaware
1660 Restoration of the English monarchy; Royal African Company founded; Council for Foreign Plantations founded
1662 English Poor Law Act regulating settlement and removal and transportation overseas; Act of Uniformity; English Guinea Company incorporated
1663 Royal Charter for Rhode Island
1664 Conventicle Act directed against Nonconformist worship
1665 Great Plague in London; New Jersey founded
1666 Fire of London: French Census in Canada
1669 South Carolina founded
1670 Hudson Bay Company founded
1671 English West Indies organized
1672 Test Act excludes Catholics from office; Declaration of Indulgence gives tolerance to Nonconformists; English Guinea Company has monopoly of slave trade (until 1698)
1676 Nathaniel Bacon leads rebellion of frontier states
1681 Royal Charter for Pennsylvania
1682 Indentured servants allowed to go to colonies in

America; Philadelphia founded; French Protestants excluded from civil service and guilds

1685 Revocation of the Edict of Nantes: Huguenots flee to Netherlands, Brandenburg and England; Monmouth's Rebellion

1688 Last Heraldic Visitation in England

1689 Act of Toleration towards Nonconformists; Dutch found Natal

1690 Irish Catholics defeated at Battle of the Boyne; English factory established at Calcutta

1691 Protestant farmers settled in Ireland; Poor Law Act

1692 13 February, Massacre of Glencoe

1696 Board of Trade and Plantations founded

1697 Poor Law Act

1698 African trade opened to all British subjects

1701 Act of Settlement re the Protestant Hanoverian succession to the English throne

1707 Act of Union between England and Scotland

1709 First mass German emigration to Pennsylvania

1710 English South Sea Company formed

1714 Landholders to take oath of allegiance and renounce Roman Catholicism

1715 Jacobites beaten at Preston and Sheriffmuir; disarmament of Scots clans ordered

1717 Roman Catholics to register their estates with Clerks of the Peace

1729 Baltimore founded; North and South Carolina become Crown Colonies

1732 Georgia founded by James Oglethorpe

1733 English becomes the language in legal records

c. 1740 Wesleyans (Methodists) founded

1746 16 April, Battle of Culloden: Jacobites finally beaten; Highland dress banned (until 1782)

1748 French religious persecution of Protestants

1752 Gregorian calendar adopted by Britain and her dominions in Asia, Africa, America and Europe

1754 Anglo/French war in North America

1755 British standing Army introduced

1759 18 September, English win Battle of Quebec

1760 British seize Montreal

1763 Peace of Paris: British get St Vincent, Tobago, Dominica, Grenada, Senegal, Canada, Nova Scotia, Cape Breton and Florida

1765–6 Stamp Act in the thirteen colonies

1769–70 James Cook's first voyage round the world: finds East Australia

1774 Kentucky settled; First Congress of thirteen colonies (except Virginia) at Philadelphia; Quebec Act establishes rights of French Canadians

1775–83 American Revolutionary War

1775 British hire 29,000 German mercenaries for American war; Battle of Bunker Hill won by British; Scots clans recognized as subsisting groups

1776 4 July, Declaration of American Independence; Americans driven out of Canada

1778 3 September, Peace of Versailles; Britain recognizes the United States of America and recovers her West Indian possessions, France gains St Lucia, Tobago, Senegal, Goree and parts of East Indies, Spain gets Florida

1787 First fleet of convicts sails to New South Wales,

Australia; settlement of Sierra Leone as an asylum for Negro waifs and slaves

1788 New York the federal capital of America

1789 14 July, Fall of the Bastille; French Revolution; revolution in Austrian Netherlands; Belgium declares independence

1790 First American federal Census

1791 6 May, Canadian Constitution Act; Upper and Lower Canada separated; Jews admitted as French citizens; Catholic Relief Act

1792 22 September, French Republic declared; Returns of aliens made to Quarter Sessions

1793 Anglo/French war

1794 French religious persecution; abolition of slavery in French colonies

1795 Ceylon surrendered by Dutch to Britain

1798–9 Irish Rebellion

1800 Act of Union between Britain and Ireland

1801 First United Kingdom Census

1802 First protective law against child labour in Britain

1803 Transportation of convicts starts to Port Phillip, Australia

1805 21 October, Battle of Trafalgar

1807 Sierra Leone and Gambia become Crown Colonies; abolition of slavery in British Empire

1808 Importation of slaves into USA prohibited

1812 USA declares war on Britain and invades Canada; Jews emancipated in Prussia; transportation of convicts starts to Tasmania

1813 Abolition of East India Company's monopoly in India

1814 Civil courts instituted in New South Wales, Australia; Cape of Good Hope a British colony

1815 18 June, Battle of Waterloo; Treaty of Ghent between Britain and America

1819 British arrive in South Africa (Cape); British found Singapore

1820 Liberia founded for repatriation of Negroes

1822 Irish Potato Famine

1823 Monroe Doctrine closing American continent to colonial settlement by non-Americans, and preventing European powers from interfering in political affairs of USA.

1824 Scottish wills proved in Sheriffs' Courts (previously in Commissariat Courts)

1825 Trade Unions recognized as legal in Britain

1828 Test and Corporation Acts (1672 and 1661) repealed, thus removing restrictions for civil and military office

1829 Catholic Emancipation Act

1832 Reform Bill extends British franchise

1833 Slaves freed in British possessions

1834 Start of colonization of Victoria, Australia; Poor Law (Amendment) Act

1835 Impressment to Royal Navy ends

1836 South Australian colony founded; Tithe Commutation Act

1837 Mackenzie's Rebellion in Canada; Mormons arrive in England (emigration to Missouri and Illinois); Central registration starts in England and Wales; Natal Republic founded by Dutch settlers

1839 New South Wales and New Zealand incorporated
1840 Maori chiefs hand over sovereignty of New Zealand to Britain; Upper and Lower Canada united
1842 Chartist Riots in manufacturing districts of England; Hong Kong ceded by Chinese and becomes British colony
1843 Slavery abolished in India; Natal proclaimed British colony; establishment of Free Church in Scotland
1844–7 Transportation of convicts starts to Norfolk Islands
1845–7 Irish Famine
1847 Liberia becomes independent Negro state
1848 Revolutions in Sicily, France, Venice, Parma, Milan, Sardinia, Austria, Hungary, Bohemia and Germany; Mexico cedes California, New Mexico, Texas, Nevada, Utah, Arizona, parts of Colorado and Wyoming to USA; slavery abolished in French colonies
1849 US Gold Rush; Transportation of convicts to New South Wales ends; Cape Colony forbids landing of convicts
1850 Denmark sells Gold Coast to Britain; Australian Constitution Act; Transportation of convicts starts to West Australia; Fugitive Slave Act in USA
1851 Gold discovered in Australia; Victoria a separate Australian colony; Great Exhibition in London
1852 South African Republic established
1853–5 Peak of German emigration
1853 Transportation of convicts to Tasmania ends
1854–6 Crimean War
1854 Orange Free State constituted
1855 Emigration from north Scotland on large scale; central registration starts in Scotland
1856 Tasmania a self-governing colony
1857 Indian Mutiny; East India Company powers and territories transferred to British Crown; Ottawa declared Canadian capital
1858 Jurisdiction of wills transferred in England and Wales to Principal Probate Registry
1859 Suez Canal begun; Queensland separates from New South Wales
1860–1 Maori Rising in New Zealand
1860 Italian unification
1861–5 American Civil War
1864 Irish central registration starts
1865 Slavery abolished in USA
1868 Transportation of convicts to Australia ends
1869 Suez Canal opened; disestablishment of the Irish Church
1870–3 Franco–Prussian War
1870 United Germany; Diamonds found in Orange Free State
1871 Dutch colonies on Guinea coast granted to Britain; Basutoland joined to Cape Colony; purchased commissions abolished in British Army
1872 Holland cedes Gold Coast to Britain
1873–4 Ashanti War
1877 Britain annexes Transvaal
1878 Britain acquires Cyprus from Turkey
1879 Zulu War

1880 Transvaal declared a republic
1882 USA bars entry of Chinese immigrants
1884 Germany occupies South West Africa, Togoland and Cameroons
1885 Germany annexes Tanganyika and Zanzibar; Congo established under Belgians; Gold discovered in Transvaal
1886 Britain annexes Upper Burma; Royal Charter for Niger Company
1888 British Protectorates of North Borneo, Brunei and Sarawak; Royal Charter for East India Company
1889 Royal Charter for South Africa Company
1891 Nyasaland a British Protectorate
1894 Uganda a British Protectorate
1899–1902 Boer War in South Africa
1900 Britain annexes Tongan Islands, Orange Free State and Transvaal
1905 Pogrom against Jews in Russia
1907 Immigration to USA restricted
1910 Union of South Africa a British Dominion
1911 National Insurance Act in Britain
1914–18 First World War
1914 Irish Rising in Dublin
1917 Russian Revolution
1919 Peace Conference in Paris and Treaty of Versailles; Hapsburg dynasty exiled from Austria—end of Austro–Hungarian Empire
1921 Irish Peace agreement: Ireland divides into Ulster and Free Republic
1922 Britain recognizes Egyptian independence; Mussolini marches on Rome; Emergency Quota Immigration Act in America
1923 Union of Soviet Socialist Republics established
1924 Chinese Civil War; American Indians declared US citizens
1926 General Strike in Britain
1929 Great Depression starts
1931 Spanish Revolution
1932 All places of worship closed in Russia
1933 30 January, Hitler Chancellor of Germany; 1 April, official Anti-Semitic Day; Concentration camps opened and systematic persecution of Jews starts in Germany
1935 Jews outlawed in Germany
1936 Italy annexes Abyssinia; Spanish civil War
1938 Libya annexed by Italy; Anti-Jewish legislation in Italy; Violent persecution of German Jews
1939–45 Second World War
1939 Albania annexed by Italy
1940–1 Anti-Jewish laws in France; The London Blitz
1941–3 Germans invade Russia
1942 Belgians deported to labour in Germany
1943 Jews massacred in Warsaw
1945 Americans bomb Hiroshima; World Zionist Congress demands million Jews to be sent to Palestine
1946 Philippine Republic inaugurated; Vietminh hostilities start in French Indo-China; Hungary and Albania become republics
1947 Britain withdraws from Palestine; Partition of India and Pakistan; Burma leaves the Commonwealth; Romania a republic

1948 Israel independent; Ceylon a British dominion; North Korean People's Republic founded; Czechoslovakia turns communist; law against Roman Catholic Church in Romania

1949 Eire leaves the Commonwealth; Chinese People's Republic set up; Indonesia independent from the Netherlands

1950–3 Korean War

1950 India becomes a republic; Nationalist Chinese in Taiwan

1951 Tibet annexed by China

1953 Armistice in Korea; Constitution of Federal People's Republic of Yugoslavia; Egypt a republic; Federation of Rhodesia and Nyasaland; Anti-Jewish campaign in Russia; Polish Catholic Church brought under State control

1954 Cambodia independent from France

1955 South Vietnam a republic

1956 Egypt nationalizes the Suez Canal; Hungarian Rising against Russia; Pakistan an Islamic Republic; Sudan independent

1957 Malaysian Federation and Ghana independent; Tunisia a republic

1959 Castro seizes power in Cuba; Hawaii admitted to USA; Singapore a self-governing state; unsuccessful Tibetan rising against Chinese

1960 Ghana and Somalia republics; Nigeria and Cyprus independent; Belgian Congo independent

1961 India annexes Goa; South Africa withdraws from the Commonwealth; Sierra Leone and Tanganyika independent

1962 Jamaica, Trinidad and Tobago independent; Algerian ceasefire; Yemeni Revolution

1963 Kenya and Zanzibar independent; Federation of Rhodesia and Nyasaland dissolved

1964 Kenya a republic

1965–75 American involvement in Vietnam

1965–6 Indo-Pakistan war

1966 British Guiana independent; Malawi a republic; British withdraw from Libya

1966–79 Unilateral Declaration of Independence by Rhodesia

1967–70 Nigerian war

1967 Six Day War between Israel, Egypt, Syria and Jordan

1968 British leave Aden; Czechoslovakian unrest

1969 Kenya and Uganda withdraw citizenship from British Asians

1970 Guyana (British Guiana) a republic; Tonga and Fiji independent

1971 Bangladesh a republic; Amin takes over in Uganda

1972 Pakistan withdraws from the Commonwealth; Ceylon a republic

1974 Military coup in Cyprus by Turks; Angola independent; Haile Selassie deposed in Ethiopia

1976 Reunification of Vietnam proclaimed

1979 Boat People flee Cambodia and Vietnam

Appendix II
Registration Districts

This list gives the numbers of the registration districts for births, marriages and deaths in England and Wales, as used in the indexes at the General Register Office, London. The numbers are arranged geographically; although the name of the registration district may seem unfamiliar the number will help to identify the locality.

1837–1851

I, II, III	London and Middlesex
IV	London and Surrey
V	Kent
VI	Bedfordshire, Berkshire, Buckinghamshire and Hertfordshire
VII	Hampshire and Sussex
VIII	Dorset, Hampshire and Wiltshire
IX	Cornwall and Devonshire
X	Devonshire and Somerset
XI	Gloucestershire, Somerset and Warwickshire
XII	Essex and Suffolk
XIII	Norfolk and Suffolk
XIV	Cambridgeshire, Huntingdonshire and Lincolnshire
XV	Leicestershire, Northamptonshire, Nottinghamshire and Rutland
XVI	Oxfordshire, Staffordshire and Warwickshire
XVII	Staffordshire
XVIII	Gloucestershire, Shropshire, Staffordshire, Warwickshire and Worcestershire
XIX	Cheshire, Derbyshire and Flintshire
XX	Lancashire
XXI	Lancashire and Yorkshire
XXII, XXIII	Yorkshire
XXIV	Durham and Yorkshire
XXV	Cumberland, Westmorland, Lancashire and Northumberland
XXVI	Brecknockshire, Carmarthenshire, Glamorganshire, Herefordshire, Monmouthshire, Pembrokeshire, Radnorshire and Shropshire
XXVII	Anglesey, Caernarvonshire, Cardiganshire, Denbighshire, Flintshire, Merionethshire and Montgomeryshire

1852–1946

1a, 1b, 1c	London and Middlesex
1d	London, Kent and Surrey
2a	Kent and Surrey
2b	Hampshire and Sussex
2c	Berkshire and Hampshire
3a	Berkshire, Buckinghamshire, Hertfordshire, Middlesex and Oxfordshire
3b	Bedfordshire, Cambridgeshire, Huntingdonshire, Nottinghamshire and Suffolk
4a	Essex and Suffolk
4b	Norfolk
5a	Dorset and Wiltshire
5b	Devonshire
5c	Cornwall and Somerset
6a	Gloucestershire, Herefordshire and Worcestershire
6b	Staffordshire, Warwickshire and Worcestershire
6c	Warwickshire and Worcestershire
6d	Warwickshire
7a	Leicestershire, Lincolnshire and Rutland
7b	Derbyshire and Nottinghamshire
8a	Cheshire
8b, 8c, 8d, 8e	Lancashire
9a, 9b, 9c, 9d	Yorkshire
10a	Durham
10b	Cumberland, Northumberland and Westmorland
11a	Glamorganshire, Monmouthshire and Pembrokeshire
11b	Denbighshire, Flintshire, Merionethshire, Montgomeryshire and Radnorshire

Appendix III
Useful Addresses

1. United Kingdom and Ireland

(a) Major Repositories

Public Record Office,
    Chancery Lane, London WC2A 1LR

Public Record Office,
    Census Section, Portugal Street, London WC2

Public Record Office,
    Ruskin Avenue, Kew, Richmond, Surrey TW9 4DU

    Note: The archives in the PRO at Chancery Lane currently include central legal records, Nonconformist chapel registers, Prerogative Court of Canterbury and Estate Duty wills, and old taxation records. Portugal Street houses only the Census records. The Kew office archives include Army and Navy records, Foreign and Home Office, Board of Trade and Inland Revenue papers, and old maps.

General Register Office,
    St Catherine's House, 10 Kingsway, London WC2B 6JB

Principal Probate Registry,
    Somerset House, Strand, London WC2R 1LP

British Library,
    Great Russell Street, London WC1B 3DG

Colindale Newspaper Library,
    Colindale Avenue, London NW9

Guildhall Library,
    Aldermanbury, London EC2P 2EJ

Greater London Record Office,
    40 Northampton Road, London EC1

India Office Library and Records,
    Foreign and Commonwealth Office, 197 Blackfriars Road, London SE1 8NG

House of Lords Record Office,
    House of Lords, London SW1A 0PW

College of Arms,
    Queen Victoria Street, London EC4

Historical Manuscripts Commission,
    Quality House, Quality Court, Chancery Lane, London WC2

National Library of Wales,
    Aberystwyth, Dyfed SY23 3BU

General Register Office,
    New Register House, Edinburgh EH1 3YT

Court of the Lord Lyon,
    New Register House, Edinburgh EH1 3YT

Public Record Office of Northern Ireland,
    66 Balmoral Avenue, Belfast BT9 6NY

General Register Office,
    49–55 Chichester Street, Belfast BT1 4HL

Public Record Office,
    Four Courts, Dublin 7

General Register Office,
    8 – 11 Lombard East, Dublin 2

Genealogical Office,
    Dublin Castle, Dublin

(b) Principal Genealogical Societies

The Society of Genealogists,
    14 Charterhouse Buildings, London EC1M 7BA

The Federation of Family History Societies,
    c/o Mrs A. Chiswell, 96 Beaumont Street, Milehouse, Plymouth, Devon

The Association of Genealogists and Record Agents,
    c/o Mrs M. Gandy, 31 Alexandra Grove, London N12 8HE
    The Association publishes a list of its members.

National Pedigree Index,
    c/o Society of Genealogists, 37 Harrington Gardens, London SW7

Heraldry Society,
    28 Museum Street, London WC1

Scots Ancestry Research Society,
    20 York Place, Edinburgh EH1 3EP

Irish Genealogical Research Society,
    c/o Glenholme, High Oakham Road, Mansfield, Notts.

Ulster Historical Foundation,
    66 Balmoral Avenue, Belfast BT9 6NY

(c) Printed Directories of Addresses

Royal Commission on Historical Manuscripts, *Record Repositories in Great Britain*, 1979 (HMSO)
    This is the basic source for addresses and telephone numbers of all the national and local repositories of Great Britain, including all the County Record Offices and many specialized collections.

ASLIB (Association of Special Libraries and Information Bureaus), *A Guide to sources of Information in Great Britain and Ireland*, Vol. 1 (4th ed.), 1977; Vol. 2 (3rd ed.), 1970

Burchall, M. J. and Warren, J., *National Genealogical Directory*, 1979.
    Lists surnames of families currently being researched, with names and addresses of their searchers.

Directory of British Associations, 5th ed., 1977–8

Downs, R. B., *British Library Resources: A Bibliographical Guide*, 1973

HMSO, *Abstract of Arrangements Respecting Registration of Births, Marriages and Deaths*, 1952
    Gives full details of registers kept in the UK, Commonwealth and Republic of Ireland.

The Libraries, Museums and Art Galleries Year Book

Robert, S., Cooper, A., Gilder, L., *Research Libraries in the United Kingdom*, 1978

Whitaker's Almanack

2. United States of America

(a) Principal Repositories

National Archives,
    Pennsylvania Avenue, Washington DC 20408

Library of Congress,
    Washington DC 20540

(b) Principal Genealogical Societies

American Society of Genealogists,
    1228 Eye Street NW, Washington DC 20005

National Genealogical Society,
    1921 Sunderland Place NW, Washington DC 20005

The Genealogical Society,
    50 E. North Temple Street, Salt Lake City, Utah 84150

(c) Printed Directories of Addresses

American Association of State and Local History, *Directory of Historical Societies and Agencies in the United States and Canada*, 1959

American Library Directory, 1978

Directory of Special Libraries and Information Centers, 1974

Encyclopedia of Associations, 1984

Lansing Mid-Michigan Genealogical Society, *A Brief Guide to American Genealogical Societies and Periodicals*, 1975

Meyer, M.K., *Directory of Genealogical Societies in the United States of America and Canada*, 1976

US Government Printing Office, *Where to Write for Birth and Death Records* (Public Health Service Publication no. 630A)

US Government Printing Office, *Where to Write for Marriage Records* (Public Health Service Publication no. 630B)

US Government Printing Office, *Where to Write for Divorce Records* (Public Health Service Publication no. 630C)

3. Europe and Commonwealth

The listing here is selective

(a) Principal Repositories

The addresses of the major public archives of all the countries in the world are listed in the *International Directory of Archives*, published as a special issue of the periodical *Archivum* (Vols. 22 – 23, 1972 – 3).

(b) Genealogical Societies
Listed in alphabetical order of countries

AUSTRALIA
Society of Australian Genealogists,
    120 Kent Street, Observatory Hill, Sydney, New South Wales 2000

AUSTRIA
Heraldisch-Genealogisch Gesellschaft 'Adler',
    Haarhof 4a, 1010 Vienna

BELGIUM
L'Office Généalogique et Héraldique de Belgique,
    Parc du Cinquantenaire, B – 1040 Brussels

CANADA
The Family History Association of Canada,
    P.O. Box 398, West Vancouver, BC V7V 3P1

Note: there is no national Canadian genealogical society

DENMARK
Samfundet for Dansk Genealogi og Personalhistorie,
  Stenshøj 12, Brunnshåb, 8800 Viborg

FRANCE
Centre d'entr'aide généalogique,
  69 rue Cardinal Lemoine, F – 75005 Paris

EAST GERMANY
Zentralstelle für Genealogie in der DDR,
  Georgi-Dimitrof-Platz 1, DDR 701 Leipzig

WEST GERMANY
Deutsche Arbeitsgemeinschaft genealogischer Verbände e.V.,
  Steintorwall 15, D33 Braunschweig

ITALY
Istituto Storice Famiglie Italiane,
  Via Cavour 31, 50129 Firenze

THE NETHERLANDS
Centraal Bureau voor Genealogie,
  Prins Willem Alexanderhof 20, Postbus 11755, 2502 AT
  's-Gravenhage

C. W. Delforterie and W. W. Van Resandt's *Wenken en adressen
voor genealogisch onderzoek in het buitenland* (1973), gives details
of genealogical societies and central and Census registration
throughout the world where the Dutch have been involved.

NEW ZEALAND
The New Zealand Society of Genealogists,
  P.O. Box 8795, Auckland 3

NORWAY
Norsk Slektshistorisk Forening,
  Villarn 18, Oslo 3

PORTUGAL
Instituto Portugues de Heraldica,
  Largo do Carmo, Lisboa

SOUTH AFRICA
Genealogical Society of South Africa,
  Postbus 3057, Coetzernburg, SA 7602

Heraldry Society of Southern Africa,
  P.O. Box 4839, Cape Town 8000

SPAIN
Instituto Internacional de Genealogica y Heraldica,
  Apartado de Correos 12.079, Madrid

SWEDEN
Foreningen for Slaktforskning,
  Olof Hermelins Vag 7, Stocksund

(c) Printed Directories of Addresses

Directory of European Associations, 1976

Directory of National Organisations (published by the Standing
  Conference for Local History, 26 Bedford Square, London
  WC1), 1978

Esdaile, A. J. K., *National Libraries of the World*, 1957

Lewanski, R. C., *European Library Directory*, 1968

The World of Learning, 30th edn, 1979
  Details of archives, libraries and research institutes
  throughout the world.

Bibliography

General Introductions to Family History

BEARD, T. F. and DEMONG, D., *How to Find your Family Roots*, 1977

CAMP, A. J., *Everyone Has Roots*, 1978

CLARE, W., *Simple Guide to Irish Genealogy*, 1938; 3rd edn., ed. by R. ffolliot, 1967

DOANE, G. H., *Searching for your Ancestors*, 1973

HAMILTON-EDWARDS, G. K. S., *In Search of Ancestry*, 1976

HAMILTON-EDWARDS, G. K. S., *In Search of Scottish Ancestry*, 1972

IREDALE, D., *Discovering your Family Tree*, 3rd edn., 1977

IREDALE, D., *Enjoying Archives*, 1973

STEEL, D. J. and TAYLOR, L., *Family History in Schools*, 1973

STEVENSON, N. C., *Search and Research*, 1959

UNETT, J., *Making a Pedigree*, 1971

WILLIS, A. J., *Genealogy for Beginners*, 1976

Bibliographies

DOWNS, R. B., *British Library Resources: a Bibliographical Guide*, 1973

FILBY, P. W., *A Select List of Books: American and British Genealogy and Heraldry*, 1970

HARRISON, H. G., *Select Bibliography of English Genealogy*, 1937

KAMINKOW, M. J., *A New Bibliography of British Genealogy*, 1965
Updates Harrison's *Select Bibliography*

MULLINS, E. L. C., *A Guide to the Historical and Archaeological Publications of Societies in England and Wales, 1901–1933*, 1968

MULLINS, E. L. C., *Texts and Calendars, an Analytical Guide to Serial Publications*, 1958
Records published by local and national societies

SCHREINER-YANTIS, N., *Genealogical Books in Print*, 1975

WALFORD, A. J., *Guide to Reference Material*, Vol. 2, 1975
Short bibliography of genealogical and heraldic books

WEDEN, F. *Familiengeschichtliche Bibliographie*, 1928–
Bibliography of German personal and family history

General Guides to Sources

American Society of Genealogists, *Sources for Genealogical Research*, 1973

ANDREWS, C. M., *Guide to the Material for American History to 1783, in the Public Record Office of Great Britain*, 2 vols., 1912

BARRY, J. G., *The Study of Family History in Ireland*, 1967

BOND, M. F., *The Records of Parliament: A Guide for Genealogists and Local Historians*, 1964

BOND, M. F., *Guide to the Records of Parliament* [in the House of Lords Record Office], 1971

B.R.A., *Handlist of Scottish and Welsh Record Publications*, 1954

Central Bureau for Genealogy, The Hague, *Searching for your Ancestors in the Netherlands*, 1972

COLKET, M. B. and BRIDGES, F. E., *Guide to Genealogical Records in the National Archives* [in Washington D.C.], 1964

CRICK, B. R. and ALMAN, M., *Guide to Manuscripts Relating to America in Great Britain and Ireland*, 1961

EVERTON, G. B., *Handy Book for Genealogists*, 6th edn., 1971

FALLEY, M. D., *Irish and Scotch–Irish Ancestral Research*, 1961–2

GALBRAITH, V. H., *An Introduction to the Use of Public Records*, 1934

GREENWOOD, V. D., *The Researcher's Guide to American Genealogy*, 1973

HANDLIN, O. and others, *Harvard Guide to American History*, 1954
List of publications of records, colony by colony

HANSEN, N. T., *Guide to Genealogical Sources—Australia and New Zealand*, 1963

HMSO, *British National Archives*, 1980
List of printed records from the Public Record Office

HMSO, *The Records of the Colonial and Dominions Offices*, 1964 (PRO Handbook No. 3)

KIRKHAM, E. K., *Research in American Genealogy*, 1962

LIVINGSTONE, M., *A Guide to the Public Records of Scotland*, 1905

LOMBARD, R. J. J., *Handbook for Genealogical Research in South Africa*, 1977

New York Public Library, *Research Libraries. Dictionary Catalog of the Local History and Genealogy Division*, 1971

NICKSON, M. A. E., *The British Library: Guide to the Catalogues and Indexes of the Department of Manuscripts*, 1975

Norwegian Ministry of Foreign Affairs, Oslo, *How to Trace your Ancestors in Norway*, 5th edn., 1980

PAMA, C., *Genealogy in South Africa*, 1969

PINE, L. G., *Genealogist's Encyclopaedia*, 1969

Public Archives of Canada, *Tracing your Ancestors in Canada*, 1972

Public Records Office leaflets, particularly:
1 Records of Birth, Marriage and Death
2 Censuses of Population
4 Probate Records
5 Change of Name
6 Immigrants
7 Emigrants
8 Records of the Registrar General of Merchant Shipping and Seamen
9 British Military Records
10 Militia Muster Rolls 1522–1640
11 English Local History
12 Inclosure Awards
13 Tithe Records
16 The American Revolution
17 The Records of the Foreign Office 1782–1947
18 Admiralty Records
21 Domesday Book
25 Private Conveyances
26 Apprenticeship Records
34 The Death Duty Registers

ROBERT, S., COOPER, A. and GILDER, L., *Research Libraries and Collections in the United Kingdom*, 1978

ROTTENBERG, D., *Finding our Fathers*, 1977
  A Guidebook to Jewish Genealogy
Royal Ministry for Foreign Affairs, Stockholm, *Finding your Forefathers: Some Hints for Americans of Swedish Origin*, 1976
RUBINCAM, M., *Genealogical Research Methods and Sources*, 1966
RYE, W., *Records and Record Searching*, 1969
SANDISON, A., *Tracing Ancestors in Shetland*, 1978
SMITH, C. N. and A. P-C., *Encyclopaedia of German–American Genealogical Research*, 1976
SMITH, F. and GARDNER, D. E., *Genealogical Research in England and Wales*, 3 vols., 1957–64
THOMSON, J. M., *The Public Records of Scotland*, 1922
WHYTE, D., *Introducing Scottish Genealogical Research*, 1979

Newspapers

Ayer Directory of Publications ... Newspapers ... Magazines 1869–1976, 1977
FERGUSON, J. P. S., *Scottish Newspapers Held in Scottish Libraries*, 1956
GREGORY, W., *American Newspapers 1821–1936*, 1937
The Times, *Tercentenary Handlist of English and Welsh Newspapers, Magazines and Reviews 1620–1920*, 1920

Guides to Genealogical Periodicals

CAPPON, L. J., *American Genealogical Periodicals: A Bibliography with a Chronological Finding-List*, 1964
Genealogical Periodical Annual index, 1962–
JACOBUS, D. L., *Index to Genealogical Periodicals*, 1932–53
KONRAD, J., *Directory of Genealogical Periodicals*, 1975
  (The principal British and American genealogical periodicals are the *Genealogists' Magazine* (1925–) *The American Genealogist* (1922–) and the *New England Historical and Genealogical Register*, 1847– .)

Places and Place-names

EKWALL, B. O. E., *Concise Oxford Dictionary of English Place-names*, 1960
EVERTON, G. B., *Genealogical Atlas of the USA*, 1966
FIELD, J., *English Field-names*, 1972
LEWIS, S., *Topographical Dictionary of England*, 4 vols., 1848–9
LEWIS, S., *Topographical Dictionary of Ireland*, 2 vols., 2nd edn. 1846
LEWIS, S., *Topographical Dictionary of Scotland*, 2 vols., 2nd edr 1846
LEWIS, S., *Topographical Dictionary of Wales*, 2 vols., 3rd edn., 1845
LUCAS, C. P., *A Historical Geography of the British Colonies*, 190
MASON, O. (ed.), *Gazetteer of Britain*, 1977

Chapter 1: Genealogy in the Past and its Uses

(a) Genealogy in History

ANDERSON, J., *Royal Genealogies*, 1732
BERKNER, L. K. and MENDELS, E. F., *Inheritance Systems, Fam Structure, and Demographic Patterns in Western Europe (1700–1900)*, mimeograph, 1973
BETHAM, W., *Genealogical Tables of the Sovereigns of the World*, 1795
GOODY, J., THIRSK, J. and THOMPSON, E. P., *Family and Inheritance*, 1976
MILLER, A. M., *Studies in Greek Genealogy*, 1968
PALMER, S. J. (ed.), *Studies in Asian Genealogy*, 1972
  History and sources in China, Japan, Korea and India, and Chinese and Japanese in America
ROUND, J. H., *Family Origins and Other Studies*, 1930
ROUND, J. H., *Peerage and Pedigree*, 1910, reprinted 1970
TOYNBEE, J. M. C., *Death and Burial in the Roman World*, 1971
WAGNER, A. R., *English Genealogy*, 1972
WAGNER, A. R., *Pedigree and Progress*, 1975

(b) Some Uses of Genealogy

GALTON, F., *Hereditary Genius*, 1869
GALTON, F., *Index to Achievements of Near Kinsfolk of some of the Fellows of the Royal Society*, 1904
GUN, W. T. J., *Studies in Hereditary Ability*, 1928
HOLLINGSWORTH, T. H., *Historical Demography*, 1969
HOSKINS, W. G., *The Midland Peasant*, 1957
  Study of Wigston Magna, Leicestershire
LASLETT, P., *The World we Have Lost*, 2nd edn., 1971
LASLETT, P. and WALL, R., *Household and Family in Past Time*, 1972
SPUFFORD, M., *Contrasting Communities, English Villagers in the 16th and 17th Centuries*, 1974
SQUIBB, G. D., *Founder's Kin, Privilege and Pedigree*, 1972
SQUIBB, G. D., *Visitation Pedigrees and the Genealogist*, 2nd edn., 1978
WRIGLEY, E. A., *An Introduction to English Historical Demography*, 1966

Chapter 2: Tracing your Ancestors

(a) Printed and Manuscript Pedigrees

American and English Genealogies in the Library of Congress, 1910, 1919
BARROW, G. W., *The Genealogist's Guide*, 1977
  Updates both Marshall and Whitmore
BRIDGER, C., *Index to Printed Pedigrees ... [of English Families]*, 1867, reprinted 1969
Catalogue of American Genealogies in the Library of the Long Island Historical Society, 1935
BURCHALL, M. J. and WARREN, T., *National Genealogical Directory*, 1979
  Lists surnames of families currently being researched, with names and addresses of their searchers
FERGUSON, J. P. S., *Scottish Family Histories Held in Scottish Libraries*, 1960
GATFIELD, G., *Guide to the Printed Books and Manuscripts Relating to English and Foreign Heraldry*, 1892
GRANT, F. J., *Index to Genealogies, Birthbriefs and Funeral Escutcheons in the Lyon Office, Edinburgh*, 1908
KAMINKOW, M. J., *Genealogical Manuscripts in British Libraries*, 1967
KAMINKOW, M. J., *Genealogies in the Library of Congress: a Bibliography*, 1972; supplement 1972–6, 1977
MARSHALL, G. W., *The Genealogist's Guide*, 1903 and 1967
  Alphabetical list of pedigrees in print
O'HART, J., *Irish Pedigrees*, 2 vols., 1892
PAGET, G., *Genealogies of European Families from Charlemagne to the Present Day*, 6 vols., 1957
PRYCE, F. R., *A Guide to European Genealogies, exclusive of the British Isles*, 1965

RIDER, F., *American Genealogical Index*, 1942–52
STUART, M. and BALFOUR PAUL, J., *Scottish Family History*, 1930
THOMSON, T. R., *A Catalogue of British Family Histories*, 1976
WHITMORE. J. B., *A Genealogical Guide*, 1953
 Updates Marshall's *Genealogist's Guide*
WHITMORE, W. H., *The American Genealogist*, 1967
 Catalogue of American genealogies, alphabetically arranged

(b) Central Registration and Censuses

DUBESTER, H. J., *State Censuses: An Annotated Bibliography of Censuses of Population Taken after the Year 1790 by States and Territories of the United States*, 1969
A Century of Population Growth from the First Census of the United States to the Twelfth, 1790–1900, 1909
 Includes maps
Gendex Corporation, *The Census Compendium*, 1972
GIBSON, J. S. W., *Census Returns 1841, 1851, 1861, 1871 on Microfilm: A Directory of Local Holdings*, 1979
HMSO, *Abstract of Arrangements Respecting Registration of Births, Marriages and Deaths*, 1952
 Full details of registers kept in the United Kingdom, Commonwealth and Republic of Ireland
HMSO, *Guide to Official Sources: Census Reports of Great Britain 1801–1931*, 1951
KIRKHAM, E. K., *A Handy Guide to Census Searching in the Larger Cities of the United States*, 1974
KIRKHAM, E. K., *A Survey of American Census Schedules 1790–1950*, 1961

(c) Parish Registers

BLOXHAM, V. B. and METCALFE, D. F., *Key to Parochial Registers of Scotland*, 1970
BURKE, A. M., *Key to the Ancient Parish Registers of England and Wales*, 1908
COX, J. C., *The Parish Registers of England*, 1908
GRH, Edinburgh, *Detailed List of the Old Parish Registers of Scotland*, 1872
HUMPHERY-SMITH, C. R., *Parish Maps of the Counties of England and Wales*, 1977
KIRKHAM, E. K., *A Survey of American Church Records, Major Denominations before 1880*, 1971
Local Population Studies, *Catalogue of Original Parish Registers in Record Offices and Libraries*, 1974, supplements 1976 and 1978
STEEL, D. J. (ed.), *National Index of Parish Registers*, Vol. 1, *Sources for Births, Marriages and Deaths before 1837*, 1976
STEEL, D. J. (ed.), *National Index of Parish Registers*, Vol. 12, *Sources for Scottish Genealogy and Family History*, 1971

(d) Parish Church and Chest

BAGLEY, J. J. and A. J., *The English Poor Law*, 1966
BURGESS, F. B., *English Churchyard Memorials*, 1963
COX, J. C., *Churchwardens' Accounts*, 1913
EVANS, E. J., *Tithes and the Tithe Commutation Act 1836*, 1978
JORDAN, W. K., *The Charities of Rural England*, 1961
Memorials of the Dead in Ireland, 1888–
OWEN, D. M., *The Records of the Established Church in England*, 1970
STEPHENSON, M., *A List of Monumental Brasses in the British Isles*, rev. edn., 1977
SUMMERS, P., *Hatchments of Britain*, 1974
TATE, W. E., *The Parish Chest*, 1963
WHITE, H. L., *Monuments and their Inscriptions*, 1978
 Practical guide to identification of styles of stone, and
decipherment of inscriptions

(e) Dissenters

AGNEW, D. C. A., *Protestant Exiles from France*, 2 vols., before and after 1681, 3rd edn., 1886
ESTCOURT, E. and PAINE, J. D., *English Catholic Nonjurors of 1715*, 1885
FREEDMAN, M., *A Minority in Britain*, 1955
 Jewish history
HENSHAW, W. W., *Encyclopaedia of American Quaker Genealogy*, 6 vols., 1936–50
MAGEE, B., *The English Recusants*, 1938
Registrar General, *List of Non-Parochial Registers and Records in the Custody of the Registrar General of Births, Deaths and Marriages*, 1841, 1859
SMILES, S., *The Huguenots*, 1868
 Historical survey, including migrations
STEEL, D. J. (ed.), *National Index of Parish Registers*, Vol. 2, *Sources for Nonconformist Genealogy and Family History*, 1972
STEEL, D. J. (ed.), *National Index of Parish Registers*, Vol. 3, *Sources for Roman Catholic and Jewish Genealogy and Family History*, 1973
TURNER, G. L., *Original Records of Early Nonconformity*, 1911
 Includes list of dissenters after the 1664 Conventicle Act

(f) Wills and Inventories

CAMP, A. J., *Wills and their Whereabouts*, 1974
GIBSON, J. S. W., *Wills and where to Find them*, 1974
STEER, F. W., *Farm and Cottage Inventories of Mid Essex 1635–1749*, 1969

Chapter 3: Using the Sources

(a) Types of Record Repository

ESDAILE, A. J. K., *The British Museum Library*, 1946
HMSO, *Guide to the Contents of the Public Record Office*, 3 vols., 1963–68
Royal Commission on Historical Manuscripts, *Record Repositories in Great Britain*, 1979
 A comprehensive listing of national and local repositories; see also the directories listed in Appendix III.

(b) Handwriting

BUCK, W. S. B., *Examples of Handwriting 1550–1650*, 1973
EMMISON, F. G., *How to Read Local Archives 1550–1700*, 1978
GRIEVE, H. E. P., *Examples of English Handwriting 1150–1750*, rev. edn., 1966
HECTOR, L. C., *The Handwriting of English Documents*, 1966
JOHNSON, C. and JENKINSON, H., *English Court Hand 1066–1500*, 1915

(c) Reading Latin

BAXTER, J. H. and JOHNSON, C., *Medieval Latin Word-list*, 1934
GOODER, E. Q., *Latin for Local History: An Introduction*, 1961
MARTIN, C. T., *The Record Interpreter*, 1976
 Latin abbreviations and words
NEWTON, K. C., *Medieval Local Records: A Reading Aid*, 1971

(d) Dating

CHENEY, C. R., *Handbook of Dates for Students of English History*, 1970

(e) Analysing Evidence and Writing the Family History

BARNETT, M., *How to Publish Genealogical and Historical Records*, 1971
PALGRAVE-MOORE, P. T. R., *How to Record your Family Tree*, 1979
PHILLIMORE, W. P. W., *How to Write the History of a Family*, 1887
PUGH, R. B., *How to Write a Parish History*, 1959

Chapter 4: How our Ancestors Lived

(a) General Works on Social History and Local Sources

BAGLEY, J. J., *Historical Interpretation*, Vol. 1, *1066–1540*; Vol. 2, *1540–* , 1972
    Contains reference to local original and printed source material
EMMISON, F. G., *Archives and Local History*, 1966
EMMISON, F. G. and GRAY, I., *County Records*, 1948
HEARNSHAW, F. J. C., *Municipal records*, 1918
HOSKINS, W. G., *Local History in England*, 2nd edn., 1972
KAMINKOW, M. J., *American Local Histories in the Library of Congress*, 1974/6
KUHLICKE, F. and EMMISON, F. G., *English Local History Handlist: A Short Bibliography and List of Sources for the Study of Local History and Antiquities*, 1965
LONGMATE, N., *The Workhouse*, 1974
MUNBY, L. M., *Short Guides to Records*, 1962
PUGH, R. B., *Victoria County History of the Counties of England: General Introduction*, 1970
RICHARDSON, J., *The Local Historian's Encyclopaedia*, 1974
STEPHENS, W. B., *Sources for English Local History*, 1973
TAYLOR, G., *The Problem of Poverty 1660–1834*, 1969
WEST, J., *Village Records*, 1962

(b) Legal Records

BURKE, J. (ed.), *Osborn's Concise Law Dictionary*, 6th edn., 1976
GARRETT, R. E. F., *Chancery and Other Legal Proceedings*, 1968

(c) Records of Landownership and Residence

BATEMAN, J., *The Great Landowners of Great Britain and Ireland* (1876), 1971
DIBBEN, A. A., *Title Deeds*, 1968
GRIFFITH, R., *General Valuation of Ireland 1844–50*, 1849–58
HONE, N. J., *The Manor and Manorial Records*, 1925
IREDALE, D., *Discovering your Old House*, 1977
KIRKHAM, E. K., *The Land Records of America and their Genealogical Value*, 1972
Return of Owners of Land of One Acre and Upwards ... England and Wales, 2 vols., 1875; Ireland, 1876.

(d) Maps

EVANS, E. J., *The Contentious Tithe 1750–1850*, 1976
HARLEY, J. B., *Maps for the Local Historian, a Guide to the British Sources*, 1972
HMSO, *Maps and Plans in the Public Record Office*, Vol. 1, *British Isles*, 1964; Vol. 2, *North America and West Indies*, 1974
NCSS, *The Historian's Guide to Ordnance Survey Maps*, 1964
THIRSK, J., *Tudor Enclosures*, 1959
TOOLEY, R. V., *Maps and Map-makers*, 4th edn., 1970

(d) Taxation Records

BERESFORD, M. W., *Lay Subsidies and Poll Taxes*, 1963
WARD, W. R., *The English Land Tax in the Eighteenth Century*, 1953

(e) Army and Navy Records

Army List, 1760–
    Annual lists of officers in the British Army, by regiment
BARNETT, C., *Britain and Her Army 1509–1970*, 1970
DALTON, C., *English Army Lists and Commission Registers 1661–1714*, 6 vols., 1892–1904
FOTHERGILL, G., *The Records of Naval Men*, 1910
GROENE, B. H., *Tracing your Civil War Ancestor*, 1977
HAMILTON-EDWARDS, G. K. S., *In Search of Army Ancestry*, 1977
HIGHAM, R. (ed.), *British Military History, A Guide to Sources*, 1972
LLOYD, C., *The British Seaman, 1200–1860, a Social Survey*, 1968
MARSHALL, J., *Royal Naval Biography*, 6 vols., 1823–30
National Genealogical Society (USA), *An Index of Revolutionary War Pension Applications*, 1966
National Maritime Museum, *Commissioned Sea Officers of the Royal Navy 1660–1815*, 3 vols., 1954
O'BYRNE, W. R., *A Naval Biographical Dictionary*, 1849
POWELL, W. H., *List of Officers of the Army of the United States from 1779 to 1900*, 1900, reprinted 1967

(f) Trades and Professions

CARR-SAUNDERS, A. M. and WILSON, P. A., *The Professions*, 1933
FROW, E. and E., and KATANKA, M., *The History of British Trade Unionism: A Select Bibliography*, 1969
GOSDEN, P. H. J. H., *The Friendly Societies in England 1815–75*, 1961
GOSS, C. W. F., *The London Directories 1677–1855*, 1932
JACOBS, P. M., *Registers of the Universities, Colleges and Schools of Great Britain and Ireland*, 1964
McGRATH, P. V., *The Merchant Venturers of Bristol: A History*, 1975
MATTHIAS, P., *English Trade Tokens*, 1962
NORTON, J. E., *Guide to National and Provincial Directories of England and Wales, excluding London, published before 1856*, 1950
READER, W. J., *Professional Men: The Rise of the Professional Classes in 19th Century England*, 1966
SPEAR, D., *Bibliography of American Directories through 1860*, 1961
UNWIN, G., *The Guilds and Companies of London*, 4th edn., 1963

(g) Landed and Titled Families
    (See also titles mentioned in the text)

Annuaire de la Noblesse de France et de l'Europe, 1843– (English edition 1953–)
A. and C. Black's Titles and Forms of Address, 1971
BRYDGES, E., *Collin's Peerage*, 1812
BURKE, J. B. and A. P., *Genealogical and Heraldic History of the Colonial Gentry*, 1970
Burke's Distinguished Families of America, 1948
Burke's Landed Gentry of Ireland, 1899, 1904, 1912, 1958
LODGE, J., *Peerage of Ireland*, 1754
PAUL, J. B., *The Scots Peerage*, 9 vols., 1904–14
SHAW, W. A., *Knights of England*, 1906, reprinted 1971
WALFORD, E., *County Families of the United Kingdom*, issued annually 1870–1921

Most countries have their own official directories and dictionaries of outstanding men and women of the past.

Chapter 5: Emigration and Travel

(a) Early Emigration

BANKS, C. E., *The English Ancestry and Homes of the Pilgrim Fathers*, 1962

BANKS, C. E. and BROWNELL, E. E., *Topographical Dictionary of 2,885 English Emigrants to New England 1620–50*, 1974

BRIDENBAUGH, C., *Vexed and Troubled Englishmen, 1590–1642*, 1976

COWAN, H. I., *British Emigration to British North America: The First Hundred Years*, rev. edn., 1961

FORBES, H. M., *Gravestones in Early New England and the Men who Made Them, 1653–1800*, 1927

HOTTEN, J. C., *Original Lists of Persons Emigrating to America 1600–1700*, 1874

LIBBY, C. T., NOYES, S. and DAVIS, W. G., *Genealogical Dictionary of Maine and New Hampshire*, 1928–38
Origins of settlers

MYERS, A. C., *Immigration of Irish Quakers into Pennsylvania 1628–1750*, 1902, reprinted 1969

PRENDERGAST, J. P., *The Cromwellian Settlement of Ireland*, 3rd edn, 1922

SAVAGE, J., *Genealogical Dictionary of the First Settlers of New England*, 4 vols., 1969

SHERWOOD, G. F. T., *American Colonists in English Records*, 2 vols., 1932–3, reprinted 1969
Early shipping lists

SMITH, J. M. (ed.), *Seventeenth Century America: Essays in Colonial History*, 1959
Analysis of emigration from British ports

WATERS, H. F., *Genealogical Gleanings in England*, 2 vols., 1969
Taken largely from wills and legal records, and references to connections overseas

WHITTEMORE, H., *Genealogical Guide to the Early Settlers of America*, 1898
Contains detailed calendar of dates

(b) Later Emigration

CHADWICK, E. M., *Ontarian Families*, 1894

COLEMAN, T., *Passage to America*, 1972
Nineteenth-century emigration

CRESSWELL, D., *Early New Zealand Families*, 1956

DICKSON, R. J., *Ulster Emigration to Colonial America 1718–75*, 1966

HENDERSON, A., *Australian Families*, 1941

HOCKLY, H. E., *The Story of the British Settlers of 1820 in South Africa*, 1949
Historical survey, including list of those in the parties sailing in 1819/20

JOHNSON, S. C., *A History of Emigration from the United Kingdom to North America 1763–1912*, 1913

JONES, E. M., *Roll of the British Settlers in South Africa*, 1969

LANCOUR, H. and WOLFE, R. J., *Bibliography of Ship Passenger Lists 1538–1825: A Guide to Published Lists of Early Immigrants to North America*, 1966

MOWLE, P. C., *A Genealogical History of Pioneer Families of Australia*, 1969

RUPP, I. D., *A Collection of Upwards of 30,000 Names of German, Swiss, Dutch, French and Other Immigrants in Pennsylvania from 1727 to 1776*, 1975

STERN, M. H., *Americans of Jewish Descent, A Compendium of Genealogy*, 1960, reprinted 1971
Mainly concerning settlers prior to 1840

TAYLOR, P. A. M., *Expectations Westward. The Mormons and the Emigration of their British Converts in the 19th Century*, 1965

Historical survey of migration to and within America

WHYTE, D., *Dictionary of Scottish Emigrants to the USA*, 1972

WANG, S-WU, *The Organisation of Chinese Emigration 1848–1888*, 1969
American and Australian immigrants and methods of passage

(c) Immigration

BERTHOFF, R. T., *British Immigrants in Industrial America 1790–1950*, 1953

BURN, T. S., *The History of the French, Walloon, Dutch and other Foreign Protestant Refugees Settled in England*, 1846

HANSEN, M. L., *The Immigrant in American History*, 1942

HMSO, *Index to Names: Certificates of Naturalization 1844–1900*, 1908

KIRK, R. E. G. and E. F., *Returns of Aliens in London 1523–1625*, 1900–1908

NEAGLES, J. C. and L. L., *Locating your Immigrant Ancestor, A Guide to Naturalization Records*, 1974

PAGE, W., *Denizations and Naturalizations of Aliens in England 1509–1603*, 1893

REAMAN, G. E., *The Trail of the Huguenots, in Europe, the United States, South Africa and Canada*, 1964

SHAW, W. A., *Letters of Denization and Acts of Naturalization for Aliens in England and Ireland, 1701–1800*, 1923; supplement by W. and S. Minet, 1932

(d) Convicts

BATESON, C., *The Convict Ships 1788–1868*, 1959

JOHNSON, W. B., *The English Prison Hulks*, rev. edn., 1970

KAMINKOW, M. and J., *Original List of Emigrants in Bondage from London to the American Colonies 1719–44*, 1967

ROBSON, L. L., *The Convict Settlers of Australia*, 1965

SMITH, A. E., *Colonists in Bondage: White Servitude and Convict Labor in America 1607–1776*, 1947

(e) Slaves

BERNARD, J., *Marriage and Family among Negroes*, 1973

CALDWELL, G. B., *History of the American Negro and his Institutions*, 1920

HUGGETT, F. E., *Slaves and Slavery*, 1975
History of slavery with details of dates and dealers

RICHARDSON, P., *Empire and Slavery*, 1968

ROSE, J. and EICHOLZ, A., *Black Genesis: A genealogical guide*, 1978

WOODSON, C., *Free Negro Heads of Families in the United States Census of 1830*, 1925

(f) Trade and Travel

BRIDENBAUGH, C. and R., *No Peace beyond the Lines: The English in the Caribbean 1624–90*, 1972

The Guildhall Library, *Parish Registers: A Handlist: Pt. III A Guide to Foreign Registers and Register Transcripts of Anglican Communities Abroad ...*, 1972

KINGSBURY, S. M., *The Virginia Company of London Records*, 4 vols., 1906–35

LAWRENCE-ARCHER, J. H., *Monumental Inscriptions of the British West Indies*, 1875

OLIVER, V. L., *Caribbeana*, 6 vols., 1909–19
Pedigrees and notes concerning the British in the West Indies

WRIGHT, P., *Monumental Inscriptions of Jamaica*, 1966

(g) British in India

BAXTER, I. A., *A Brief Guide to Biographical Sources* [In the India Office Library and Records], 1979
HODSON, V. C. P., *List of the Officers of the Bengal Army 1758–1834*, 1927–47
WILKINSON, T., *Two Monsoons: The British in India*, 1976

Chapter 6: Names

ADAM, F., *The Clans, Septs and Regiments of the Scottish Highlands*, 1960
  Includes alphabetical list of clan septs and dependents, and a tartan clan map
BAHLOW, H., *Deutsches Namenlexikon: Familien- und Vornamen nach Ursprung und Sinn erklärt*, 1967
BARDSLEY, C. W., *A Dictionary of English and Welsh Surnames, with Special American Instances*, 1968
BLACK, G. F., *Surnames of Scotland*, 1946
DAVIES, T. R., *A Book of Welsh Names*, 1952
DAUZAT, A., *Dictionnaire étymologique des noms de famille et prénoms de France*, 1951
GARDINER, A., *The Theory of Proper Names*, 1954
GEIPEL, G., *The Viking Legacy*, 1971
  Scandinavian names and surnames in Britain
GUPPY, H. B., *Homes of Family Names in Great Britain*, 1968
JOSLING, J. F., *Change of Name*, 1974
KAGANOFF, B. C., *A Dictionary of Jewish Names and their History*, 1978
MACLYSAGHT, E. A. E., *The Surnames of Ireland*, 1969
MASANI, R. P., *Folk Culture Reflected in Names*, 1966
MOORE, A. W., *Manx Names*, 1903
PHILLIMORE, W. P. W. and FRY, E. A., *Index to Changes of Name 1760–1901*, 1968
PUCKETT, N. W. N., *Black Names in America: Origins and Usage*, 1928
REANEY, P. H., *A Dictionary of British Surnames*, 1958
REANEY, P. H., *The Origin of English Surnames*, 1967
ROSENTHAL, E., *South African Surnames*, 1965
SMITH, E. C., *New Dictionary of American Family Names*, 1973
SMITH, E. C., *Personal Names: A Bibliography*, 1967
UNBEGAUN, B. O., *Russian Surnames*, 1972
WITHYCOMBE, E. G., *The Oxford Dictionary of English Christian Names*, 1977
WOULFE, P., *Irish Names and Surnames*, 1923
YONGE, C. M., *History of Christian Names*, 1967

Chapter 7: Heraldry

(a) Heraldry

BROOKE-LITTLE, J. P., *An Heraldic Alphabet*, 1973
BROOKE-LITTLE, J. P. (ed.), *Boutell's Heraldry*, rev. edn., 1978
BURKE, J. B., *The General Armory of England, Scotland, Ireland and Wales*, 1884
DENNYS, R. O., *The Heraldic Imagination*, 1975
DE RENESSE, COMTE T., *Dictionnaire des Figures Héraldiques*, 7 vols., 1894–1903
ELVIN, C. N., *A Hand-book of Mottoes . . .*, 1860, reprinted 1971
ELVIN, C. N., *Dictionary of Heraldry*, 1889, reprinted 1969
FAIRBAIRN, J., *Fairbairn's Book of Crests of the Families of Great Britain and Ireland*, 1968
FOX-DAVIES, A. C., *A Complete Guide to Heraldry*, 1969
FOX-DAVIES, A. C., *Armorial Families*, 1970
  Only those arms officially recorded are included
GODFREY, W. H. and WAGNER, A. R., *The College of Arms: A Monograph*, 1963
Harleian Society, Vols. 66, 67 and 68, *Grantees of Arms Named in Docquets and Patents to 1898*, 1915–17
INNES OF LEARNEY, T., *Scots Heraldry*, 1956
LOW, C., *A Roll of Australian Arms*, 1971
MOULE, T., *Biblioteca Heraldica Magnae Britanniae*, 1822, new edn., 1966
PAPWORTH, J. W. and MORANT, A. W. W., *Papworth's Ordinary of British Armorials*, 1961
  Arms listed A–Z under heraldic charges
PAUL, J. B., *An Ordinary of Arms Contained in the Public Register of All Arms and Bearings in Scotland 1672–1901*, 1969
RIETSTAP, J. B., *Armorial général; précédé d'un dictionnaire des termes du blason*, 1965
SAFFROY, G., *Bibliographie généalogique, héraldique et nobilaire de la France*, 4 vols., 1968–79
SKEY, W., *Heraldic Calendar*, 1846
  Irish grants of Arms from the time of Edward VI
WAGNER, A. R., *A Catalogue of English Medieval Rolls of Arms*, 1950
WAGNER, A. R., *Heralds and Ancestors*, 1978
WAGNER, A. R., *Heralds of England*, 1967
WAGNER, A. R., *Heralds and Heraldry in the Middle Ages*, 1956
WAGNER, A. R., *The Records and Collections of the College of Arms*, 1974
WRIGHT, C. E., *English Heraldic Manuscripts in the British Museum*, 1973
ZIEBER, E., *Heraldry in America*, 1895, 1909

(b) Orders and Decorations

BARBER, R., *The Knight and Chivalry*, 1974
HIERONYMUSSEN, P., *Orders, Medals and Decorations of Britain and Europe*, 1967
HOOD, J. and YOUNG, C. T., *American Orders and Societies and their Decorations*, 1917
WEHRLICH, R., *Orders and Decorations of All Nations*, 1965

Appendix I: Calendar of Dates

STEINBERG, S. H., *Historical Tables 58 BC–AD 1972*, 1973
STEINBERG, S. H. and EVANS, I. H., *Steinberg's Dictionary of British History*, 1974
POWICKE, F. M. and FRYDE, E. B., *Handbook of British Chronology*, 2nd edn., 1972

Index